FUNDAMENTALS OF HEALTH INSURANCE

PART A

The Health Insurance Association of America
Washington, DC 20004-1109

ISBN 1-879143-36-4

TABLE OF CONTENTS

FIGURES, TABLES, AND EXHIBITS

CHAPTER 6

Exhibits

FOREWORD

The HIAA Insurance Education Program aims to be the leader in providing the highest quality educational material and service to the health insurance industry and other related health care fields.

To accomplish this mission, the Program seeks to fulfill the following goals:

1. Provide a tool for use by member company personnel to enhance quality and efficiency of services to the public;
2. Provide a career development vehicle for employees and other health care industry personnel; and
3. Further general understanding of the role and contribution of the health insurance industry to the financing, administration, and delivery of health care services.

The Insurance Education Program provides the following services:

1. A comprehensive course of study in Fundamentals of Health Insurance, Long-Term Care Insurance, Managed Care, Disability Income Insurance, and Fraud;
2. Certification by examination of educational achievement for all courses;
3. Programs to recognize accomplishment in the industry and academic communities through course evaluation and certification, which enables participants to obtain academic or continuing education credits; and
4. Development of educational, instructional, training, and informational materials related to the health insurance and health care industries.

PREFACE

Fundamentals of Health Insurance: Part A and *Fundamentals of Health Insurance: Part B* introduce students to the basic concepts underlying group and individual health insurance. These books are an introduction to the technical as well as socioeconomic aspects of health insurance.

Previously, the HIAA Insurance Education Program had separated group and individual health insurance into two different courses of study. HIAA's revised program, as reflected in the new texts, deals with group and individual insurance within the same course of study. The restructured program allows for ensuing courses to parallel insurance company trends toward specialization in one or more product lines.

Other HIAA books in the curriculum provide students the opportunity to delve more deeply into these product lines, such as medical expense, managed care, specialized or supplemental medical expense, disability income, and long-term care insurance, and into issues of industrywide concern, such as health care fraud and abuse.

Health insurance is the term used to define a broad array of coverages for payment of benefits as a result of sickness or injury. Although all of the above coverages are discussed to some degree in this book, more attention is given to medical expense insurance and disability income insurance because so many millions of Americans have these coverages.

The contents of this book are educational, not a statement of policy. The views expressed or suggested in this and all other HIAA textbooks are those of the contributing authors or editors. They are not necessarily the opinions of HIAA or of its member companies.

ACKNOWLEDGMENTS

Chapter 1: History of Health Insurance
Terry R. Lowe
State Farm Mutual Automobile Insurance Company

Chapter 2: The Insurance Industry
Marilyn Finley
UNUM Life Insurance Company of America

Chapter 3: Health Insurance Coverages
John Boni
Physicians Mutual Insurance Company

Chapter 4: The Insurance Contract
Bernard E. Peskowitz
NYLCare Health Plans, Inc.

Chapter 5: Marketing and Sales of Health Insurance Products
Elizabeth M. Denning
Guardian Life Insurance Company

Chapter 6: Underwriting of Health Insurance Risks
Elizabeth M. Denning
Guardian Life Insurance Company

Reviewers
Bruce Boyd
Bruce Boyd Associates

Marianne Miller
Health Insurance Association of America

Editor
Jane J. Stein
The Stein Group

ABOUT THE AUTHORS . . .

John Boni has served over 20 years in sales and marketing divisions of the insurance industry—beginning as a field agent and advancing to sales and product management in his company's corporate headquarters. Currently, Boni is a product design analyst at Physicians Mutual Insurance Company where his responsibilities include the development of individual and group health and life insurance products.

Elizabeth M. Denning is a vice president of disability sales and marketing at Guardian Life Insurance Company of America. Her 25-year career covers claims administration, underwriting, agent training, and development of sales and marketing materials for disability insurance. She has served on HIAA's Individual Insurance Education Subcommittee, the Disability Insurance Training Council, the Accident and Health Club of New York, and the Eastern Claims Conference.

Marilyn Finley is a director of product development for UNUM Life Insurance Company of America's individual disability division where she is accountable for the design and delivery of the company's new and enhanced products. She also negotiates regularly with state insurance departments on issues of compliance. Previously, as a representative of UNUM's field and customer services departments, Finley supported sales of individual disability products.

Terry R. Lowe has enjoyed a 20-year career in the health insurance industry with particular emphasis in the area of claims. Currently, he is superintendent of training for State Farm Insurance Companies' life and health claims and is chair of the Health Insurance Association of America's Insurance Education Curriculum Subcommittee. Lowe has written and edited numerous health insurance industry publications.

Bernard E. Peskowitz has enjoyed a long career in contract development for the insurance industry working, over a period of time, for several large companies. Currently, as assistant vice president of NYLCare Health Plans, Inc., he is responsible for overseeing compliance and contract development for large and small group life, accident and health, and managed indemnity products.

Chapter 1

HISTORY OF HEALTH INSURANCE

■ Introduction

Some people think of health insurance as a recent development in human history. But concern for financial loss resulting from accident and illness can be traced to ancient civilizations. In fact, one of the earliest forms of health insurance may well have been the ancient Chinese custom of paying the doctor while in good health and discontinuing payment during periods of illness. Health insurance, limited primarily to disability income in case of accident, existed in the early history of Rome. This tradition continued in Europe in the Middle Ages, and by the 17th century there were laws providing sickness insurance for seamen and dismemberment insurance for soldiers.

Health insurance today is a broad array of coverage providing for the payment of benefits as a result of sickness or injury. It includes insurance for losses from medical expense, accident, disability, and accidental death and dismemberment (AD&D). This chapter traces the history and development of individual and group health insurance, starting in

1

19th century England and concentrating on its development in the United States.

■ Early Development of Individual Health Insurance

As the middle of the 19th century approached, the English railroads were plagued with bad publicity because of accidents. Railroad management sought a means of alleviating the public's fear of train travel. The Railroad Passengers' Assurance Company of London was established in 1848 to help the railroads deal with this situation. The company issued the first travel accident insurance in the form of an extra stub on a railroad ticket. This coverage provided benefits for accidental death or severe injury during the trip.

It soon was apparent to the founders of the Railroad Passengers' Assurance Company that simple train travel accident insurance was too limited, so the company extended its charter to cover all types of accidents. The company made another contribution to the insurance business with its "Premium Tables for Personal Accident Insurance." These tables proved to be quite accurate and are used today as the basis for rating certain accident risks in England.

In spite of its name, the Accidental Death Insurance Association of London, established in 1850, offered coverages for bodily injuries that did not result in death. (It also offered medical expense coverage, but this innovation presented problems that led to its early abandonment.) The company's major contribution was the establishment of a system of classifications for accident risks under which different premiums were charged according to the person's occupation.

It used the following classifications:

Class 1—Professional persons;
Class 2—Master tradespersons not doing manual labor;
Class 3—Mechanics, or the "working" risks; and
Class 4—All others, the "hazardous" risks.

Unlike its early competitor, the Railway Passengers' Assurance Company, which prospered and grew, the Accidental Death Insurance Association was the victim of fraudulent claims against which it was unsuccessful in defending itself. It abandoned further efforts in the insurance field.

Accident Insurance in the United States

Accidents were first insured in the United States by the Franklin Health Assurance Company of Massachusetts, founded in 1850. Established with $50,000 paid-in capital, it offered coverage for injury resulting from railway and steamboat accidents under a policy issued at a premium rate of 15 cents for a 24-hour term. A $200 benefit was paid if injury "detained" the insured for ten days. For total disability lasting two months, a $400 benefit was paid.

In the early 1860s, J. G. Batterson, a Hartford architect traveling in England, learned about an insurance stub that was added on to tickets issued by the Railroad Passengers' Assurance Company. As a result of his visit and consultations with English innovators, he established the Travelers Insurance Company of Hartford. This company initially insured travel accidents only. Its first policy was an oral agreement that covered a Hartford post office employee during travel from home to the office. The company issued its first printed policy to Batterson himself on April 1, 1864. Soon after, Travelers amended its charter to cover all types of accidents, issuing its first general policy on July 1, 1864. The establishment of Travelers and the issuance of its first policies is important because those policies were the direct ancestors of present-day accident insurance.

The success of Travelers in its first years of operation impressed other groups that soon entered the field. By 1866 there were 60 companies and associations writing accident insurance. Competition, often involving rate cutting, became intense; in many cases companies failed because of unsound rates. Action was required to protect both insurers and insureds. In 1865 Travelers established the Railway Passengers' Assurance Company of Hartford, and within it consolidated the travel

accident business of ten other companies. Of the 70 companies organized between 1865 and 1869, only Travelers remained by 1871.

During the decade 1864–1874, rail and sea disasters gave further impetus to the development of accident insurance. In 1864 alone, 140 railroad accidents took 404 lives and injured 1,846 persons. Between 1867
and 1871, 526 steamship disasters in American waters took 1,437 lives.
Claims resulting from these disasters almost ruined many insurance companies, but a number were able to survive by borrowing money. The
insurance industry capitalized on the publicity of the accidents, which
helped make the nation more aware of accidents and the need to protect against financial losses due to them.

By 1870 the insurance business had become large enough to run into
difficulties that had to be solved if the industry was to survive and
grow. The original simple policies had become highly complicated and
hedged with restrictions. Many fraternal societies and other groups offering insurance failed because of ignorance about insurance principles
and poor management. Unscrupulous promoters, interested primarily in
fast profits, cheated on claim settlements. Some states forced insurers
with headquarters in other states to pay heavy license fees and to invest
a large portion of assets in weak state bonds. All these factors had an
adverse influence on the insurance industry's image, reliability, and
financial stability.

In spite of these setbacks, by the late 1870s the health insurance business was beginning to find itself, and several strong companies were
established. For example, in 1876 the Knickerbocker Casualty Company,
later renamed Fidelity and Casualty Company of New York, was formed.
The oldest fraternal group, the Iowa State Traveling Men's Association,
was formed in 1880, and Woodmen Accident was founded in 1890. In
1891 the Aetna Life Insurance Company added accident insurance to its
product list.

Sickness Insurance in the United States

Sickness insurance actually was written in the United States before accident insurance. The first insurer in this field was the Massachusetts

Health Insurance Company of Boston, which was established in 1847. A number of other companies followed suit, but many failed largely because there were no reliable statistics on the frequency of sicknesses or diseases on which to base premiums. The early sickness policies offered very limited coverage and did not serve as a basis for later developments.

For all practical purposes, experimentation in the sickness insurance field began in 1890 when the St. Lawrence Life Association began writing accident and sickness insurance under one contract. The Federal Life and Casualty Company started writing similar coverage the following year.

The **stock companies,** led by Fidelity Life and Casualty, began to offer accident and sickness coverage in the late 1890s. Fidelity issued a conservative combination accident and sickness policy that restricted coverage for sickness to about 15 specified diseases. It contained a seven-day waiting period and limited benefits to 26 weeks. Fidelity and other stock companies began to expand coverage. By 1903 all diseases and surgical benefits were covered, and by 1908 the seven-day waiting period generally was eliminated.

■ Expansion and Growth of Individual Health Insurance

Pre–World War I

The trend toward broadened coverage continued in the early part of the century. For example, insurers extended disability provisions from 26 weeks to 52 weeks and then to 104 weeks; in 1913 they introduced lifetime disability benefits. Insurers also began writing policies that they had to renew, with premium rates that the insurers could not raise. The marketplace, too, expanded, and many new companies were formed. In some instances, existing fire insurers formed companion casualty companies, and several life insurance companies entered the health insurance field.

At the same time, adverse conditions existed. The policies had heavy restrictions and were filled with fine print. There was little or no cooperation among insurers to improve the condition of the insurance business. Legal requirements were lax, and so was supervision. Competition was cutthroat, and insurers assumed amounts of monthly disability indemnity beyond the bounds of good underwriting practice. Moreover, insurers tended to ignore hazards, such as the automobile and war, which had huge potential for accident and disability claims that could put them out of business.

As might be expected, the shaky financial backing and questionable practices that characterized some of these new insurance companies led to official investigations. These investigations had a great impact on the future course of the health insurance business and resulted in much-needed reforms.

The Armstrong investigation of 1905, although directed at life insurance practices, had strong repercussions in the health insurance field, including:

- much greater regulatory control over the entire insurance industry;
- more and more statutes regarding policy provisions and insurer operations; and
- growing competition, with some business diverted from the larger, established insurers to smaller, newer insurers throughout the country.

The health insurance industry also benefited from the development of a model law by the National Convention of Insurance Commissioners in 1912, which was designed to make the operating provisions in health insurance contracts more uniform. This model law, the Standard Provisions Law, was adopted in 27 states.

Trends and Developments: 1918–1940

The health insurance business experienced little growth in the years immediately following World War I. However, life insurance companies exerted some effort to meet public needs by offering certain health benefits, such as accidental death and disability income, as riders on life insurance policies.

The collapse of the stock market in October 1929, followed by the Great Depression, affected the health insurance industry profoundly. Sales fell sharply and many policies lapsed. Loss ratios climbed alarmingly, especially in the field of sickness disability coverages, where there was widespread exaggeration of the extent of disability. Often the policy benefits were the only income available to the policyholder or they were greater than what could be earned on a job.

Accidental death and monthly indemnity risks were a staggering source of loss. Noncancellable business, including the total and permanent disability income riders issued by life companies, presented a major problem for insurers. Renewal of coverage could not be refused, nor could premiums be raised, even though the insurers were losing money on the coverage. Suicide losses also climbed.

The health insurance industry would have been adversely affected by the Depression even with proper foresight. The industry's problems were compounded by the following:

- improper underwriting, primarily by underwriting only physical aspects of the risk and almost completely ignoring other hazards, such as risks from nonphysical, personal characteristics of the insured that could increase the possibility or intensify the severity of a loss;

- writing increasingly large amounts of monthly indemnity, particularly in noncancellable policies and in life insurance riders that provided disability benefits; and

- inadequate premiums resulting from insufficient claim experience on which to base rates.

As a result of the bad times during the Depression, health insurers retreated from the liberal coverages and underwriting practices that had been prevalent. Conservative coverages and practices were instituted throughout the industry. Some companies withdrew completely from the health insurance field. Several that remained would no longer issue sickness disability coverage, and those that did used longer elimination periods. Commissions were reduced sharply to discourage sales. The sale of noncancellable coverage was almost entirely discontinued, and virtually every life insurer gave up its disability income riders.

While the Depression had adverse effects on the industry, it also contributed to the industry's advancement. All the troubles forced the health insurance industry to reappraise its coverages and underwriting practices. Insurers became more willing to share information about their claim experience, and the availability of this information helped actuaries to calculate premium rates more accurately. This change resulted in a far more stable health insurance industry. Insurers introduced other changes and innovations more cautiously while still attempting to meet the social and economic needs of the public.

For example, because of the severely depressed economic situation, many people were not able to pay for proper medical care. At the same time, hospitals faced severe financial problems because of patients who could not pay their bills. As a response to this situation, insurers developed a hospital and medical expense insurance product line. Previously this coverage had been a fringe benefit of disability income insurance.

During and after the Depression, a new era of health insurance began. Some of the innovations and changes that were introduced in the 1930s included:

- emphasis in private insurance on reimbursement for hospital, surgical, and medical expenses;
- introduction of blanket accident expense policies; and
- introduction of coverage for the entire family.

Growth Years: 1940–1960

After World War II, health insurance as a whole entered a period of dynamic growth exceeding that of any other form of insurance. Many life insurance companies reentered the health insurance field.

Innovations that had previously appeared gained new significance. People were looking for broad coverages and guaranteed benefits.

To meet this need the individual health insurance industry expanded hospital and medical expense policies and made greater use of renewal guarantees. Disability income policies took on a new importance as the buying public recognized their value, particularly if the policies were noncancellable or guaranteed renewable. By the close of the 1940s, existing coverages were being broadened and new ones introduced. A new industry consciousness of responsibility to the public led more and more insurance companies and agents to turn their attention to the health field.

The beginning of a new decade in 1950 witnessed the continued growth and expansion of the individual health insurance industry. Contributing to the expansion was an increasing public awareness of the staggering loss of national income from accident and sickness. With the public showing a greater interest in health insurance, the National Association of Insurance Commissioners (NAIC), which replaced the National Convention of Insurance Commissioners, developed the model Uniform Policy Provisions Law (UPPL) in 1950. The law, or the essence of it, was adopted by all states.

New companies continued to enter the health insurance field rapidly. Particularly noticeable was the movement of an increasing number of life insurers into the health insurance field, not just with riders but with separate accident and sickness policies administered by full-scale health insurance departments. New coverages began to appear, such as comprehensive major medical and paid-up hospitalization policies. Insurers also launched a major effort to underwrite coverage for risks formerly considered uninsurable because of age or physical impairment.

Up to this time, the U.S. federal government had been involved in health insurance only minimally. But in 1956 it became involved on a larger scale when Congress established the Social Security Disability Insurance (SSDI) program. Involvement increased in 1965 with the enactment of two health insurance programs, Medicare for the elderly and Medicaid for the poor. For more information about Medicare, see

Chapter 3: Health Insurance Coverages in this book; for more information about both Medicare and Medicaid, see Chapter 5: Government Regulation in *Fundamentals of Health Insurance: Part B.*

Educational Activity

During the 1950s expanded health insurance coverage gave the industry the impetus to develop educational and training programs for agents.

- The Disability Insurance Training Council (DITC) was established to conduct annual disability income clinics on university campuses.
- The Chartered Life Underwriters (CLU) program began to incorporate health insurance information.
- The American College, sponsor of the CLU program, introduced a health certificate course.
- The Life Underwriter Training Council (LUTC) began offering a special health insurance training program to be conducted at local levels.

In addition, the Health Insurance Association of America (HIAA) was formed in 1956 to absorb the memberships of two smaller industry associations that had existed for more than 50 years. This consolidation enabled the health insurance industry to broaden its activities in research and statistics and to provide more widespread dissemination of valuable industry information. HIAA has developed an extensive health insurance curriculum, including specially written textbooks. By completing and passing exams in specific courses, students can achieve the professional designations of Health Insurance Associate and Managed Healthcare Professional.

■ Individual Health Insurance Today

The growth that characterized individual health insurance in the 1950s and 1960s settled into a more controlled expansion, with greater emphasis on refinement of products and delivery systems. Changes in individual health insurance evolved in response to consumer needs, cost containment activities, and legislative mandates.

Needs Met by Health Insurance

Everyone needs insurance to ease the financial burden caused by adverse changes in health. These costs can be so expensive that very few people could afford to pay for medical expenses or cope with the loss of income due to disability. Health insurance helps fulfill these needs by:

- providing protection against the cost of medical care;
- providing a set amount of income replacement; and/or
- providing a lump-sum payment for losses.

The Need for Medical Expense Insurance

The cost of medical care can reach substantial amounts. Hospital charges well over $10,000 can be incurred in a few days. Surgery, including hospital and doctors' bills, easily can reach or exceed $20,000. The expenses of a hospital stay of 30 days or more can be devastating.

Given these costs, people need to protect themselves with health insurance to make sure they are covered for major medical bills through group plans or individual policies. Even so, costs for simple treatments can place a severe financial burden on individuals and, in extreme cases, can force people to declare personal bankruptcy. Supplemental health insurance—for example, to cover out-of-pocket costs for hospitalization—can help pay some of these additional costs. Supplemental plans are discussed in Chapter 3.

The Need for Disability Income Insurance

Many people have difficulty living within their income even while healthy. Working adults need disability income insurance

(continued on next page)

(continued from previous page)

because of the potential financial burden of not being able to earn a full salary because of sickness or injury. Assume that a 30-year-old person is injured and not able to work, and that the injury does not shorten his or her life span. If this person's monthly earnings are $3,000, the salary loss each year is $36,000. The total amount of earnings lost between age 30 and the normal retirement age of 65 will be $1,260,000. This is certainly an amount worth insuring.

The Need for Long-Term Care Insurance

The U.S. population is aging, and the likelihood of needing long-term care insurance increases with age. In addition, smaller sized families, divorce, and the geographic dispersion of families may result in more older people being in situations where there are no family care givers and formal paid care is the only alternative. It is estimated that a person aged 65 faces a 43 percent chance of entering a nursing home during his or her lifetime.

Charges for skilled care in a nursing home can reach or exceed $40,000 per year, and formal care at home can be quite expensive. Long-term care insurance can help meet these expenses. These policies generally offer daily benefits to help pay for nursing home charges and formal care at home provided by a nurse or home health aide. Because nursing home charges continue to escalate yearly, many long-term care policies offer benefits to help pay for the increasing cost of care.

Medical Expense Insurance

Starting in the 1950s individual health insurance for various expenses incurred for medical care became more readily available for persons under age 65. Private insurers now offer individual comprehensive coverage, integrating basic and major medical coverages in a single policy with a deductible and with an unlimited maximum benefit. More recently, new coverages, such as long-term care insurance, have become available.

Disability Income Insurance

During the 1970s and 1980s a substantial liberalization occurred in the field of individual disability income insurance, which provides benefits when an insured is unable to work because of illness or injury. Policies that are noncancellable and guaranteed renewable to age 65 became more available. As earnings of prospective insureds increased because of inflation, insurers began to offer:

- policies with larger monthly benefits;
- options guaranteeing the insured the right to increase benefits in later years, regardless of his or her physical condition; and
- a cost-of-living provision under which the monthly benefit is increased periodically while the insured is disabled.

Disability insurance for coverage of individuals presenting other than a normal or standard risk also has developed rapidly in recent years. Formerly, such insurance generally was available only with certain conditions excluded, although increased premiums were used for some conditions such as obesity, amputations, and impaired vision. As an alternative to excluding coverage for an impairment, insurers now offer disability income policies at non-standard rates. Premiums can be as much as 200 percent or more of the standard premium, based on the degree of impairment.

■ Group Insurance Development

In 1911 Montgomery Ward and Company negotiated an insurance plan to provide weekly benefits for its employees who were unable to work because of sickness or injury. This plan generally is considered the first group health insurance policy. During the following years many large insurers established group health insurance products.

13

Accidental Death and Dismemberment Insurance

From 1911 to 1917 the only available form of group health insurance was short-term disability income insurance for temporary disability resulting from a nonoccupational accident or sickness. During this period it became apparent to insurers that they might offer an important service to employees by providing benefits for accidental death or permanent disability as a result of the accidental loss of sight or limbs. Since nonoccupational accidental losses did not fall under workers' compensation laws, individual life and health insurance policies offered this type of indemnity. By 1917 group accidental death and dismemberment insurance was offered as a supplemental group coverage.

Disability Income Insurance

Short-term disability income insurance did not change substantially in the first 40 years or so following the negotiation of the Montgomery Ward contract. Insurance covered only temporary disabilities, and rarely did the plans have a term that exceeded one year. Most plans provided coverage for 13 or 26 weeks.

Beginning in 1942, four states (Rhode Island, 1942; California, 1946; New Jersey, 1948; and New York, 1949) stimulated the growth of group disability income coverage by adopting plans that made temporary disability benefits compulsory. Hawaii and Puerto Rico also adopted compulsory disability plans in 1969. Interest in such plans by other states has since decreased; the spread of voluntary plans has removed most of the motivation for states to enact compulsory disability benefit programs.

In the 1940s a few insurance companies began experimenting with an extension of short-term disability income insurance that resulted in what is known today as long-term disability income insurance. The early long-term disability plans, which provided coverage for up to five years, were devised primarily for the protection of certain classes of higher-salaried employees, such as those in management and supervisory groups. Today, plans covering all active full-time employees and providing coverage up to normal retirement age for disabilities resulting from accidents or sickness are common.

14

Basic Medical Expense Benefits

Proposals to provide compulsory hospital-surgical, medical expense benefits were explored during the early 1900s, but even Samuel Gompers, then president of the American Federation of Labor, rejected compulsory health insurance as being too paternalistic. Not until 1911, when Great Britain passed a National Health Insurance Act, did the concept of providing medical care expense benefits generate significant interest in the United States. In the early 1920s individual hospitals in Rockford, Illinois; Grinnell, Iowa; New Bedford, Massachusetts; and Brattleboro, Vermont, offered hospital expense benefits on an individual prepaid basis.

The principle of group prepayment for hospital expenses (premiums paid in advance for specific services covered in full) originated at Baylor University Hospital in Dallas, Texas. In 1929, some 1,500 school teachers who were members of a mutual benefit society were covered for 21 days a year for semi-private room and board and necessary hospital services and supplies. At the beginning of the Depression, hospitals were faced with declining revenues and welcomed the Baylor group concept. The Depression also focused public interest to a greater degree than before on the problem of meeting the cost of medical care.

The Baylor Plan is considered the forerunner of what later became known as the Blue Cross plans. Other individual hospital prepayment programs were developed in New Jersey, Minnesota, and North Carolina in 1931. The first citywide plan was offered by hospitals in Sacramento, California in 1932, Washington, D.C. in 1934, and New York City in 1935. By 1935 the shift from hospital expense benefit programs of individual hospitals to communitywide programs became common.

Hospital, Doctor, and Medical Expense Benefits

In 1934 the General Tire & Rubber Company asked The Equitable Life Assurance Society of the United States to add hospital expense benefits to its existing group insurance program. About the same time, Occidental Life of California added hospital expense benefits to an existing short-term disability income insurance policy for a large chain of grocery stores.

15

The development of group hospital expense benefits was a significant step in helping employees meet the cost of medical care. The next step was coverage for surgeons' fees and physicians' charges for in-hospital, home, and office visits. Private insurers introduced group surgical expense benefits in 1938, followed by group medical expense benefits to cover physicians' visits in 1943. The first Blue Shield Surgical-Medical Plan (California Physicians' Service) developed a statewide, prepaid, medical society–sponsored plan in 1939.

Major Medical Expense Benefits

Although beneficial for most illnesses and accidents, basic medical expense coverages developed during the 1930s and 1940s were inadequate for prolonged confinements and expensive procedures. To provide insurance against such catastrophic medical events, the Liberty Mutual Insurance Company introduced "major medical" in 1949 to supplement basic medical care expense benefits. This dramatic new approach to medical care expenses resulted in a 90 percent enrollment of the members of the Elfun Society (a voluntary association of approximately 4,000 General Electric management employees) when the first group major medical expense benefits plan was written in 1949.

Insurers originally wrote major medical expense benefits policies as a supplement to their own basic medical care coverages or to coverages provided by Blue Cross/Blue Shield. Today, major medical insurance encompasses virtually all types of medical care expenses, both in and out of a hospital.

Dental Expense Insurance

As early as 1945 the American Dental Association (ADA) adopted recommendations for experimental prepayment dental plans on a nonprofit basis. In so doing the ADA was aware that individuals who visit their dentists regularly can budget the cost of dental needs to some extent. The ADA recognized also that only scant factual information was available on whether dental plans could be financially sound.

Experimental dental prepayment programs, initiated cautiously in the 1950s, provided dental care benefits to select groups. In August 1959 the first comprehensive group dental expense insurance plan, covering all types of services, was written by the Continental Casualty Company.

Other Health Benefits

Other group health insurance benefits were developed over the years, including credit health insurance in 1950; vision care benefits in 1957; extended care facility benefits (skilled nursing facilities) in 1959; prescription drug benefits in 1964; and hospice care, home health care, and long-term care benefits in the 1980s.

■ Factors Influencing the Growth of Group Health Insurance

Multiple economic, social, and political forces affected the growth of group insurance. By the beginning of the 20th century, American society was becoming increasingly industrialized and urbanized; traditional family obligations to care for the old and the sick were weakening. Also, dissatisfaction with public measures for the relief of the ill, the old, and the destitute was growing. These general trends set the stage for development of group insurance.

Other factors responsible for the rapid and extensive growth of group insurance included union demands, favorable tax treatments, expanded benefits, consumer demands, and changing demographic needs.

Wage Controls During World War II

During World War II the federal government imposed industrial wage and price controls in an effort to control inflation. Since employer contributions to fringe benefits, including insurance plans, were not controlled, employers turned to group insurance and pension plans to supplement wages as a means of attracting and retaining employees.

Union Demands Through Collective Bargaining

The Wagner Act (National Labor Relations Act of 1935) gave employees the right to organize unions and bargain collectively with their employers over wages, hours, and other conditions of employment. However, the real impetus for negotiated employee benefit plans occurred in 1948 when the National Labor Relations Board ruled, in a dispute between the United Steelworkers' Union and the Inland Steel Company, that the term *wages* "must be construed to include emoluments of value, like pension and insurance benefits."

In upholding this ruling in its notable decision of 1949, the Supreme Court removed any doubt about the right of labor to bargain collectively over wages, hours, or other conditions of employment, including retirement and insurance plans. The decision clearly established that group insurance and other benefits are within the scope of collective bargaining, engendering much of the post–World War II growth of employee benefit plans.

Although they are not required to do so, most employers extend the benefits negotiated for their union employees to their nonunion employees. Today, all workers—union and nonunion, alike—recognize insurance benefits as an integral part of an employee compensation package.

Favorable Federal Tax Treatment

The premiums paid by an employer for employees' group insurance are treated as a business expense. The premiums paid by the employer do not constitute taxable income to the employees except under specific conditions for some amounts of life insurance.

An employee who itemizes federal income tax deductions may deduct contributions for medical and dental care expense insurance subject to the overall requirements for medical and dental expense deductions. Under the present federal income tax law, medical and dental care expense insurance is limited to coverage such as hospitalization, doctors' fees, and medicines. It does not include premiums for accidental death and dismemberment insurance or short-term and long-term disability income insurance.

Recent federal legislation, the Health Insurance Portability and Accountability Act of 1996, effective January 1, 1997, allows, with certain limitations, the tax deductibility of long-term care insurance premiums and services as medical expenses. This same legislation incrementally increases the percentage of health insurance premium expenses that self-employed individuals can deduct, regardless of the amount of other medical expenses, to a maximum of 80 percent in the year 2006 and thereafter.

Social Legislation

State and federal laws have had a marked effect on the group health insurance business. The states and territories with compulsory temporary disability benefits legislation mentioned earlier permit health insurers to write short-term disability income coverage to meet the requirements of these laws (except for Rhode Island, which has a state fund). California and New Jersey state funds are conducted in a way that places insurers at a competitive disadvantage, and state funds there provide most of this coverage. Private insurers can provide statutory benefits and do compete with the funds in New York, Hawaii, and Puerto Rico, and sometimes in New Jersey.

Also, half of the states have increased the number of people with health insurance by enacting laws establishing health plans for people who were categorized as uninsurable. In addition to the premium paid by insureds, these plans sometimes are financed through statewide pools to which all insurers operating in the state are required to contribute. Through this mechanism, premiums for small groups and individuals are kept at affordable levels.

On the federal level, legislation such as Social Security disability benefits, Medicare, Medicaid, and the Health Maintenance Organization Act of 1973 has affected the growth of group health insurance and the design of products provided by insurers. For example, some long-term disability income insurance plans supplement the benefits available under the Social Security program.

Extension of the Group Insurance Concept

Since World War II, group insurance has been extended to cover a wider array of products and people. Insurers have group plans for trade associations, professional associations, and multiple-employer trusts, and they extend group medical expense coverages to retired persons and their dependents. Insurers also convert group medical expense coverages to individual policies.

Impact of Consumerism

Consumerism, a powerful influence in the marketplace since the 1960s, is a social movement supporting the rights and powers of buyers in relation to sellers. Consumer advocates want buyers to have adequate information about a product or service, including quality, quantity, advantages, disadvantages, guarantees, and prices.

Reflecting consumer concerns, various states have legislated group health insurance coverage for alcoholism, drug addiction, home health care, mental and nervous disorders, newborn children, handicapped children, and continuation of survivors' health benefits. Insurers, too, are offering new benefits to address those concerns. Additionally, state legislatures have enacted laws mandating minimum health insurance benefits and confidentiality of medical care information. Federal legislation requires that employers make continuation of coverage available for terminated employees. Major recent federal legislation places significant limits on the ability of insurers and employers to deny coverage under group and individual plans based on pre-existing health conditions.

It is natural that the insurance business should be subjected to consumer scrutiny, both because of the fiduciary nature of the business (the insurer is entrusted with the responsibility of acting in the interest of beneficiaries) and because it affects so many people in important and meaningful ways throughout their lives.

Expansion of Benefits

Another factor contributing to the growth of group insurance has been the expansion through the years of its benefits to solve various coverage and cost problems. For example, basic health insurance originally provided 21 days at a limited amount per day for coverage in the hospital and a maximum surgical schedule of $200 to $300. Now major medical coverage reimburses for an unlimited number of hospital days and reasonable and customary charges, often with a $1 million maximum or greater.

Population Demographics

Most employee benefit plans were designed to meet the needs of the traditional family unit of the 1940s and 1950s—a male employee with a nonworking wife and two or three minor children. Today's work force and family structure is quite different, with more women working and a significant increase in households headed by single mothers.

In response to changing demographics, group insurance has developed a number of new benefits. Flexible benefit plans offer a wide range of benefits and let participants select the ones that best meet their needs. Benefit options often include life insurance, long-term disability, medical care, dental care, vision care, and flexible spending accounts.

Another demographic change is an increasingly aging population. A good part of the work force is retired or will soon be retiring. Over the years, many employers have added postretirement medical insurance benefits to their existing group pension benefits. More recently, however, because of a new financial accounting standard requiring these benefits to be recognized as an employer liability, employers often modify their plans to include reduced retiree benefits, more stringent eligibility conditions, and increased retiree pension contributions.

21

Demand and Cost of Medical Care

The introduction and wide use of many highly effective drugs, advances in diagnostic services, and new lifesaving surgical procedures have greatly increased the use of medical care services and facilities. Increased demand is also a result of such factors as the greater availability and diversity of medical care services and facilities with widespread reimbursement by third-party payers, the change in the public image of the hospital from a place to die to a place to sustain life, and the more frequent use of the hospital for diagnostic and nonsurgical purposes.

A broader degree of health education through the use of mass media, the school system, medical societies, employers, labor unions, health insurers, voluntary agencies, and all levels of government also has served to expand public awareness of health matters and, consequently, has increased the demand for medical care and treatment. Meanwhile the more technical and highly specialized nature of medical care has resulted in increases in the price of that care. In recent years the medical care component of the consumer price index has increased at about twice the rate of the average of all goods and services.

This combination of greater demand and rising cost has caused a growing interest in managing health costs. One approach taken by insurers and employers is to institute utilization review programs, to ensure that health care services are being used appropriately. Another is the establishment of managed care arrangements such as health maintenance organizations (HMOs) and preferred provider organizations (PPOs).

The cost of financing health care has had an enormous impact on the health insurance industry. Employees are sharing an increasing portion of the cost of health insurance through use of deductibles and coinsurance.

Catastrophic illnesses such as the acquired immune deficiency syndrome (AIDS) also have left their mark on the health insurance industry. The use of managed health care concepts, such as medical case management, and support for research and education are two of the industry's responses to such illnesses.

Competition

The highly competitive marketplace also has influenced the development of group insurance. To stay competitive, the group insurance market has to continually develop new products, concepts in coverage, and funding vehicles. These new products provide alternatives for the buyer of group insurance.

Quality of services provided is an increasingly important factor in obtaining and retaining group insurance policyholders. The ability of the insurance company to communicate the plan effectively and to provide sound administration, computer capability, and prompt, accurate claim payments is vital to the satisfactory operation of the group plan and to retaining policyholders.

Another competitive factor is an insurer's ability to negotiate discounted contracts with hospitals and physicians. These concessions create a distinct cost advantage over insurers that do not have discounted arrangements.

There is another competitive factor—the self-funded or partially self-funded employee benefit plan. The desire to improve cash flow and reduce tax liabilities has led many employers to the self- or partially self-funded approach to insurance. Thus, many private insurers have developed administrative services only (ASO) relationships with self-insured plans.

■ Current Status of the Health Insurance Industry

Most Americans have some sort of health insurance, either through the private sector or through government programs. (Figure 1.1) In 1994 approximately 180 million Americans—about 70 percent of the population—were protected by one or more forms of private health insurance. This represents tremendous growth in the industry. In 1940 it was estimated that only about 12 million persons had private coverage. The number of people with private insurance has remained relatively stable since the mid-1980s.

Health Insurance (HI) Status of Americans, 1995

	Nonelderly		Elderly	
	Millions	**Percentage**	**Millions**	**Percentage**
Total population	231.9	100.0%	31.7	100.0%
With private health insurance	163.9	70.7	21.8	68.7
Employer coverage	147.9	63.8	11.1	35.1
Other/private	16.0	7.9	10.6	33.5
With public health insurance	38.4	16.6	30.6	96.6
Medicare	4.1	1.8	30.5	96.4
Medicaid	29.0	12.5	2.8	8.9
CHAMPUS/VA	7.4	3.2	1.2	3.6
Uninsured	40.3	17.4	0.3	0.1

Figure 1.1

SOURCE: Employee Benefit Research Institute tabulations of data from the March 1996 Current Population Survey.

More than 1,000 private insurance companies in the United States write individual and group health policies. The predominant form of health insurance sold today is group insurance. Of those people under age 65 with private coverage, approximately 94 percent have group insurance, and 6 percent have individual insurance. Group and individual health insurance premiums total nearly $125 billion a year. (Tables 1.1a and 1.1b)

While traditional medical expense policies providing fee-for-service reimbursement are offered through commercial insurance companies and Blue Cross and Blue Shield plans, these insurers also sponsor health maintenance organizations and account for over one quarter of all HMO enrollment.

Table 1.1a

Group Health Insurance Premiums of Insurance Companies by Type of Coverage (Billions)

Year	Total group	Hospital/ medical	Dental	Medicare supplement	Loss of income
1980	$ 36.8	$28.2	$3.2	$0.0	$5.3
1981	42.5	33.0	4.1	0.1	5.2
1982	50.0	39.6	4.8	0.1	5.5
1983	54.9	44.4	5.3	0.1	5.1
1984	60.8	49.6	5.7	0.5	5.0
1985	64.4	52.7	6.2	0.6	4.8
1986	65.9	53.0	6.2	1.8	5.0
1987	74.0	59.9	6.8	1.8	5.5
1988	87.6	71.9	7.8	2.5	5.5
1989	96.1	79.3	7.8	3.0	6.0
1990	100.2	82.4	7.8	3.4	6.6
1991	103.0	85.0	7.6	4.2	6.2
1992	110.4	90.4	8.1	5.3	6.6
1993	110.2	90.3	8.1	6.0	5.8
1994	114.1	93.7	8.1	6.6	5.7

SOURCE: Health Insurance Association of America, Annual Survey of Health Insurance Companies.

Table 1.1b

Individual Health Insurance Premiums of Insurance Companies by Type of Coverage (Billions)

Year	Total individual	Hospital/ medical	Loss of income
1980	$ 6.9	$ 4.9	$2.0
1981	6.5	4.7	1.8
1982	8.3	5.8	2.5
1983	8.3	6.3	2.0
1984	9.6	7.2	2.4
1985	10.8	7.9	2.9
1986	9.6	6.7	2.9
1987	10.1	7.0	3.1
1988	10.6	7.4	3.2
1989	11.8	8.2	3.6
1990	12.7	8.9	3.8
1991	13.3	10.0	3.3
1992	14.6	10.3	4.3
1993	14.5	10.7	3.8
1994	15.2	11.7	3.5

SOURCE: Health Insurance Association of America, Annual Survey of Insurance Companies.

Table 1.2

Distribution of Persons with Private Insurance by Type of Insurer (Millions)

Type of insurer	1990	1991	1992	1993	1994
All insurers	181.7	181.0	180.7	180.9	182.2
Insurance companies (net)	83.1	78.0	76.6	74.7	75.8
Group	88.7	83.3	82.1	80.9	82.4
Fully insured	40.9	36.2	33.8	33.3	36.8
ASO	30.8	35.3	35.9	37.2	37.4
MPP	16.9	11.8	12.4	10.4	8.2
Individual	10.2	9.9	8.5	7.4	7.0
Blue Cross/Blue Shield	70.9	68.1	67.5	65.9	65.2
Self-insured	49.7	54.8	56.5	60.5	61.8
HMO	36.5	38.7	41.4	45.2	51.1
Blue Cross/Blue Shield	4.6	4.7	5.8	6.7	7.6
Insurance companies	5.4	6.0	6.1	6.5	7.3
Other	26.5	28.0	29.5	32.0	36.2

SOURCE: Health Insurance Association of America, Annual Survey of Health Insurance Companies.

A growing number of health insurance plans are self-insured—those where an employer or union assumes all or part of the financial responsibility for the claims incurred. An additional expanding area for the private health insurance business is providing administrative services only (ASO) to self-insured plans. Under such arrangements, a fee is paid by the self-funding group to process claims and provide other administrative services. Another approach for private insurers is the minimum premium plan (MPP). This is a combination approach to funding an insurance plan, and it is aimed primarily at premium tax savings. Under an MPP an employer self-funds a fixed percent (e.g., 90 percent) of the estimated monthly claims and the insurance company insures the rest. (Table 1.2)

Health care benefits are available also through various government programs. These include Medicare for persons over age 65 and those with certain disabilities, and Medicaid for a portion of the indigent population as well as certain categories of the medically needy.

Despite the development of government programs, recent years have witnessed a dramatic growth in the number of people without health insurance. In 1994 there were an estimated 41 million persons without heath care insurance. A number of factors are responsible for the increase in uninsureds, including the erosion of Medicaid coverage for the poor, demographic shifts, more part-time workers, loss of jobs due to corporate downsizing, and a shift of workers to service industries that are less likely to offer group health insurance. There may be some decrease in the number of uninsured persons because the new Health Insurance Portability and Accountability Act of 1996 guarantees access to insurance to certain individuals leaving group coverage.

■ Emerging Trends

Insurers have developed health insurance products to reflect changes in the socioeconomic environment. Both the range of benefits and the scope of coverages have increased to meet changing needs. This process can be expected to continue as public demands rise. As insurers gain more experience and knowledge, even more diverse forms of coverage may evolve.

Competition and the need to control costs has led to various alternative combinations and forms of health insurance delivery options. Managed care, which is fast becoming the leading form of health insurance delivery, integrates the financing and delivery of appropriate health care services. (Figure 1.2) Providers in managed care plans offer standardized health services to enrollees at set costs that generally are lower than traditional fee-for-service arrangements. Sometimes insurers or employers join in these arrangements. In all managed care arrangements there are more guidelines on utilization and cost monitoring than in traditional settings.

Some of the more common managed care arrangements are:

■ **Health Maintenance Organization (HMO).** This health care arrangement provides comprehensive health care services for a

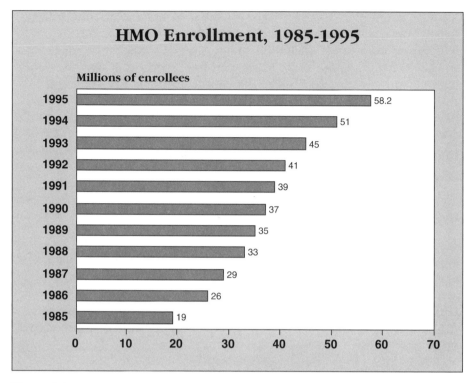

Figure 1.2

SOURCE: Group Health Association of America, December 1994.

specified group of enrollees at a fixed prepayment. HMOs often use a primary care physician as a gatekeeper or manager to coordinate the care of enrollees to maximize efficiency and effectiveness in the delivery of care. Members are not reimbursed if they use non-HMO providers.

■ **Preferred Provider Organization (PPO).** This managed care arrangement combines features of standard fee-for-service indemnity plans and HMOs. A PPO has contracts with networks or panels of providers that agree to provide medical services and to be paid according to a negotiated fee schedule. Individuals who are enrolled in a PPO can get care from a nonaffiliated provider, but that option carries a financial penalty, usually an increased coinsurance amount.

■ **Point-of-Service (POS) Plan.** This plan, which is sometimes called an HMO-PPO hybrid or an open-ended HMO, combines features of HMOs and PPOs. It uses a network of participating providers under contract. Enrollees choose a primary care physician who controls referrals for medical specialists. If an enrollee receives care from a POS provider, the enrollee pays little or nothing out-of-pocket as in an HMO and does not file claims. Care provided by out-of-plan providers is reimbursed, but there is no predetermined fee and enrollees must pay a deductible and higher coinsurance amounts.

Other specialized managed care arrangements include prescription drug programs, in which network pharmacies or mail-order pharmacies provide discounted services to enrollees using services, and dental specialty programs, some of which operate like an HMO while others operate more like a PPO. There are many emerging managed care arrangements for skilled care facilities, hospice programs, home health care, and rehabilitation facilities. For more information about managed care see Chapter 1: Managing the Cost of Health Care in *Fundamentals of Health Insurance: Part B*. The HIAA Insurance Education curriculum includes a two-part course on managed care.

■ Summary

The health insurance industry has enjoyed substantial growth throughout its history because of its importance to individuals and to the well-being of the national economy. The growth of group insurance plans has been influenced strongly by the numerous changing economic, social, and political forces in the past several decades. To meet consumer demands and to respond to changing demographics, health insurers have expanded—and continue to expand—the types of benefits available. Insurers also have been responsive to rising health care costs and the highly competitive marketplace by creating alternative forms of health insurance delivery to suit the needs of both the consumer and the buyer of health insurance. The health insurance business will continue to grow and change, responding to the needs of those to whom it helps provide protection and financial security.

■ Key Terms

Accident insurance

Accidental death and
dismemberment
(AD&D) policies

Administrative
services only (ASO)

Armstrong
investigation

Baylor Plan

Blue Cross/Blue Shield
plans

Competition

Dental expense
insurance

Disability income
insurance

Flexible benefit plan

Group hospital
expense benefits

Guaranteed renewable
policy

Health maintenance
organization (HMO)

Long-term care
insurance

Major medical
expense insurance

Managed health care

Medicaid

Medical expense
insurance

Medicare

National Association
of Insurance
Commissioners
(NAIC)

Noncancellable policy

Preferred provider
organization (PPO)

Riders

Self-insured

Sickness insurance

Standard Provisions
Law

Supplemental medical
insurance

Uniform Policy
Provisions Law
(UPPL)

Wagner Act

Chapter 2

THE INSURANCE INDUSTRY

■ Introduction

Despite exercising caution, people cannot completely avoid danger. Sickness, accidents, death, fire, earthquake, tornado, lightning, theft, and criminal assault are some of the hazards we face. The consequences that may result from these hazards vary from unpleasant to disastrous.

The impact of these occurrences is not only physical; there are economic consequences as well. An illness may result in thousands of dollars of health care bills. An injury may prevent a person from earning a salary for a period of several years, perhaps for a lifetime. The burning of a home may represent the loss of most of the owner's wealth. And the death of a spouse or head of the household may have long-term economic consequences for the family and loved ones.

Although the focus of this textbook is health insurance, this chapter takes a broader look at insurance. It covers the basic principles of insurance and the structure of the industry in the United States and Canada.

■ How Insurance Works

The financial loss that can result from sudden and unexpected events is minimized through the use of insurance. Insurance is a plan of risk management that, for a price, offers the insured an opportunity to share the costs of possible economic loss through an insurance company.

Insurance operates by spreading a risk over a number of people so that the many people who could have the loss, but do not, help to repay the loss of those few who do. Those who want to be protected from such losses purchase insurance from an insurer. They pay the insurer a stated amount of money called a premium. Out of the pool of funds contributed by all insured persons, the insurer pays all or a portion of the financial loss sustained by anyone who has the kind of misfortune insured against.

Principles of Insurance

Certain conditions exist that are prerequisites for the successful operation of insurance concepts. These include:

- uncertainty of loss;
- measurability, or the ability to place a dollar value on what is to be insured;
- a large number of insureds;
- a significant size of potential loss; and
- an equitable method of sharing the risk.

Uncertainty of Loss

A basic principle of insurance is the uncertainty that a loss beyond the control of the insured will occur. A sick person cannot buy insurance against hospital expenses when he or she is in an ambulance on the way to the hospital. Such a case would require the insurer to charge the insured the full amount that it would soon be called upon to pay, plus a charge for its services. Insurance is possible only for an event that is unpredictable.

Measurability of Loss

Insurers have to be able to place an exact dollar value on a loss, such as the cost of a surgical procedure or hospitalization or the damage to a car involved in a collision. If the loss is not precisely measurable, some other way must be found to establish what the insurer will pay. For example, if a person dies prematurely, it may not be possible to determine just what that person would have earned during a normal working life. In this case, the valuation is made ahead of time. The insured purchases a life insurance policy for a stated amount, such as $25,000 or $100,000, which the insurer agrees to pay in case of the insured's death.

Large Number of Insureds

Insurance is based on the concept of spreading risk across large numbers of insureds. An insurer would not want to provide health insurance if it were insuring only one person. It would have no way of knowing whether this particular person would incur a serious and costly illness. But if an insurance company covers thousands of people through group and/or individual insurance programs, it can make a reasonable estimate of the total number of people who will incur medical expenses. For example, statistics show that of 100,000 persons of a certain age, a predictable number will be hospitalized.

Significant Size of Potential Loss

The potential loss must be large enough to make a significant impact on the financial well-being of the insured. No one needs to purchase insurance to cover the cost of a ballpoint pen. If it is lost or broken, it can easily be replaced without affecting one's budget. But paying a hospital bill of several thousand dollars could bankrupt many people. Similarly, many people may never recover financially if the most valuable thing they own—a house, a car, or their earning power—is destroyed. It is against catastrophic losses that insurance is most necessary.

Some people want to have insurance to cover even a $50 loss. For someone living on a very low income, even this seemingly insignificant amount may be difficult to pay. Insurers can and do provide insurance for people who want coverage for low-cost items, but it is not a very efficient use of insurance. The insurer must collect funds from its insureds that are sufficient to cover not only the losses insured against, but also its own expenses of handling the transaction and a reasonable profit. It costs the insurer almost as much to pay a $50 claim as to pay a claim many times larger. The efficient use of premium dollars is to purchase insurance to cover potential losses that will significantly affect the insured's financial status.

Equitable Sharing

Insurers charge premiums in proportion to the risk involved. The person with a large potential loss should pay more than one whose potential loss is small.

The Concept of Risk

The term *risk* has several meanings in the insurance industry. It can identify the person being insured, the peril insured against, or the chance of loss assumed by the insurer.

An additional distinction is made between speculative risk and pure risk. A person who puts up money to start a business or invests in securities such as stocks faces a speculative risk. All or part of the investment may be lost if the business fails or the securities decline in value, but the investor really hopes to make a profit. Insurance cannot be purchased to cover the possibility that a business will lose money through its operations. The owner receives the possibility of gain in return for the risk taken. In such a case, owners rely on their skill to earn a profit rather than experience a loss.

For a pure risk there is no possibility of gain or profit. There is only the possibility of no loss, or a loss due to unforeseen and unexpected hazards beyond the control of the one for whom the risk exists. This is the kind of risk that insurance is designed to cover.

People use various methods to manage the possibility of loss that occurs in the course of everyday living. Risk management techniques include:

- elimination of the risk by avoiding its cause;
- reduction of risk by engaging in activities to prevent loss or minimize loss if it should occur;

- assumption of risk; and
- transferring all or a part of the risk to another entity, such as an insurance company, in return for payment of a premium.

Insurance Contrasted with Gambling

One final distinction needs to be made. Insurance is not gambling. Insurance, in fact, is the opposite of gambling. The gambler faces the possibility of a substantial financial loss by an illness, accident, fire, or similar unexpected event and does not purchase insurance. The way to avoid the gamble is to buy insurance. For a relatively small, budgetable premium, an insured person avoids the possibility of a big loss that could be ruinous.

■ Major Types of Insurance

There are four major types of insurance offered by the insurance industry. They usually are referred to in two categories: life and health, and property and casualty.

Life and Health Insurance

Life and health insurance is personal insurance and is available on either an individual or group basis. There are more than 2,000 life insurance companies in the United States; more than 1,000 of these companies also sell health insurance. An additional 165 property and casualty insurance companies sell health insurance as well.

Life Insurance

Life insurance is broken down into a number of types of policies. Ordinary life insurance is the most widely purchased and is available in two basic types: permanent (also known as whole life) and term. Whole life policies build up cash value and are used by many people as a way to save money. Term policies generally offer protection for a specified period of time and most do not build up cash value. Another form of life insurance, credit life insurance, may be used to pay down the balance of loans that may be outstanding if a borrower dies.

Life insurance benefits are paid to the person named as beneficiary in the event of the death of the insured. Still another form of life insurance, annuity contracts, guarantees payments to a designated party for a specific time period or for life. Annuities often are used to provide retirement income or income for a surviving spouse.

Health Insurance

Health insurance (sometimes called accident and health or sickness and accident insurance) is designed to ease the financial burden caused by adverse changes in health from either sickness or injury. Health insurance is designed to protect against the risk that health care services will be needed or that an individual will be unable to work due to an illness or injury.

Health insurance covers many health care expenses including medical, hospital, surgical, and dental expenses, and protection from loss of income while the insured is disabled.

Property and Casualty Insurance

Property and casualty insurance is designed to provide protection for actual physical items as well as liability from specific events. Both individuals and businesses purchase property and casualty insurance to protect their investments and provide protection against loss. More than 3,000 insurance companies in the United States sell some form of property and casualty insurance.

Property Insurance

Property insurance is available to protect homes and their contents, commercial and industrial buildings, equipment, furniture, fixtures, inventories, business records, supplies, automobiles, and other physical items. Under property insurance, two types of property losses are covered:

- direct (lost, stolen, damaged, or destroyed); and

- indirect (the expense of temporary housing, loss of rental income, and loss of profits).

Casualty Insurance

Casualty insurance covers liability or specific losses arising from events, accidents, or occurrences in which people are killed, injured, or become ill. Casualty insurance consists primarily of liability coverage, designed to protect against injury or damage claims made by other persons. Other forms of casualty insurance cover crime (burglary and robbery), fidelity bonds, surety bonds, boiler and machinery coverage, and aviation.

Reinsurance

Reinsurance is the method used by an insurer to reduce its liability by transferring part of the coverage for a policyholder or a block of business to another insurer. Under reinsurance (a term meaning "to insure again"), one insurer (the ceding or direct-writing insurer) purchases insurance from another insurer (the reinsurer) to cover part of the loss against which it protects its policyholder. The reinsurer is, in a sense, the silent partner of the original insurer.

The action of reinsuring does not relieve the original insurer from any of its liability for the person insured nor is the contractual right of the insured affected by reinsurance. No contract exists between the policyholder and the reinsurer. The insured individual looks to the original insurer for payment in case of loss, and the original insurer can look to its reinsurer, if one was used.

If the dollar amounts of the reinsured portion of the risk is large, the reinsurer may pass on or cede a portion of the liability it has accepted from an insurer to another reinsurer. This transaction is called retrocession. A reinsurer would choose to retrocede its business for many of the same reasons a direct-writing company would seek reinsurance.

There are two major types of reinsurance arrangements: automatic reinsurance and facultative reinsurance.

- *Automatic reinsurance* is a type of reinsurance in which the insurer must cede and the reinsuring company must accept all risks within certain contractually defined areas. For example, if the reinsurance treaty between the two insurers calls for the reinsurer to accept risks over $1,000, all cases that exceed that limit will be reinsured.

- *Facultative reinsurance* refers to a type of reinsurance in which the reinsurer can accept or reject any risk presented by an insurance company seeking reinsurance. In other words, the reinsurer has the ability to evaluate and make a determination for each risk.

Reasons for Reinsurance

The primary function of reinsurance is the transfer of risk from the ceding insurer to the reinsurer. However, the act of reinsuring all or part of a particular risk serves several other purposes. For example, reinsurance is of particular value to the small health insurer or to the insurer who just entered the field. Reinsurers provide these insurers with the benefit of their underwriting experience and help prevent wide fluctuations in operating results.

Reinsurance also enables an insurer to accept a greater variety of risks. By sharing these risks with a reinsurer, the ceding insurer obtains an adequate spread wherein the law of averages can operate. It allows the ceding company to plan for an orderly growth of business. A relatively few high amounts of major medical or long-term disability expense, for example, can turn a stable, profitable health portfolio into a losing block of business. It may take many years to make the affected coverage profitable again. Reinsurance operates to provide insurers, particularly small and medium-sized insurers, with a degree of financial stability when exposed to catastrophes or unusual loss experience.

Advantages of Reinsurance

Because certain types of insurance involve a substantial risk on one individual, reinsurance becomes a particular advantage. Although any claim may be paid out over a long period of time, the ceding insurer must set up a substantial claim reserve. Relief from both the large monthly payments, as well as the reserve obligation, can be obtained through reinsurance.

Some less well-defined and often overlooked results come from a reinsurance transaction. For example, the reinsurer can help an insurer maintain a competitive position, experiment with new coverages, and advise and assist the ceding insurer when technical problems arise. Other ways a reinsurer usually can help a ceding insurer's underwriting department are:

- classifying occupations;

- assisting in the underwriting of difficult cases;

- supplying underwriting manuals (medical and nonmedical) for insurers that do not have their own;

- recommending whether changing medical and nonmedical requirements is feasible; and

- providing training for underwriters through seminars conducted by the reinsurer.

In addition to underwriting, the reinsurer is knowledgeable about and has had experience with many types of problems involving claims, administration, actuarial science, product development, and market analysis. In recent years, reinsurers have expanded the services they offer to their partners to include such items as actuarial consulting, marketing assistance, and technology improvements. This makes the relationship between the reinsurer and the insurer even closer and provides an opportunity for both parties to grow.

Status of Health Reinsurance

There are far fewer health reinsurers than life reinsurers. The individual health reinsurance market began to develop in the 1960s, primarily because of the tremendous growth of issue limits under disability income and major medical policies. With such growth, even the largest direct insurers have elected to share or spread the risk with a reinsurer. The life reinsurance market has been around for a long time because life insurance limits historically have been high enough to warrant reinsurance.

U.S. Life and Health Insurance Industry

Life and health insurance is a major business in the United States. Its assets and the number of people it employs make important contributions to the nation's economy.

Assets

Current assets for the life and health insurance industry are nearly $2 trillion. (Approximately 95 percent of all health insurance business is conducted by life insurance companies, so the assets are reported together.) These assets are split between government securities, corporate securities (such as stocks and bonds), mortgages, real estate, and policy loans. (Table 2.1)

Number of People Employed

The insurance industry employs more than 3 million people in the United States, with 23 states having direct employment of more than 25,000 persons. The top five states correspond to the five most populous states: California, New York, Illinois, Texas, and Pennsylvania. The states that have the most insurance employment relative to their total employment are Connecticut, Nebraska, Iowa, Massachusetts, and Illinois. The majority of persons employed by the insurance industry work directly for insurance carriers. Others work for insurance agencies, brokerage operations, or other service organizations, such as rating bureaus, or are independent claims adjusters, appraisers, and loss control service providers. (Figure 2.1)

Nearly 900,000 agents, brokers, and service personnel are employed in the life and health insurance industry. Their wages added nearly $30 billion to the nation's payroll in 1992.

Table 2.1

Life and Health Insurance Company Assets

		Distribution of Assets of U.S. Life and Health Insurance Companies						
	Government	Corporate securities			Real	Policy	Misc.	
Year	securities	Bonds	Stocks	Mortgages	estate	loans	assets	Total
			AMOUNT (000,000 omitted)					
1917	562	1,975	83	2,021	179	810	311	5,941
1920	1,349	1,949	75	2,442	172	859	474	7,320
1925	1,311	3,022	81	4,808	266	1,446	604	11,538
1930	1,502	4,929	519	7,598	548	2,807	977	18,880
1935	4,727	5,314	583	5,357	1,990	3,540	1,705	23,216
1940	8,447	8,645	605	5,972	2,065	3,091	1,977	30,802
1945	22,545	10,060	999	6,636	857	1,962	1,738	44,797
1950	16,118	23,248	2,103	16,102	1,445	2,413	2,591	64,020
1955	11,829	35,912	3,633	29,445	2,581	3,290	3,742	90,432
1960	11,815	46,740	4,981	41,771	3,765	5,231	5,273	119,576
1965	11,908	58,244	9,126	60,013	4,681	7,678	7,234	158,884
1970	11,068	73,098	15,420	74,375	6,320	16,064	10,909	207,254
1975	15,177	105,837	28,061	89,167	9,621	24,467	16,974	289,304
1980	33,015	179,603	47,366	131,080	15,033	41,411	31,702	479,210
1981	39,502	193,806	47,670	137,747	18,278	48,706	40,094	525,803
1982	55,516	212,772	55,730	141,989	20,624	52,961	48,571	588,163
1983	76,615	232,123	64,868	150,999	22,234	54,063	54,046	654,948
1984	99,769	259,128	63,335	156,699	25,767	54,505	63,776	722,979
1985	124,598	296,848	77,496	171,797	28,822	54,369	71,971	825,901
1986	144,616	341,967	90,864	193,842	31,615	54,055	80,592	937,551
1987	151,436	405,674	96,515	213,450	34,172	53,626	89,586	1,044,459
1988	159,781	480,313	104,373	232,863	37,371	54,236*	97,933	1,166,870
1989	178,141	538,063	125,614	254,215	39,908	57,439	106,376	1,299,756
1990	210,846	582,597	128,484	270,109	43,367	62,603	110,202	1,408,208
1991	269,490	623,515	164,515	265,258	46,711	66,364	115,348	1,551,201
1992	320,109	670,206	192,403	246,702	50,595	72,058	112,458	1,664,531
1993	384,124	729,729	251,885	229,061	54,249	77,725	112,354	1,839,127
1994	395,580	790,559	281,816	215,332	53,813	85,499	119,674	1,942,273
1995	409,304	869,112	371,867	211,815	52,437	95,939	133,070	2,143,544

NOTE: Excludes some $600 million of policy loans securitized during 1988.
SOURCES: Spectator Year Book and American Council of Life Insurance.

Major Types of Ownership

The two most common types of commercial insurance companies are stock companies and mutual companies. A third source for insurance is fraternal societies.

In 1994 out of 1,745 life and health insurance companies in business, 94 percent were stock companies. (Table 2.2) Although there are

41

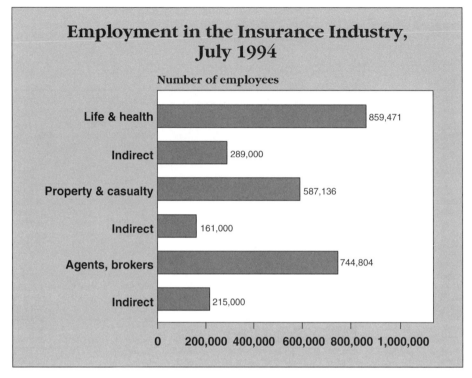

Figure 2.1

NOTE: In addition to the 2,191,411 direct employees in the industry there are 665,000 indirect employees, bringing the total industry employment figure up to 2,856,411.
SOURCE: Alliance of American Insurers, 1993.

Table 2.2

Number of U.S. Life and Health Insurance Companies in Business, Year-End, 1994

Years in business	Stock	Mutual	Total
100 years or more	10	20	31
50–100 years	128	34	162
25–50 years	504	37	541
Less than 25 years	996	15	1011
Total	1,639	106	1,745

SOURCE: American Council of Life Insurance.

significantly more stock insurance companies than mutual insurance companies in the United States, mutual companies account for approximately half of the life insurance in force, as many of the largest life insurance companies are mutual.

Stock Insurers

In a stock insurance company, the legal ownership and control is vested in the people who purchased shares of the company's stock or the stockholders. Stock purchases represent ownership in a company. The percentage of ownership that one person holds is determined by the number of shares of stock that person owns compared with the number of shares that have been issued. The stockholders share in the earnings of the company by receiving periodic (usually quarterly) payments called dividends. The size of the dividend is dependent on the number of shares an individual owns and the most recent performance of the company.

A stock insurance company is formed to sell various kinds of insurance with the expectation of profits for the stockholders who own and control the insurer. The organizing stockholders put up the necessary funds to start the insurer. A new stock insurance company must have a certain amount of capital and a certain amount of surplus funds. In most states, the minimum capital required for a stock company planning to write health insurance falls in the range of $100,000 to $1,000,000. In addition, the company must have surplus funds, in some cases up to 200 percent of the minimum capital. Well-financed stock insurance companies have an initial capital and surplus considerably in excess of the required minimum.

Stock insurers are in business to make a profit for their stockholders. As a percentage of premium, the profit does not have to be very large. However, an anticipated profit should be considered when determining premium rates.

Mutual Insurers

A mutual company has no stockholders. The ownership and control of a mutual insurance company is vested in its policyholders. Each policy owner is eligible to vote in elections of the company's board of directors and receives one vote per person, regardless of the number of policies owned or the amount of insurance purchased.

Almost all mutual insurers that now exist were organized originally as stock companies and later mutualized. This was done by the purchase of outstanding stock with surplus funds accumulated by the insurer. Before a mutual insurance company can be organized, it must have a minimum number of applications accompanied by premiums and a minimum amount of surplus funds. In some states, the requirements to form a mutual insurer are so strict that it is now virtually impossible to form a new mutual company.

Mutual insurers do not look for profit in the same manner as a stock insurer. However, they have surplus similar to the capital account of a stock insurer. The surplus is the amount set aside as a margin of safety, above the insurer's known liabilities, to guarantee the solvency and continuity of the organization through any conceivable adverse circumstances. The size of the surplus determines, to some extent, how much new business the insurer may write. It also is a measure of the financial strength and stability of the insurer.

For these reasons, mutual insurers try to have some degree of growth in their surplus. An allowance for addition to surplus can be put into premium rates in the same manner as profits are included for stock companies. After a mutual insurer's surplus has reached its optimum size, any excess amounts can be returned to the company's policyholders as dividends.

Changing Type of Ownership

A company can choose to change its ownership from a stock insurance company to a mutual insurance company and vice versa. There are a number of legal and regulatory requirements necessary to accomplish such a change, and the state insurance departments have specific rules about what needs to be done. The process can be expensive and may require a great deal of time to be invested.

If they change type of ownership, most insurance companies today switch from mutual to stock. Mutual insurers convert to a stock form by a process called demutualization. This change of ownership gives the new company several advantages:

- *Greater flexibility to buy and operate other types of companies.* If a mutual company buys a different type of company, that company must conform with regulations that affect a mutual insurance company. This is not necessarily true with a stock insurance company.

- *Increase in capital.* Companies can increase their capital by selling additional shares of stock. This enables them to buy other companies by having more resources available for such purchases. Mutual companies are more limited in the ways that they can use their surplus.

- *Greater flexibility in attracting top-level employees.* Having stock allows the company to offer stock options or shares of company stock as part of the overall compensation package.

- *Reduction in the tax burden.* Recent changes in the corporate income tax structure have placed a potentially higher tax burden on mutual insurance companies.

The disadvantages of demutualization generally lie with the cost of accomplishing such a conversion, the equitable distribution of the mutual company's surplus among policy owners, and the variation of state regulations on such a process.

Although it was once popular for stock insurance companies to convert to mutual companies, this happens with much less frequency today. The driving force behind converting to a mutual company is to have more control over the operations of the company and to be free from the demands of the stockholders.

Fraternal Societies

In addition to stock and mutual companies, fraternal societies may provide insurance for their members. Fraternal societies are social organizations. Separate laws govern the activities of fraternal societies, and the insurance is available only to members of the society. The purpose of the laws governing fraternal societies is generally the same as those governing mutual and stock companies: to ensure that the organization has the financial capacity to meet all of its insurance commitments.

Blue Cross and Blue Shield Plans

Development. With few exceptions, Blue Cross and Blue Shield plans were established starting in the 1930s as nonprofit hospital and physician prepayment service plans, not as insurance companies. Blue Cross plans were also established in Puerto Rico, Jamaica, and Canada. Blue Cross plans sponsored by local hospital groups and Blue Shield plans sponsored by local physician groups were established separately from, and, in some cases, in direct competition with, each other.

The prepaid service plan approach, when strictly implemented, assured subscribers of specific health service benefits rather than indemnification for medical expenses incurred.

In many cases, Blue Cross and Blue Shield plans enjoyed unique advantages, such as:

- preferential tax status, and

- favorable reimbursement agreements with hospitals and doctors.

In return, plans were expected periodically to offer coverage to individuals using lowered medical underwriting requirements in a practice known as "open enrollment." The same rates often were charged to subscribers regardless of their risk categories or group experience, a practice that became known as "community rating."

Also, the plans vested unique authority in their national trade associations, which became the Blue Cross and Blue Shield Association in 1982 after the merger of the Blue Cross Association and the National Association of Blue Shield Plans.

The Blue Cross and Blue Shield Association:

- licenses the local plans to use the Blue Cross and Blue Shield names and symbols and requires compliance with certain organizational, operational, and product/service standards;

- assists with the marketing of Blue Cross plan services to large national employer groups with multistate locations, thereby requiring the participation and cooperation of the local independent plans; and

■ serves as the contractor with the federal government on behalf of the individual plans.

Evolution. In more recent years, Blue Cross and Blue Shield plans have undergone significant changes, which seem to have removed many of the operational characteristics that had distinguished them from insurance companies. As a result, in 1986, Congress withdrew the Blue Cross exemption from federal income tax. Depending on state law, plans began to pay a greater share of the local, state, and premium taxes.

Blue Cross and Blue Shield plans have undergone merger and consolidation, with the over 100 independent plans existing in the 1980s having been reduced to approximately 60. That trend continues.

The organizational framework of many plans has also begun to change to allow better access to capital markets and regulatory flexibility in operations and product offerings in response to the current managed care business climate.

Today, some plans have become mutual insurance companies, while others operate publicly traded companies for their managed care and insurance business. Still others are converting to investor-owned status. Merger activities have continued at a new stage as larger plans have merged with other Plans across state lines or with commercial insurers to form regional health care conglomerates.

■ Canadian Life and Health Insurance Industry

The Canadian insurance industry differs in several important ways from the U.S. insurance industry, mostly because of the different roles of the two countries' governments concerning insurance matters. The Canadian government does not regulate the insurance industry as heavily as does the United States; in fact, the Canadian system is highly self-regulated.

However, a government-administered health care system dominates the health insurance market in Canada, whereas the United States does not have such a system. Each of the provinces in Canada provides its residents with a comprehensive program of hospitalization and medical expense coverage. These universal plans are funded by a combination of grants from provincial and federal governments, direct or general tax revenues, and, in most provinces, a small premium. Private health insurance is available and may be used to meet the needs not met by the government coverage.

Assets

In 1994 the total assets held in Canada on behalf of Canadian life and health insurance policyholders amounted to $176.3 billion. Of that total, $166 billion was held on behalf of life insurance policyholders and annuitants. The remainder was held for health insurance policyholders.

Stocks and bonds are major components of the Canadian life and health insurance industry's total asset portfolio. The industry also is a major source of financing for Canadian governments. Twenty-three percent of total assets was held in government bonds and treasury bills, with the majority held at the federal level. (Table 2.3)

Canada has a higher proportion of mutual insurance companies to stock insurance companies than the United States. The 1957 amendment to the federal Canadian and British Insurance Companies Act provided a specific procedure for mutualization, or the process of changing from a stock company to a mutual company. Canadian stock companies were encouraged to become mutual companies to avoid being taken over by foreign companies. Because mutual companies have no stock to sell, a mutual company cannot be bought by another company as easily as a stock company can. Many Canadian companies successfully avoided takeovers by foreign companies by the process of mutualization.

In 1994 nearly 100,000 people worked in the life and health insurance business in Canada.

Regulation

There is a distinct difference between the United States and Canada in the way the insurance business is regulated. Regulation of the insurance

Table 2.3

Assets of Life and Health Insurance Companies in Canada (Millions)

End of year	Bonds	Stocks	Mortgage loans	Real estate	Policy loans	Cash	Other assets	Total
1960	$ 4,064	$ 257	$ 3,108	$ 294	$ 356	$ 54	$ 223	$ 8,356
1970	5,909	1,108	6,914	737	799	166	357	15,990
1980	17,178	5,814	16,942	1,862	1,950	804	1,695	46,245
1981	19,349	5,733	18,262	2,369	2,499	1,204	2,152	51,568
1982	21,915	6,285	19,271	2,969	2,697	1,467	2,615	57,219
1983	24,677	7,966	20,857	3,557	2,681	1,069	2,773	63,580
1984	29,737	8,232	21,641	3,805	2,660	1,311	3,339	70,725
1985	35,488	8,990	23,825	4,022	2,661	1,554	3,735	80,275
1986	37,967	10,369	27,718	4,098	2,658	1,638	4,016	88,464
1987	40,398	11,055	31,227	4,644	2,665	1,896	4,605	96,490
1988	44,463	12,397	35,582	5,245	2,735	1,823	5,786	108,031
1989	46,867	14,458	41,934	6,035	2,804	1,841	6,680	120,619
1990	51,247	14,159	46,873	6,716	2,902	2,231	6,734	130,862
1991	58,301	16,967	50,099	7,954	3,056	1,922	6,769	145,068
1992	64,170	20,103	51,868	10,084	3,013	3,343	6,733	159,314
1993	69,762	23,068	52,308	10,317	3,071	6,083	6,586	171,195
1994	75,753	23,138	50,118	10,245	3,181	7,129	6,735	176,299

NOTES: Assets invested in Canada on behalf of foreign policyholders are excluded. Assets held in segregated funds are included.

SOURCES: Reports of the Superintendent of Financial Institutions, Ottawa; Canadian Life and Health Insurance Association.

business in the United States is in the hands of the states. (For more information about U.S. regulation see Chapter 5: Regulation of Health Insurance, in *Fundamentals of Health Insurance: Part B*.) In Canada regulation of the insurance business has been a joint function of the federal and provincial governments almost since the confederation of the provinces.

The British North America Act, passed by the British Parliament in 1867, is the law that provided for the formation of the Dominion of Canada. Among other things, the act divided up the powers between the federal government and the provinces. The founders of the Canadian confederation seemed to believe that the U.S. Civil War gave evidence of weakness of the federal government of the United States. To avoid this problem, they provided for a strong central government in the Dominion.

The federal government was given jurisdiction over 16 areas of regulation, including property and civil rights, provincial company charters,

49

municipal governments, and direct taxation within the provinces for provincial purposes. All residual powers—that is, those not specifically enumerated—were vested in the federal government. The federal government also received power to disallow any provincial legislation it believed to be undesirable.

Since 1867 court decisions have weakened the power of the federal government and strengthened the power of the provinces. While these decisions have created an overlapping of jurisdiction of the federal government and provincial governments in the control of the insurance business, there is not any real or substantial problem in this regard. The Canada Act of 1982, which superseded the British North America Act of 1867, did not materially affect the regulation of insurance in Canada.

Responsibility and Supervisory Control

The responsibility and supervisory control of the Canadian insurance industry is split between the federal and provincial governments.

Federal Government Role

The federal government licenses all federally incorporated Canadian insurers and all non-Canadian insurers doing business in Canada. Although the insurance companies doing business solely within the boundaries of a given province may be licensed to do business within that province without getting a federal license, most companies of that type have voluntarily submitted to federal jurisdiction. The federal government inspects insurance companies licensed by it and administers legislation concerning the deposits, solvency, and valuation of assets and liabilities of these companies. At the specific request of the Nova Scotia government, the federal government supervises all Nova Scotian provincial insurance companies.

Provincial Government Role

The provinces have the sole responsibility for legislation regarding the form of the insurance contract, advertising and consumer protection, and the licensing and regulation of agents, brokers, and adjusters. The provinces also supervise and assume responsibility for inspections relating to the solvency of insurers that are not registered with the federal government.

All insurers must be licensed by each province (except Nova Scotia) in which they operate, whether they hold a federal license or not. As part of the licensing process, the provinces require the filing of documents of incorporation. After that, the insurer must file an annual statement showing its business in the given province. The provinces do not inspect or require deposits from those insurers that are licensed by the federal government. However, because of the prestige attached to federal registry, many insurers get federal licenses even though their business is limited to one or two provinces.

■ Emerging Trends

There are three major trends in the insurance industry: mergers, joint ventures, and changes in the ability to sell insurance products.

Mergers

Insurers are merging with other insurers and acquiring existing insurance companies in an effort to:

- build scale in core businesses, and
- divest nonstrategic operations.

Especially in a mature market such as life insurance, merging with or acquiring another insurer may be the means to gain market share and survive in an increasingly competitive environment. This may be especially true of mutual companies that need to improve their competitive position relative to their stock counterparts.

The most recent activity has focused on mutual insurers as they seek to improve their competitive standing and often are faced with two choices—merge or tap into the capital market. However, organization as a stock company may facilitate the merger of companies since the stock of one company can be bought by another. Mergers and acquisitions also are driven by the need to reduce expenses in mature lines and refocus efforts in areas that are perceived as high growth sectors.

The level of mergers and acquisitions in the health and managed care arena has increased dramatically. This type of merger reflects an evolution in the marketplace, with the stronger health maintenance organizations (HMOs) acquiring smaller organizations. Through such mergers and acquisitions, the acquiring HMO increases its presence in an existing marketplace.

Additionally, some HMOs are speeding their growth by expanding their product line through the acquisition of traditional health benefit plan business, as well as companies specializing in nontraditional products, such as workers' compensation and disability insurance. Such actions bring managed care savings to these markets as well as more traditional health care.

Joint Ventures

Joint ventures have been part of the insurance industry for a long period of time. In each case an insurer forms a relationship with another entity to provide a service or product or reach a market that the insurer cannot either provide or reach alone; joint ventures can also come about when an insurer wants to leverage off the expertise of another entity.

There has been a proliferation of new types of joint ventures or alliances, including:

- insurers outsourcing certain functions to other insurers or firms specializing in functions such as administration, investment, or underwriting;
- geographic alliances between North American insurers and local companies to start up operations in other countries, particularly in developing companies; and
- private labeling of specialty products, such as long-term care, disability income, or term insurance.

As a result of the increased competition for the consumer's dollar and the investment squeeze, many insurers have realized that they do not have the resources to keep operating as full-service insurance companies. Leaders in each insurance company must reexamine their market position and decide which lines represent core competencies and should be continued and which are peripheral or represent areas where there is a lack of knowledge and skills. Alliances with other entities may provide the answer to these areas of weakness.

With the fast pace of change and the challenging environment the insurance industry is experiencing, joint ventures represent one way to continue to provide all lines while leveraging the competencies of others. In coming years more and more joint ventures are likely as companies seek to take maximum advantage of their own strengths and to form partnerships that will enhance their ability to grow and prosper.

Right to Sell Insurance

Insurers historically have been virtually the only provider of insurance benefits. Recent rulings of the courts have opened the door to expand the ability of banks to sell insurance products. Although questions remain about the regulation of banks in the sale of insurance and the ability to protect consumers, the trend is toward expanding the power of the banks to provide additional insurance.

■ Summary

The U.S. insurance industry has nearly $2 trillion in assets and provides coverage for protection against a wide range of risks, including life, health, property, and casualty. Insurers generally are organized as either a stock insurance company or a mutual insurance company. In recent years the trend has been for mutual companies to demutualize and convert to stock ownership, primarily due to the ability to raise additional capital.

As risks grow larger, more insurance transactions involve reinsurers, who agree to cover a portion of the risk for the original insurer. Reinsurance has many benefits, especially when the ceding insurer also can make use of the expertise of the reinsurer in matters such as underwriting and risk management.

The U.S. insurance industry is highly regulated at the state level. The Canadian insurance industry, which has $176 billion in assets, differs significantly in the way it is regulated. Except for health insurance, which is provided by the provinces, the government does not play a large role. Private health insurance is used to cover needs not met by the provincial plans.

■ Key Terms

Accident and health
Acquisition
Agency system
Annuity
Automatic reinsurance
Beneficiary
Blue Cross and Blue
   Shield plans
British North America
   Act
Canadian insurance
   industry
Cash value
Casualty insurance
Ceding insurer

Credit life insurance
Demutualization
Dividends
Facultative
   reinsurance
Fraternal societies
Health maintenance
   organization (HMO)
Insurance
Joint venture
Licensing
Life insurance
Merger
Mutual insurance
   company

Policyholders
Property insurance
Pure risk
Reinsurance
Retrocession
Risk
Speculative risk
Stockholders
Stock insurance
   company
Surplus funds
U.S. insurance
   industry
Valuation
Whole life

Chapter 3

HEALTH INSURANCE COVERAGES

■ Introduction

Everyone faces the risk of a costly serious illness or injury. Health insurance protects individuals or families by providing for the payment of benefits for losses that occur as a result of such illnesses or injuries.

Health care involves a wide range of facilities, services, and supplies. Coverage against these expenses varies, and there are many different plans offered in the marketplace. Operating in a competitive market, the private health insurance industry has developed a wide range of health insurance coverages to meet consumers' needs.

This chapter discusses health insurance coverages under the broad categories of medical expenses, supplemental expenses, disability income expenses, and long-term care expenses.

■ Medical Expense Coverage

Insurers offer medical expense coverage in both the group and individual markets. The purpose of medical expense coverage is to protect an individual insured, and members of that insured's family when applicable, from eligible medical care costs. The two major types of medical expense coverage are major medical and hospital-surgical plans.

Major Medical Insurance

Major medical insurance plans provide broad coverage and substantial protection from large, unpredictable, and therefore, unbudgetable medical care expenses. They cover most medical expenses up to a high maximum benefit. These plans may contain internal limits on benefits identified on a per procedure, service category, or confinement basis and usually are subject to a deductible and coinsurance.

There are two basic major medical mechanisms for reimbursing covered expenses: supplemental and comprehensive. Comprehensive major medical is used more frequently.

Supplemental Major Medical Insurance

Supplemental major medical insurance covers certain expenses initially left unpaid by a basic plan of hospital-surgical-medical benefits. After satisfying the deductible, the supplemental major medical plan pays the remaining covered expenses, usually on a percentage basis (e.g., 80 percent). The total cost to the insured is the amount of the deductible plus the percentage of expenses not reimbursed under the major medical formula.

Comprehensive Major Medical

A comprehensive major medical plan uses one reimbursement formula for total covered expenses without distinguishing between those expenses that would otherwise be covered under a basic plan and those expenses to be covered as major medical expense benefits. An example of a comprehensive major medical plan is one that provides reimbursement of 80 percent of all combined covered expenses in a calendar year, after a deductible of $500 or $1,000, up to a maximum benefit limit of $1 million.

The main features of comprehensive major medical are simplicity of plan design and avoidance of overlapping coverages. The size, type, and application of the deductible; full coverage of certain expenses; and a dollar limit on out-of-pocket expenses to be borne by the insured are decided by the group policyholder and the underwriting practices of the insurer.

Features of Major Medical Plans

Both supplemental and comprehensive plans have common provisions, such as deductibles, coinsurance, overall maximum benefits, and covered expenses. Many types of medical care services and supplies—from the professional services of physicians, osteopaths, and other recognized medical practitioners to physical therapy—are common to all types of plans. In addition, plans may provide coverage of expenses incurred in skilled nursing facilities as well as home health care expenses and hospice care expenses.

Deductible

A deductible is the amount of covered expenses that must be incurred and paid by the insured before benefits become payable by the insurer. The primary purpose of a deductible is to lower premium costs by avoiding unnecessary utilization and eliminating small claims and the expense of handling them.

In conjunction with a deductible is an accumulation period. This is the period of time during which incurred medical care expenses accumulate sufficiently to satisfy the deductible.

Common deductibles are the all cause, per cause, corridor, and integrated types.

All cause deductible. The all cause deductible includes all expenses incurred, regardless of the number of illnesses or accidents, that are accumulated to satisfy the deductible. The calendar year (January 1 to December 31) is used almost universally as the accumulation period for

57

the all cause deductible. The all cause deductible approach is simple to administer and is considered the easiest for the insured to understand.

Per cause deductible. The per cause deductible is the flat amount that the insured must pay toward eligible medical expenses resulting from each illness or accident before the insurance company makes any benefit payments. The benefit period for each cause starts with the first expense that is used to satisfy the deductible and normally ends one or two years after the date it starts.

Once the benefit period ends, the deductible must be satisfied again to start a new benefit period for that cause. Under the per cause approach, small claims for minor, unrelated illnesses or accidents often are eliminated.

Corridor deductible. This deductible is used with supplemental major medical plans. It operates as a corridor between the basic plan and the major medical plan. Medical expenses that exceed the amounts covered in the basic plan are covered in the supplemental major medical plan after the corridor deductible is satisfied.

Integrated deductible. Less common than the corridor deductible is an integrated deductible that is the greater of a fairly high amount, such as $1,000, or the basic plan benefits. For example, if the basic plan paid $1,500, a $1,000 deductible automatically would be satisfied and supplemental benefits would be payable. On the other hand, if the basic plan only paid $700, then $300 would be needed to satisfy the $1,000 deductible before supplemental medical benefits would be payable.

Coinsurance

Coinsurance is the arrangement by which the insurer and the insured share a percentage of covered losses after the deductible is met. For every dollar of covered expenses incurred after the deductible, the insurer typically pays 80 cents and insured pays 20 cents. Many plans apply a dollar limit (e.g., $1,000) to the coinsurance to be borne by the insured during any one calendar year. In managed care plans, however, the term *coinsurance* refers to the amount, usually five or ten dollars, paid by the patient at the time service is rendered by a participating provider. Coinsurance is used to control plan costs, to retain the insured's financial interest in the cost of services, and to curtail unnecessary utilization of services.

Overall Maximum

Each major medical policy has a maximum benefit limit payable by the insurer. The maximum may be written as lifetime (all cause) or per cause.

Covered Expenses

Major medical plans provide coverage for specified medical care services and supplies. The following are common to most types of plans:

■ professional services of physicians and other recognized medical practitioners;

■ hospital charges for semi-private room and board and other necessary services and supplies;

■ physical therapy;

■ routine nursing care;

■ ambulatory surgical center;

■ anesthetics and their administration;

■ diagnostic X-rays and laboratory procedures;

■ X-ray or radium treatments;

■ mammography screening;

■ oxygen and other medicinal or therapeutic gases and their administration;

■ blood transfusions, including the cost of blood (when not replaced by blood donors);

■ drugs and medicines requiring a physician's prescription;

■ local ambulance service;

■ rental of durable medical equipment required for therapeutic use;

- artificial limbs or other prosthetic appliances, except replacement of such appliances;

- casts, splints, trusses, braces, and crutches; and

- rental of a wheelchair or hospital-type bed.

General Exclusions and Limitations

Plans also exclude or limit services and supplies. A provision that eliminates coverage for a certain risk is called an exclusion; one that limits coverage in a particular area is called a limitation. The limitation for dental benefits, for example, often is expressed on a lifetime or per-year basis.

Medical expense plans commonly exclude or limit benefits for the following:

- care received from any government or by any government agency;

- occupational accidents and sickness;

- cosmetic surgery;

- pre-existing conditions;

- dental care and treatment;

- jaw joint disorders;

- eye refractions and the purchase or fitting of eyeglasses or hearing aids;

- transportation (except for local ambulance service);

- health examinations or periodic check-ups;

- mental or nervous disorders;

- custodial care;

- body manipulation and subluxation;

- charges beyond allowable benefit amounts;

- elective items; and

- injuries incurred in a war, declared or undeclared, including armed aggression or resistance to aggression.

Hospital-Surgical Insurance

Insurers sell many different hospital-surgical policies, which vary considerably in the expenses covered and the degree to which they are covered. The most complete policies include:

- daily room and board;
- miscellaneous hospital expense;
- outpatient, diagnostic X-ray, and lab expense;
- surgical expense;
- maternity expense; and
- physician's in-hospital expense.

Daily Room and Board

A major expense of hospital confinement is that of daily room and board and general nursing care. This benefit generally is considered the basic benefit provision in a hospital-surgical policy. The wide variety of daily maximums offered by insurers enables an insured to select a policy that adequately meets the insured's individual or family needs. Such needs will vary depending on where the insured lives. Most insurers have moved away from the concept of stated room and board maximums (e.g., $100 a day) by reimbursing on the basis of the hospital's actual charges for a semi-private room.

Miscellaneous Hospital Expense

Hospital charges for necessary services and supplies (other than daily room and board) furnished during a period of inpatient confinement are covered by the miscellaneous hospital expense provision. The most common services and supplies include:

- laboratory services;
- X-ray examinations;
- medicines and drugs;
- surgical dressings; and
- operating room.

Table 3.1

Surgical Schedule

Cardiovascular system	Percentage of maximum surgical benefit
Repair of heart valve, mitral	32.0
Aortic, pulmonic or tricuspid	50.0
Catheterization of heart, independent procedure	4.0
Double valve procedure, replacement and/or repair by valvuloplasty or replacement	70.0
Triple valve procedure, replacement and/or repair	80.0
Excision and graft, thoracic aorta	48.0
Repair aneurysm of aorta	56.0
Aortography	2.7
Coronary angioplasty (endarterectomy, arterial implantation, or anastomosis, with bypass)	60.0

In addition, the miscellaneous hospital expense provision usually covers charges by the hospital for specialized services rendered by certain hospital-employed professionals, such as pathologists, radiologists, and anesthetists. Charges for professional ambulance service sometimes are covered under this provision.

Outpatient, Diagnostic X-ray, and Lab Expense

Many physicians' offices are well-equipped for the routine X-ray and laboratory examinations that aid in diagnosing a particular condition. The maximum amount payable under this provision can be limited to $200 or $500 for any one illness or injury. However, some policies may allow reimbursement up to the maximum benefit, which is often several thousand dollars.

Surgical Expense

This coverage provides benefits for the charges of a physician for surgical operations. One major element of this provision is the surgical schedule for common surgical procedures. It lists cash or unit allowances up to a maximum amount an insurer will reimburse, based on the severity of the operation. (Table 3.1)

62

Surgical benefits are paid regardless of where the surgery is performed. Much surgery today is performed on an outpatient basis in a freestanding surgical center or a physician's office and does not require an overnight stay in a hospital. The patient does not have to be confined to a hospital for the surgical benefits to be covered.

Most policies require a second surgical opinion for elective inpatient and outpatient surgery. If the patient has elective surgery without seeking a second opinion, the plan may not pay the surgical benefit or may reimburse the surgical benefit at a lower level.

Maternity Expense

The hospital-surgical policy often covers part of an insured's maternity expense. The benefit may be included automatically or offered as optional coverage. The typical maternity benefit has provided coverage only if conception occurred more than a certain number of days, usually thirty, after the policy's effective date. Alternatively, maternity benefits have been subject to a waiting period of ten months from the policy's effective date.

Some states have enacted legislation mandating that maternity be covered just as any other illness or health condition. The new federal Health Insurance Portability and Accountability Act of 1996 prohibits the use of any type of waiting period specific to maternity benefits.

Physician's In-Hospital Expense

The physician's in-hospital expense benefit provision reimburses for a physician's charges for nonsurgical treatment received during hospital confinement. Policies limit the amount payable for such services to a stated amount for each visit by a physician, with a limit usually on the number of visits that will be paid during one period of confinement.

Eligible Expenses

As with major medical plans, hospital-surgical policies contain definitions of eligible expenses and usual and customary charges for them.

They also contain exclusions and limitations. Many of the exclusions are similar for hospital-surgical policies. The common ones are pre-existing conditions, intentionally self-inflicted injuries, and injuries incurred during full-time active military duty or a war.

■ Supplemental Coverages

Insurers offer supplemental health coverages in both the group and individual markets. This coverage provides peace of mind for insureds, who know that they are covered for unforeseen expenses related to an illness or injury. Supplemental coverages are designed to:

- fill the gaps of medical expense coverages (e.g., deductibles, coinsurance, maximum out-of-pocket expenses);
- provide additional benefits, such as dental, prescription drugs, and vision coverage; and
- cover additional expenses as a result of a severe accident or illness.

The following supplemental coverages are described: hospital indemnity, dental, prescription drug, vision, accidental death and dismemberment, accident medical expense, specified disease, Medicare supplement, and travel accident insurance.

Hospital Indemnity Insurance

Hospital indemnity coverage pays benefits for each day the insured is confined in a hospital. This type of protection usually is offered as optional supplemental coverage to group or individual medical expense insurance. Benefits are paid from the first day of hospital confinement, for either a sickness or injury. The maximum benefit period is generally three, six, or 12 months.

The benefit normally is stated in a flat dollar amount per day, week, or month. Indemnity amounts range from $100 to $400 per day. Hospital indemnity benefits usually are paid in addition to any other benefits. Consumers purchase this type of protection to guard against significant out-of-pocket expenses from their major medical coverage, and to provide extra income when hospitalized to help pay for items such as child care expenses and noncovered charges.

Dental Insurance

Dental benefits provide reimbursement for expenses of dental services and supplies, including preventive care. The major classifications of dental services include:

- diagnostic;
- preventive;
- restorative (including fillings, inlays, and crowns);
- prosthodontics (installment and maintenance of bridgework);
- oral surgery;
- periodontics or endodontics (treatment of gums); and
- orthodontics (straightening treatment).

Benefits may be provided through a plan integrated with other medical expense insurance coverages, or a plan may be written separately from other coverages (nonintegrated or stand-alone).

Integrated Plans

Dental expenses under an integrated plan are blended into the covered expenses of a major medical benefits plan. Generally, coverage is on a usual and customary or nonscheduled basis. The deductible must be satisfied each calendar year by either or both medical and dental care expenses. The amount payable for dental and medical care expenses usually is subject to the same coinsurance percentage. Sometimes dental care expenses are separated into classes or categories of services (restorative, prosthodontics, orthodontics, and so forth), and a different coinsurance level is applied to each class.

Nonintegrated Plans

Dental expenses under a nonintegrated plan are covered separately on either a scheduled or a nonscheduled basis. Whether a nonintegrated

Table 3.2

Nonscheduled Dental Expense Plan

Calendar Year Maximum—$1,000, Calendar Year Deductible—$50
Preventive and Diagnostic Services—100% reimbursement (no deductible)
Diagnostic: Oral exams, tests and lab exams, emergency treatment
Preventive: Prophylaxis, fluoride treatments, space maintainers

Basic Services—80% reimbursement (20% payable by insured)
Radiographs, basic restoration (amalgam, silicate, acrylic), endodontics, peridontics, prosthodontics (maintenance), oral surgery, anesthesia

Major Services—60% reimbursement (40% payable by insured)
Major restoration (gold foil, gold inlays, porcelain, crowns), prosthodontics (installation)

Lifetime Maximum Amount—$1,000
Orthodontics—50% reimburement (50% payable by the insured)

dental plan is scheduled or nonscheduled, dental services often are classified so that different deductibles, coinsurance, and maximums benefits can be used for each class.

Scheduled. A schedule of dental services, similar to a surgical schedule, lists specific procedures. Reimbursement toward the dentist's charges is up to the amount specified in the schedule for each procedure. To avoid inadequate or excessive benefits, the amounts vary according to the level of charges in different areas of the country.

Nonscheduled. Nonscheduled dental plans provide reimbursement toward the dentist's charges for all covered dental services on a usual and customary basis, similar to an integrated plan. (Table 3.2)

Features of Dental Plans

Both integrated and nonintegrated dental plans have common provisions, such as deductibles, coinsurance, and maximum benefits.

Deductibles. In most plans a deductible must be satisfied by each individual during each calendar year. To encourage preventive care, even if the rest of the plan has a deductible it is not applied to preventive and diagnostic services.

66

Coinsurance.   Most dental plans are designed with some percentage of the dentist's charge to be paid by the insured to maintain interest in the cost of service provided and to avoid overutilization. Because orthodontics is a high-cost service and benefit, it usually is an option available to the policyholder. Because of the danger of adverse selection, it generally is paid at a reimbursement rate of 50 percent. Reimbursement on all other classes of dental care services may vary from 50 percent to 80 percent, the insured paying the greater percentage of the cost of major procedures than of basic procedures.

Maximum benefit.   Some nonintegrated dental programs are designed with a lifetime maximum for orthodontic benefits and include a calendar year or policy year maximum on all other dental care services. Some plans also place a lifetime maximum on periodontal care.

Limitations and Exclusions

The frequency with which certain services will be provided under a dental care expense policy is often limited. For example, typically no more than two dental cleanings and one fluoride treatment will be covered in any 12 consecutive months. Bridgework or dentures will not be replaced within a five-year period except under specific circumstances. Replacement of teeth missing prior to the effective date of the dental plan may be excluded entirely or covered at a reduced reimbursement rate.

Services performed solely for cosmetic purposes generally are excluded, as are those considered experimental. No payment is made for charges for oral hygiene instruction, missed appointments, or completion of claim forms.

Prescription Drug Insurance

Prescription drug insurance covers drugs and medicines purchased on the order of a physician, with very little or no cost to the insured. Most plans are offered through an employer on a group basis. There are two basic plans: reimbursement and service.

Reimbursement Plans

Reimbursement plans rely on the individual to pay for the prescription drugs and to submit these expenses to the insurer on a claim form completed by the pharmacist or the insured for the insurer. Payment is made to the individual based on the insurer's determination of usual and customary charges.

Service Plans

Service plans refer to a system in which payment by the insurer is made directly to the provider for the service or product covered by the insurance policy without the insured having to file a claim. Prescription drugs involve a large number of small claims and need extensive networks of participating pharmacies. Third-party administrators generally manage the plans for insurance companies because they can minimize costs through high volume and standardized forms and procedures.

Mail-order prescription drug programs also provide the insured the convenience of obtaining maintenance medication through the mail. These plans provide a 60- or 90-day supply of drugs and require the insured to make a copayment. Copayments range between $5 and $15.

Limitations and Exclusions

The following charges typically are excluded from prescription drug plans:

- devices of any type, such as a hypodermic needle or syringe, and bandages;
- contraceptive drugs or medicines, immunization agents, sera, blood or blood plasma, dietary supplements, beauty aids, or cosmetics;
- drugs that are dispensed while the individual is confined in a hospital or extended care facility; and
- a prescription that exceeds a specified number of days' supply of the drug, such as a 90-day supply if obtained from a participating mail-order pharmacy and a 30-day supply if obtained from any other pharmacy.

Vision Care Insurance

Vision care insurance is designed to provide benefits for routine preventive and corrective eye care. It usually is written to complement other basic group coverages. The primary objective is to encourage regular or periodic eye examinations so that appropriate corrective measures may be taken. Under most vision care programs, the services covered require the authorization of an ophthalmologist or optometrist.

Benefits of vision care expenses provide reimbursement for:

- eye examinations (including refraction);
- single vision, bifocal, and trifocal lenses;
- contact lenses;
- other aids for subnormal vision (such as lenticular lenses); and
- frames (limitation on the dollar amount, due to the variable cost of these items).

Vision plans reimburse insureds in one of three ways: They provide a flat dollar amount per individual (e.g., $150) toward all covered services provided in a calendar year; coverage on a usual and customary basis; or coverage based on a specified schedule.

Limitations and Exclusions

To avoid overutilization, vision plans may limit coverage to only one examination and one pair of lenses in any 12 consecutive months and one pair of frames every two years. It is also common to exclude:

- medical or surgical treatment;
- sunglasses;
- tinted lenses;
- safety glasses; and
- duplication due to breakage or loss.

69

Accidental Death and Dismemberment Insurance (AD&D)

Accidental death and dismemberment insurance is offered by group insurers. These benefits are payable when an insured person dies or loses the sight of one or both eyes, or loses one hand or a foot directly as a result of an accidental bodily injury. This coverage may be written as 24-hour or as nonoccupational insurance. Twenty-four-hour insurance provides benefits at any time for an accident or sickness incurred either on or off the job. Nonoccupational insurance does not provide benefits for an accident or sickness arising out of the insured's employment.

Description of Benefits

The typical benefit provision states that if, as a result of an accidental injury, an employee incurs, directly and independently of all other causes and within 90 days of the injury, one of the following losses, the insurance company will pay the amount of the individual's insurance, often called the principle sum, or part of it, as follows:

- For loss of life, the full principal sum is payable.
- For severance of a hand or foot at or above the wrist or ankle, one-half the principal sum is payable.
- For irrecoverable loss of sight of one eye, one-half the principal sum is payable.
- For more than one of the losses described above, the full principal sum is payable.

Multiple benefits. Multiple benefits in excess of the full principal sum are not payable as a result of any one accident, regardless of the extent of the loss. For example, if the insured loses both a hand and the sight of both eyes as a result of the same accident, only the principal sum will be payable. The amount of insurance usually is payable in a lump sum to the designated beneficiary for accidental death. For other losses, payment is made to the insured.

Limitations and exclusions. Benefits are not payable for any loss that results directly or indirectly, wholly or partly, from any of the following:

■ disease or bodily or mental infirmity or its medical or surgical treatment;

■ ptomaine or bacterial infection, except infections occurring through an accidental cut or wound;

■ suicide or intentionally self-inflicted injury;

■ war or any act of war; and

■ drugs, unless taken as prescribed by a physician.

Types of AD&D Plans

There are four types of accidental death and dismemberment plans: group life supplement, voluntary, business trip, and dependents.

Group life supplement. When included with group life insurance, the AD&D principal sum is usually the same as the amount of the group life insurance. However, if the life insurance is continued after retirement, accidental death and dismemberment coverage normally terminates at that time.

Voluntary. An elective benefit that is not part of a group life insurance program is available, called voluntary AD&D. Insureds generally pay their premiums through payroll deduction.

Business trip. This coverage, sometimes called travel accident insurance, is designed for employers who give supplementary accident protection for their employees while traveling on company business. The cost of this coverage usually is paid entirely by the employer. Generally, three types of business trip accident plans are offered:

■ Comprehensive or all risk plan, which provides 24-hour protection from the time the employee leaves home or place of business until the return from a business trip;

■ Common carrier plan, which covers accidents only when the employee traveling on business is boarding, alighting from, or struck by a specified type of vehicle, such as a public conveyance that is licensed and being used for transportation of passengers; and

■ All-conveyance plan, which includes coverage while traveling on busi-ness in, boarding, alighting from, or struck by a motor vehicle, air-plane, or other conveyance, including personally owned or company-owned vehicles.

Dependents. AD&D for dependents may be provided under a plan covering employees. It is written on a 24-hour basis regardless of how the coverage is provided for employees. Eligible dependents include the employee's spouse and unmarried children, up to a specified age.

Accident Medical Expense Insurance

Insurers offer various types of supplemental or ancillary accident medi-cal expense policies. Generally, the coverage applies only if the expenses are incurred within a specified time (usually three or six months) from the date of the accident. Benefits are subject to an overall maximum benefit for any one accident. Some insurers offer individual accident medical plans that exceed these benefit levels. Some plans have small deductibles (e.g., $25); others provide first dollar coverage.

The benefits, whether group or individual, cover necessary treat-ment following an accidental injury. Typically the following benefits are included:

■ treatment by a physician;

■ hospital care;

■ registered nursing care (RN); and

■ X-ray and laboratory examinations.

Specified Disease Insurance

The most common type of specified disease policy is cancer insurance and it accounts for the largest portion of the market. Many insurers offer one or more cancer policies to individuals and families to meet their need for supplemental cancer protection.

Cancer insurance is purchased to fill the gaps in medical insurance (e.g., deductibles, coinsurance, and noncovered expenses). It also provides protection against additional expenses—food and lodging while traveling to another city for treatment, child care expenses, and transportation costs often related to treating cancer patients.

Some cancer policies provide benefits much like a major medical policy. These policies pay benefits for items such as cancer screening tests; daily room and board; physician visits; nursing; and drugs and medicines. Maximum benefits of $50,000 to $150,000 are common. These benefits usually are paid in addition to any other type of medical insurance.

Medicare Supplement Insurance

The health insurance needs of people aged 65 and over are taken care of, to a great extent, by the federal government's Medicare program. However, because of the deductible and coinsurance, senior citizens are not fully protected against the considerable loss that may result from long-term hospitalization or prolonged medical expenses. Medicare supplement insurance helps pay some of these costs. To put the need for Medicare supplement insurance into perspective, the basic Medicare benefits are described.

Medicare Benefits: Part A

Part A, hospital insurance, is provided automatically to persons aged 65 and older who are eligible for Social Security retirement benefits. It is financed by the earnings tax paid by employers and employees. Part A provides for benefits for hospitalization, skilled nursing facilities, home health services, and hospice care.

A person who is hospitalized must pay an initial deductible ($736 in 1996), after which Medicare pays 100 percent of the hospital charges for the first 60 days of confinement. From the 61st to the 90th day, the patient is responsible for paying a portion of each day's confinement expense—the copayment amount ($184 in 1996). From the 91st to the 150th day, a patient may use a lifetime reserve (the copayment during

73

this period is $368 per day). This 60 days of coverage may only be used once during a person's lifetime. After the copayment period has elapsed, the patient becomes responsible for paying the entire expense.

After a hospital stay of three days, Part A pays for service in an approved skilled nursing facility for up to 100 days per spell of illness. The program pays the first 20 days with no coinsurance. For days 21 through 100, Medicare pays for a portion of any eligible expenses that remain after a daily copayment ($92 in 1996).

Home health services may be provided for a limit of 21 days (intermittent or consecutive). Hospice benefits for terminally ill patients are paid for a lifetime limit of 210 days. All blood that the patient needs, after a deductible of the first three pints, also is covered.

Medicare Benefits: Part B

Part B, supplementary medical insurance, is a voluntary program. Twenty-five percent of the premiums are paid by the participant; the balance of the premium is paid by the government. Part B provides benefits such as physicians' treatments, surgical procedures, hospital outpatient services, and medical supplies.

After the application of a calendar year deductible, Medicare pays 80 percent of charges it deems reasonable for service provided in the geographic area in which the service was provided. The patient is responsible for paying the deductible, the 20 percent copayment amount of the Medicare allowed charges, plus the full balance of any charge in excess of the Medicare-allowed charge.

Medicare Supplement Policies

As of November 1991 all Medicare supplement policies were required to be standardized into ten plans labeled A through J. Insurance companies marketing these plans must offer Plan A, which is generally referred to as the core plan. They may offer any or all of the other nine plans. (Table 3.3)

Table 3.3

Standardized Medicare Supplement Policies

Benefits	"Core" A	B	C	D	E	F	G	H	I	J
CORE benefits										
Part A hospital										
(Days 61–90)	X	X	X	X	X	X	X	X	X	X
Lifetime reserve										
(Days 91–150)	X	X	X	X	X	X	X	X	X	X
365 Lifetime hospital										
(Days at 100%)	X	X	X	X	X	X	X	X	X	X
Part A and Part B blood	X	X	X	X	X	X	X	X	X	X
Part B coinsurance–20%	X	X	X	X	X	X	X	X	X	X
Additional benefits										
Skilled Nursing Facility										
(Days 21–100)			X	X	X	X	X	X	X	X
Part A deductible		X	X	X	X	X	X	X	X	X
Part B deductible			X			X				X
Part B excess charges						100%	80%		100%	100%
Foreign travel			X	X	X	X	X	X	X	X
At-home recovery				X			X		X	X
Preventive medical care					X					X
Prescription drugs								Basic	Basic	Extended

Travel Accident Insurance

Most of the travel insurance sold today is for travel accident protection. It is purchased primarily at vending machines in airports, from representatives of insurers at many of the larger airports, or from travel agencies. These policies offer coverage that provides benefits in case of accidental death or dismemberment while the insured is a passenger on a common carrier such as an airplane. The protection is for a single trip, usually on a round-trip basis.

■ Disability Income Coverage

Disability income insurance is a form of health insurance sold on an individual and group basis that provides periodic payments if the insured is unable to work as a result of illness or injury. The basic benefit provides substitutes for a portion of the insured's earned income when the income is cut off because of a disability. Although the term *disability income insurance* is becoming increasingly accepted, a number of synonyms such as *income protection* and *loss of time insurance* are still used.

Total Disability Coverage

All disability income insurance policies specify certain requirements that a disability must meet in order to qualify for benefits: a covered cause of disability, physician's care, and meeting the policy's definition of total disability.

Following are two common yet different definitions of total disability.

■ During an initial period of disability, such as until the monthly indemnity is paid for a period of 24 months, an insured will be considered totally disabled if unable to engage in his or her own occupation. After this initial period, an insured will be considered totally disabled if unable to engage in any gainful occupation for which he or she is reasonably suited by education, training, and experience.

■ Due solely to injuries or sickness, an insured has a loss of time or duties and a loss of earnings of at least 20 percent.

Basic Coverage

Disability income policies are divided into two major categories: one covers only disability caused by accidental injury; the other covers both illness and injury. These two categories are similar in all respects except for the risk insured. The total amount of benefits payable under a disability income policy is determined and controlled by three policy specifications: the monthly/weekly indemnity, the elimination period, and the maximum benefit period.

Monthly/weekly benefits. The basic benefit provided by a disability income policy is the amount paid monthly (or weekly) during total disability. This amount is stated in the policy and agreed upon by insurer and insured. The amount may range from $100 to $15,000 per month, depending on the income needs of the insured and current company issue limits.

Elimination period. The elimination or benefit waiting period is that time for which no benefits are payable at the beginning of a period of disability. The most common elimination periods are 30, 60, 90, and 180 days for illness and injury. Elimination periods also help reduce the insurer's administrative costs, keeping the premiums more affordable for the insureds.

Maximum benefit period. The maximum benefit period (also called the indemnity limit) is the maximum length of time for which benefits are payable during any one period of disability. The most commonly offered maximum benefit periods are one year, two years, five years, and to age 65.

Residual Disability Coverage

Residual or permanent partial disability coverage is based on the concept of reduced earnings. Under such coverage the individual must be partially disabled (i.e., the insured is unable to perform some of his or her normal job duties or be unable to work full time).

Residual disability coverage generally applies to the insured who had been totally disabled and no longer is but, because of a continuing impairment or an accident or sickness, suffers a reduced income. When an insured returns to work at a reduced income, usually following a period of total disability, benefits continue to be payable on a reduced basis in proportion to the reduction in the insured's income prior to the disability.

Defining Earned Income

To determine the residual disability, earned income during the residual disability must be compared with income earned before the disability. *Earned income* is defined as income received from salary, wages, fees, commissions, or other remuneration earned by the insured for services performed. Earned income is determined before deduction of federal or state taxes.

If the insured is self-employed, earned income means gross income less normal and customary business expenses. Insurers normally use the average income during a 12- or 24-month period before a disability to determine the residual benefit.

Basic Qualifications

In most cases, the residual disability benefit is payable to an insured person if the person continues to be disabled or suffers an income loss arising from the same or related impairment; engages either full- or part-time in his or her regular occupation or any other occupation; earns a current income that is at least 20 percent (25 percent in some policies) less than prior monthly earned income; and continues to be under the care of a physician.

Optional Coverages

Optional coverages may be added to disability income policies. Some are added automatically; some may require additional premiums. Optional coverages include waiver of premium, short-term monthly indemnity, social insurance substitute, future increase option, and cost-of-living adjustment.

Short-Term Monthly Indemnity

This type of coverage provides for the payment of an additional amount of monthly indemnity during the first few months of total disability. This additional amount may be limited to five or six months, although some insurers pay up to one year. It is useful in providing additional income in the months before the insured becomes eligible for Social Security benefits.

Social Insurance Substitute

Many insurers offer a social insurance substitute (SIS) benefit that is intended to supply additional monthly disability benefits of up to $1,000 per month when disability benefits are not provided through social insurance programs such as Social Security disability or retirement bene-fits, workers' compensation, state no-fault insurance, and various other state disability programs. When an insured qualifies for one of these pro-grams, the monthly benefits provided by the SIS must be terminated or reduced by the amount of the monthly benefits under the social insur-ance for which he or she qualifies.

Future Increase Option (Guaranteed Insurability Option)

The amount of disability income coverage an insurer offers to an individ-ual depends partly on the person's earned income at the time of the application. As that income increases in subsequent years, additional dis-ability income insurance is needed to retain an adequate ratio of insur-ance to income.

Under the future increase option, an insured may purchase up to a des-ignated additional amount of disability income coverage at specified future option dates, regardless of medical insurability but subject to his or her income having increased sufficiently.

Return-of-Premium

An insured selecting this option and paying an extra premium is offered the opportunity to get a percentage (usually between 50 and 80 per-cent) of the total premium back after specified periods of time (e.g., every five or ten years) if he or she does not become disabled. Disability payments made to the insured will offset premiums to be returned on a dollar-for-dollar basis.

Cost-of-Living Adjustment (COLA)

Concerns regarding the effects of inflation on the buying power of monthly benefits during a lengthy disability have produced a cost-of-living adjustment benefit that can be added to basic disability income coverage. This provision increases benefit payments by a certain speci-fied percentage.

Exclusions and Limitations

The disability income policy contains a section that clearly defines those risks that are excluded completely from coverage and those for which coverage is limited. As with medical expense insurance, common exclusions and limitations are for pre-existing conditions, pregnancy, self-inflicted injuries or attempted suicide, active military duty, and war.

Business-Oriented Disability Plans

The prolonged disability of a business owner without adequate protection of his or her business can result in the economic death of the company. To solve this and related problems, insurers developed overhead expense insurance, disability buy-out funding policies, and other business-related policies.

Overhead Expense

An overhead expense policy is considered a reimbursement policy since it reimburses insureds for their share of actual business expenses incurred during total disability. Overhead expenses are defined as the usual and necessary expenses in the operation of a business or professional practice.

Usually these policies are sold only in small businesses where the business or professional practice depends on the skills of one or two people for income to meet business expenses.

Policies cover the following types of overhead expenses: monthly rent or interest on mortgage payments, employee salaries, utilities, postage, business laundry, and association or trade dues and subscriptions.

The types of overhead expenses that are not covered are an insured's salary; compensation of any person hired to perform the insured's duties (this kind of benefit might be purchased on an optional basis); cost of any goods; merchandise; inventory; payment on the principal of any indebtedness; and expenses not regularly and customarily liable before the disability occurred.

Disability Buyout (Business Interest Insurance)

This type of coverage provides the cash for the purchase of the business interest of a partner or stockholder who becomes disabled. The partners or stockholders prepare a formal buy/sell agreement in advance. This agreement provides that if one of them becomes disabled for a certain length of time, generally one to two years, the disabled person is obliged to sell his or her interest and the other partners or stockholders are obliged to buy it. The agreement specifies the price (or a formula calculating the price) at which the business interest will be sold.

Key-Employee Disability

Key-employee disability income insurance provides payments to a business for losses incurred through disability of one of its key personnel. During such a disability, a business will lose profit produced by the work previously done by the insured. Key-employee benefits are paid directly to the employer to offset the losses. Insurers usually sell this coverage only to small businesses.

■ Long-Term Care Coverage

Long-term care insurance provides a specific dollar benefit or a percent of expenses charged for nursing home care, home health care, and adult day care if a covered person suffers a loss of functional or cognitive capacity. This loss can be due to an accidental injury or sickness, but it is just as likely to result from the process of aging. Loss of functional capacity usually means a person needs human assistance to perform some of the following activities of daily living:

- bathing—getting into and out of a shower or tub;
- dressing—putting on and taking off all necessary items of clothing;
- transferring—moving between the bed and a chair or the bed and a wheelchair;
- toileting—getting to and from the toilet, getting on and off the toilet, and associated personal hygiene;

81

- eating—getting food into the body; and

- continence—voluntary control over bowel or bladder.

Insurers also consider cognitive impairment because of disease or injury or mental incapacity due to organic brain diseases.

Benefits

Long-term care plans usually pay between $50 and $300 for each day of confinement in a nursing care facility and between $20 and $150 for each day of home health care. Depending on the plan, these benefits can be paid as a flat dollar amount for each day of care or as a percent of the actual cost of service per day, up to the established maximum amount. Inflation adjustments may be provided by giving the insured the right to purchase periodic increases often based on changes in the consumer price index (CPI). The premium will be increased to reflect the additional amount of benefits and the age at which they are purchased. An alternative is a provision that guarantees an annual increase (e.g., 5 percent) and for which an initially greater premium is charged. This premium is designed to be level for the life of the policy.

The nursing facility must be licensed or legally qualified to provide nursing or assistance care or assistance in performing activities of daily living. Home health care must usually be provided through a home health agency and performed by a registered nurse, a licensed practical nurse, a vocational nurse, a home health aide, a licensed certified or registered occupational therapist, a speech therapist, or a physical therapist. Home health care must be performed in the insured's own home, a private home, a facility for the retired or aged, or a licensed or legally qualified adult day care center operating for the purpose of providing nursing, medical, and health-related social services.

Elimination Period

If an elimination period is included, generally long-term care benefits are payable after a specified period (e.g., 90 days) of consecutive days of continuous loss of functional capacity. Prior hospitalization or nursing home confinement is not required. Some insurers offer a zero-elimination period option. Some policies provide that the elimination period needs to be satisfied only once per lifetime rather than per benefit period.

Benefit Period

A benefit period begins on the first day following the end of the elimination period. It ends after a person no longer has a loss of functional capacity, generally for a period of 60 consecutive days. At the close of any benefit period, benefits for any subsequent loss of functional capacity will not be paid until a new elimination period has been completed.

Premium Waiver

Premium payments are waived when benefit payments begin. Premium payments start again on the first premium due date following the end of a benefit period.

Pre-Existing Condition Limitations

Any qualifying loss of functional capacity that is caused by a pre-existing condition is not covered unless the loss begins more than six or 12 consecutive months after the individual becomes insured.

Other Limitations

Other common limitations specific to long-term care benefits include exclusions for the following:

- mental, nervous, or emotional disorders (does not apply to organic brain disease such as Alzheimer's disease);
- any day the insured is confined in a hospital;
- alcoholism or drug addiction;
- self-inflicted injuries or attempted suicide;
- benefits provided under other types of health insurance for confinement in a nursing care facility or for home health care;

- care for which reimbursement is available under a government program; and

- care received outside the United States.

Portability

When long-term care insurance is purchased through an employer-sponsored plan, employees who leave that employer may continue coverage for themselves, spouses, and others. Premiums must be paid by the individual directly to the insurer.

■ Flexible Benefit Plans

Flexible benefit plans, also called cafeteria plans, are based on the concept of individual choice. They allow participants to select some or all of their benefits from among those the employer offers.

Objectives of Flexible Benefit Plans

Flexible benefit plans have three primary objectives: satisfaction of employees, cost control, and tax effectiveness.

Satisfaction of Employees

A benefits package can be a significant portion of an employee's total compensation. It is one of the important considerations in an employee's decision to take a job. Many employers view flexible benefit plans as state-of-the-art packages consistent with the image of a progressive, innovative company. These plans allow employees to use employer benefit dollars for those benefits they value most. The benefits needed will depend on factors such as family status, sex, age, lifestyle, health status, and income.

Cost Control

Health care is a large part of an employee benefit package. Its continuing high cost in the past decade has caused employers, insurers, providers, and government to look for ways to control it. A company's cost for traditional benefit plans usually is tied directly to rises in payroll and medical care costs. Perhaps the most far-reaching impact of flexible compensation programs is their ability to control an employer's future benefit cost increases.

Managed care techniques can be incorporated into some of the medical options, and price tags to employees can be set to encourage their selection of those options. The ability to choose promotes employees' awareness of the overall program costs. For more information about managed care see Chapter 1: Managing the Cost of Health Care in *Fundamentals of Health Insurance: Part B*.

Tax Effectiveness

Flexible benefit plans allow for easy incorporation of techniques such as pretax reimbursement accounts for the most tax-effective use of the employee's compensation dollars. With such an account an employee can fund premium contributions with pretax dollars. The employer also saves Social Security taxes on the salary-reduced dollars.

Designing a Flexible Benefit Plan

There are three basic approaches to designing a flexible benefits plan: modular, core-plus, and full-flexible. In all three approaches, an employer provides each employee with an amount of credits to apply to whichever package of benefits he or she elects. If the benefits selected cost more than the credits provided, an employee can pay the difference with pretax salary reduction.

Modular Format

This format allows the employee to choose from packages or groupings of benefits offered by the employer. Usually three or four packages are

Table 3.4

Modular Format Flexible Benefit Plan

Benefits	Option 1 package	Option 2 package	Option 3 package
Life insurance	2 × salary	1 × salary	3 × salary
LTD	50% salary	50% of salary	70% of salary
Vision insurance	None	Vision plans	None
Dental insurance	Dental	No dental	Dental
Rx	Drug plan	Drug plan	None
Medical insurance	$1,000 deductible or HMO	$500 deductible or HMO	$250 deductible or HMO

made available. Each package is designed to meet the needs of employees with different characteristics while reducing the potential hazards of adverse selection. By minimizing employee options initially, the employer can better predict participation and can introduce changes and additions gradually. (Table 3.4)

Core-Plus Format

The core-plus format provides a basic package of benefits usually paid for by the employer and covering all employees. Any number of optional benefits can be made available, funded through flexible credits provided by the employer, employee contributions, or a combination of the two. (Table 3.5)

Full-Flexible Format

The full-flexible format allows employees to choose freely from multiple options in each type of coverage independently, and it permits large and varied combinations of benefits. This helps employees customize a benefit package that meets their needs and lifestyle. (Table 3.6)

■ Emerging Trends

The marketplace for group and individual medical insurance coverage is continually evolving. Flexible benefit plans are popular with employees, and new options are likely to be added to the list of benefits offered in

Table 3.5

Core-Plus Format Flexible Benefit Plan

Benefits	Core (mandatory)	Optional benefits (voluntary)
Life insurance	1 × salary	1½ × salary
		2 × salary
		3 × salary
Dependent life insurance	None	$10,000 spouse/$5,000 child
Medical insurance	$1,000 deductible	$500 deductible
		$250 deductible
		HMO option
		PPO option
Dental insurance	None	$50 deductible/$1,000 maximum
		$75 deductible/$2,500 maximum
LTD	50% of salary	60% of salary
		70% of salary
Health care reimbursement account	None	$5 to $100 monthly employee dollars
Dependent care reimbursement account	None	$50 to $400 monthly employee dollars

Table 3.6

Full-Flexible Format Benefit Plan

Life options	Long-term disability options
Option A—1 × salary	Option A—50% of salary to $5,000
Option B— 2 × salary	Option B—60% of salary to $5,000
Option C— 3 × salary	

Medical options	Dental options
HMO coverage or comprehensive medical, $1,000,000 maximum	Option A—No participation
Option A—HMO	Option B—$1,000 maximum
Option B—$250 deductible PPO	$50 deductible
Option C—$500 deductible PPO	Option C—$2,000 maximum
Option D—No participation*	$75 deductible

*Proof of coverage by another plan is usually required.

such plans. Managed care products and services are leading the way with more innovative plans, larger networks, and unique provider arrangements. States are likely to continue to pass legislation requiring mandated benefits, guaranteed issue, and portability of coverage.

With an increasingly aging population, the chance of a person becoming disabled for significant periods of time is much more likely than in the past. Disability income insurance will continue to play a vital role in the protection of the consumer and the lifestyle that the consumer's income provides. Benefit designs will include longer elimination periods to lower costs.

Long-term care insurance has tremendous market potential. Steady growth is expected over the coming years in the number of employers adding long-term care coverage to their benefits package, particularly since recent legislation established federal income tax deductibility for long-term care insurance premiums.

■ Summary

The health insurance industry has developed a wide variety of policies and approaches to meet society's need for protection against potentially high financial loss that accompanies illness and injury. The basic products cover medical expense, medical supplements, accidental death and dismemberment, disability income, and long-term care. As health care and society's needs change and evolve, the insurance industry continues to respond to new challenges.

■ Key Terms

Accident medical
   expense
Accidental death and
   dismemberment
   (AD&D)
Activities of daily
   living (ADLs)
Adult day care
All cause deductible
Benefit amount
Benefit period
Business-oriented
   disability plans
Business trip AD&D

Cafeteria plan
Calendar year
Cognitive impairment
Coinsurance
Common carrier
Comprehensive major
   medical insurance
Copayment
Core-plus plans
Corridor deductible
Cost-of-living
   adjustment (COLA)
Covered expenses
Daily room and board

Deductible
Dental expense
   insurance
Dependents'
   accidental death
   and
   dismemberment
Disability benefits
Disability buyout
Disability income
   insurance
Eligible medical
   expenses
Elimination period

Exclusions
Flexible benefit plans
Full-flexible plans
Future increase option
Guaranteed
insurability option
Home health care
Hospice care
Hospital indemnity
Hospital-surgical-
medical insurance
Income protection
Integrated dental
plans
Limitations
Long-term care (LTC)
insurance
Loss of time insurance
Major medical
insurance

Maternity benefit
Maximum benefit
period
Medical expense
insurance
Medicare
Medicare supplement
insurance
Modular plans
Monthly benefit
Nonintegrated dental
plans
Out-of-pocket
expenses
Overhead expense
Partial disability
Per cause deductible
Permanent partial
disability
Pre-existing conditions

Prescription drug
insurance
Principal sum
Reimbursement plans
Residual disability
Skilled nursing
facilities
Social insurance
substitute (SIS)
Specified disease
insurance
Supplemental major
medical insurance
Surgical schedule
Total disability
Travel benefits
Usual and customary
Vision care insurance
Voluntary AD&D
Waiver of premium

89

Chapter 4

THE INSURANCE CONTRACT

■ Introduction

An insurance policy is a written agreement between an insurer and a policyholder by which the insurer agrees to compensate the policyholder for a loss in return for the premiums paid to the insurer. The policy spells out all the terms and conditions of the arrangement and the rights and obligations of the parties.

An insurance policy often is equated with an insurance contract. However, a contract may exist even without issuance of an actual policy if the actions of the parties and the documents involved otherwise satisfy the legal requirements. On the other hand, even if an insurer issues a policy, the contract might not be legally enforceable against the insurer if fraud or material misrepresentation exists in the application or if either party fails to meet any of the essential elements for the formation of a contract.

The parties to the contract are not totally free to reach any agreement they wish. Laws and regulations govern the types of forms that must be used and stipulate some types of provisions a policy must contain (required provisions) and some a policy may contain (optional provisions). This chapter discusses the legal principles, laws, and regulations that help to shape the insurance contract. It also provides an overview of the key elements in group and individual medical expense insurance contracts to give the reader an appreciation for one aspect of health insurance contract structure and content. While many aspects are similar, contracts for other health insurance—disability income, accidents, accidental death and dismemberment, and long-term care—contain features that relate to the specific coverages.

■ Features of an Insurance Contract

Before discussing the specific components of medical expense insurance contracts, it is necessary to understand the general nature of contracts—what makes them binding, the legalities of policy language, and basic types of contracts.

Binding Contract

All contracts need certain essential elements to make them binding: offer and acceptance, consideration, meeting of the minds, and capacity of the parties to contract.

Offer and Acceptance

The first component in formulating any contract occurs when one party extends to another party an offer or an invitation to make an offer. If no further action is required of the party making the initial proposal, an offer is extended. If further action is required, the proposal is regarded as an invitation to the other party to make an offer.

The application for insurance is always an integral part of the offer process. A proposed policyholder who completes an application and pays the required premium has made an offer to the insurer that the insurer may accept or reject. If a premium is not paid when the application is completed, the applicant is not making an offer to the insurer but instead is inviting the insurer to make an offer.

Whenever an offer is made, the second component—acceptance by the other party—must occur for creation of a contract. If the insurer rejects the offer but makes an alternative proposal (e.g., the insurer will only accept the risk at a higher premium rate or with an exclusion in the policy), the alternate proposal is considered a counteroffer. There is no binding contract unless the applicant accepts the counteroffer.

If the prospective policyholder makes the offer, the insurer accepts the offer when it approves the application and issues the policy that was applied for. If the insurer makes the offer, the offer will be in the form of a policy; the prospective policyholder will accept that offer by taking receipt of the policy and paying the premium.

Consideration

The term *consideration* refers to what each party gives or gives up in exchange for what the other party gives or gives up. It may include a broad range of acts or promises to be done or not to be done. For a contract to be valid, a consideration must be exchanged from each party to the other. The consideration of the applicant for insurance consists of the statements made in the application and the payment of the appropriate premium. The consideration of the insurer is its promise to pay the benefits provided by the policy.

Meeting of the Minds

Both parties to a contract must reach a meeting of the minds—an agreement and an understanding concerning their respective obligations and rights under the contract. If the parties do not understand the terms of the agreement through no fault of their own, the validity of the contract may be questioned.

For example, if the insurer is not given a fair opportunity to evaluate the risk because material information was misstated or withheld, the insurer may challenge the validity of the policy and seek to nullify it. (In the insurance business, such a nullification is called a rescission.) Medical history is a prime example of material information that, if withheld, could be cause for rescission. An insured also may challenge the validity of a contract and seek to rescind or modify it if he or she was induced to enter into the contract by misleading advertising or agent misrepresentations.

Capacity to Contract

To form a valid contract, both parties must have the ability to understand its terms. Without this capacity there can be no meeting of the minds. Generally, persons who have attained the age of majority (age eighteen in most states) have the legal capacity to enter into health insurance contracts on themselves or others in whom they have an insurable interest. Law usually considers that minors (those under the legal age) lack the capacity to contract except for a very limited number of items that are referred to in law as necessaries. Health insurance does not fall into this category, so any insurer that contracts with a minor runs the risk that the minor may void the contract before attaining the age of majority. Regardless of age, persons who are mentally incompetent do not have the capacity to form a contract of insurance or to exercise ownership rights under the contract.

Policy Language

Insurance departments of most states in which group or individual health insurance policies are sold must approve the language used in policy forms. Most states have enacted legislation requiring that some, if not all, insurance policies meet certain minimum readability standards. The intent of these laws is to simplify the language and format of policy contracts so that the average consumer can comprehend the document.

Contracts of Adhesion

Insurance contracts are referred to as contracts of adhesion—that is, contracts that are offered on a take-it-or-leave-it basis by a party of superior strength and knowledge to a party of limited resources and little expertise. Traditional contract language has acquired clear and precise meaning through time and court interpretation. In interpreting insurance contract language, the courts have recognized that the parties do not have equal bargaining power. Therefore, insurance contracts generally are construed by the courts in a manner most favorable to the policyholder and most often rule in favor of the insured whenever ambiguities exist.

Doctrine of Reasonable Expectations

Certain state courts have developed a theory of contract interpretation called the doctrine of reasonable expectations. This doctrine, applied primarily to insurance contracts, holds that the actual language of the contract may not be the controlling factor if circumstances suggest that the policyholder expected something different from what the written contract states. If the court considers the policyholder's expectations more reasonable than the conclusion arrived at by strict adherence to the contract language, it may find ambiguities in the contract and render its decision in accordance with the policyholder's reasonable expectations.

Types of Contracts

There are certain features of health insurance contracts that refer to the conditions of the parties involved. Insurance contracts can be unilateral, conditional, or aleatory.

Unilateral Contract

A unilateral contract is one in which only one of the parties to the contract makes a promise or promises. In an insurance contract the policyholder makes no promise to do or to pay anything. Policies remain in force if insureds pay premiums when due, but they do not promise to do so. The policy will lapse if a premium is not paid when due, but the insurer cannot sue the policyholder for failure to perform under the contract. The health insurance contract is one-sided; it contains legally enforceable promises by the insurer but none by the insured.

Conditional Contract

A conditional contract provides that the insurer will pay the benefits provided by the policy only if an event insured against occurs. Performance under the contract is conditional upon the occurrence of a covered loss.

Aleatory Contract

Under an aleatory contract one of the parties may recover a great deal more in value than has been parted with, depending upon the occurrence of some future contingent event. For example, under a disability income policy the insured could sustain a serious injury after the payment of only one premium and become entitled to total disability benefits and waiver of subsequent premiums for many years.

■ Medical Expense Insurance Policy Application

The application for a medical expense insurance policy furnishes information that is critical for identifying risk and underwriting it appropriately. There are differences in the information furnished on group and individual medical expense insurance policy applications.

Group Medical Expense Insurance Application

Applicants for group medical expense insurance can use either a long- or a short-form application. The long form shows the details of employee eligibility as well as the types and amounts of coverage. It gives the underwriter much of the information needed to evaluate the group and provide the benefit plan desired. When a short form is used, detailed information about the new plan usually is furnished to the underwriters on worksheets completed by group field personnel.

In either case the policyholder receives the final application with the policy. This application states that the policy has been approved by the insurer and its terms accepted by the policyholder. Signed by the policyholder and attached to the policy, it becomes a part of the contract.

96

Whatever the form of the application—short form or long form—the insurer must give its approval.

An agent cannot pass on the acceptability of any insurance or modify or expand the issued contract. Insurance applied for becomes effective when an insurer's home office approves the application and all legal requirements regarding issuance have been met. Group insurance also requires the enrollment of a minimum number or percentage of eligible persons from the applicant group to spread the risk across a broader population and minimize adverse selection. (See Chapter 6)

Individual Medical Expense Insurance Application

The individual medical expense insurance application has three sections:

- Part one identifies the applicant and any other persons proposed for coverage by name, address, and date of birth.

- Part two contains information about the coverage desired, including the type of policy and the nature, amount, and duration of benefits.

- Part three contains information of importance to underwriting, primarily that relating to past medical history. It also calls for information about other insurance coverage in force, occupation and earnings, and other factors pertinent to risk.

The insurer can reasonably expect applicants to know when they last consulted a physician or whether they ever were told they had a specific disease. Other questions that may not be answerable on a precise, factual basis are phrased to permit an answer that is accurate to the best of the applicant's knowledge.

An insurer may rescind the application if the information it contains is inaccurate or incomplete. If an answer on the application is ambiguous or incomplete to the extent that it merits further inquiry, the insurer's responsibility is to obtain clarification at the time of underwriting and before policy issue. Failure to do so may prevent the insurer from rescinding the policy once issued, even if it later learns that the ambiguous answer contained false information.

The application contains a statement that the information provided by the applicant is true to the best of the signer's knowledge and belief. Customarily, the clause states that the insurance applied for becomes effective when the first premium is paid and the policy is delivered to the applicant. It may also include, except in a few states, a statement that coverage will not become effective unless the applicant is in good health at the time of policy delivery.

The agent who solicits the application witnesses the applicant's signature. The signature of the agent on the application serves two purposes: to verify that the applicant signed the application in the presence of the soliciting agent and to fulfill the regulatory requirement of some states that the application identify the soliciting agent.

■ Characteristics of Group Medical Expense Insurance Contracts

The group medical expense insurance contract, a master policy between the insurer and the policyholder, describes not only the benefits of the group insurance plan but also the terms and conditions under which they are provided. The contract represents mutual agreement to these terms and conditions by both parties—insurer and policyholder.

The contract is based on a good-faith business relationship. Drafting the precise benefit descriptions, reviewing them with the policyholder, and, where necessary, filing them with the insurance department involved and receiving approval require a considerable amount of time.

Terms and Conditions

Certain terms and conditions characterize a group policy, including:

- types and levels of benefits available to eligible persons in the group;
- requirements a group member must meet to become insured;
- provisions relating to claim, administrative, and legal aspects;
- circumstances under which coverage may terminate; and

■ benefits that may be available to insureds after coverage has terminated.

Format for Issuance

A policy may combine in one contract all the health coverage of the plan—medical expense, disability, accidental death and dismemberment, and other benefits. This method avoids duplication of policy provisions that are common to all coverages.

Alternatively, an insurer may issue a separate policy for each major line of coverage. The definition of a major line differs somewhat among insurance companies, but it usually means group medical insurance, dental insurance, life insurance, accidental death and dismemberment insurance, short-term or long-term disability income insurance, and long-term care insurance.

Supplemental major medical insurance usually is written as part of a hospital expense policy. However, it is written as a separate policy when the basic benefits are provided by an insurer other than the one that underwrites the major medical plan. Dental insurance may be written as a separate policy or offered as a supplemental benefit under a major medical plan.

Contract Revision

Policyholders often wish to revise the type or levels of benefits in their plans and may want changes in other provisions as well. To effect these changes, insurers use policy riders to describe the changes to the group insurance policy.

The policyholder signifies acceptance of the revision described in the rider by signing and returning it to the insurer. Some insurers issue contract amendments that do not require policyholder acceptance when the policyholder itself requests a change that involves a liberalization of the plan. A revision that reduces benefits, however, requires the policyholder's signature.

■ Group Medical Expense Insurance Contract Provisions

Group medical expense insurance contracts contain a number of specific definitions and provisions. Some provisions are general; others apply to either the policyholder or the persons insured under the contract.

Definitions

As in any contract, the terms used in a group policy should be easy to understand. To achieve this goal, policies define key words and phrases that are used. Without definitions there can be disagreement over what constitutes treatment or even illness. Persons insured will attach their own meanings to these terms unless the definitions are established clearly in the contract.

Because of legislation, court decisions, and insurance industry efforts to provide more liberal coverage, the definitions of many of the terms used in the contract continually change. For example, the definition of a physician originally recognized only those licensed to practice medicine and surgery. It has been expanded to include other licensed medical practitioners whose services are required to be covered by law and who render such services within the scope of his or her license (e.g., psychologists and chiropractors).

In contrast, the definition of dependents varies little among insurance companies. Dependents usually are defined as follows:

■ the spouse of an employee, provided that the employee and spouse are not legally separated and that the spouse is not on active service in any branch of the armed forces or merchant marine of any country;

■ an unmarried child of an employee (including a stepchild) who is principally dependent on the employee for support and maintenance and is under age 19; who is over age 19 but under age 23 (and in some cases up to age 26) and a registered student in regular, full-time school and legally residing with the employee; and/or who is incapable of self-sustaining employment by reason of mental retardation or a physical handicap and who became incapable prior to attaining the age limit in the contract.

General Provisions

In addition to definitions, a number of general provisions appear in a group medical expense insurance contract.

Entire Contract

The policy and the application of the policyholder (and insured persons, if required) are the entire contract between the policyholder and the insurance company. Statements on the application made by the policyholder and any other insureds are considered representations. This means the statements are made before the policy is issued and are relied upon in determining whether and in what form to issue a policy. No statement made by any insured person can be used to challenge the validity of a contract (contest) due to possible misrepresentation on the application unless a copy of the application has been furnished to that person or his or her beneficiary.

Validity of Statements

There are several circumstances under which misstatements occur in a group medical expense insurance policy. Insurers have established methods for dealing with these misstatements.

Misstatements about age.   If the age of any individual insured under a group policy has been misstated and as a result the person is insured for an amount different from that provided by the plan for a person at the correct age, the person's insurance is adjusted to the correct amount. The premiums also are adjusted.

Clerical error.   If an error or omission occurs in the administration of a group policy, what the person's insurance should be is considered the correct basis or amount. Failure of the policyholder to report a termination, however, will not result in continued insurance coverage on the individual.

Record Keeping

The insurance company or the policyholder, depending on the type of administration agreed upon, maintains records of all persons insured, including information such as their names, ages, amounts of insurance, and insurance effective date.

Notice, Proof of Loss, and Payment of Claims

The health insurance statutes of some states require that insurers include provisions about claims payment in all health insurance policies. These provisions generally apply to:

- the time limit for submitting a notice of claim to the insurance company, usually 20 days from date of loss;
- the time limit for submitting proofs of loss, usually 90 days; and
- the time that the insurance company has to make payment, usually 60 days after proof of loss has been filed.

Assignment of Benefits

Medical expense policies usually state that no assignment is binding on the insurer unless it is in writing and has been filed at the home office. Although group medical benefits normally are payable directly to the insured, most contracts permit the insured to assign benefits to the providers of medical care services. Even in the absence of a specific contract provision permitting an assignment of benefits, insurers commonly not only accept such assignment but actually promote their use by making a space for them on the claim forms that the insured completes.

Other Provisions

Group contracts contain provisions concerning the payment of benefits if the insured is a minor, is otherwise not competent to give a release,

102

or if the insured person has died while some benefits remain unpaid. Unassigned benefits usually are paid to the surviving spouse, to any surviving children, or to the executors or administrators of the insured's estate.

Provisions Relating to the Policyholder

The group contract includes provisions that relate specifically to the policyholder.

Effective Date

The effective date of the group contract is established by agreement between the policyholder and the insurer. Usually, this date is shown on the face page of the policy and applies to all of its sections unless there is a special arrangement to have one or more of the coverages become effective at some later date. Group insurance transferred from one insurer to another places the effective date of the new contract immediately following the termination date of the old one to provide continuous coverage for persons insured when the transfer occurs.

Information Required of the Policyholder

Under the contract the policyholder is required to furnish certain information concerning persons becoming insured or changes in classification or status that have a bearing on the amount of insurance coverage.

Premium Payments

The frequency of premium payment is stated in the contract. Almost all group policyholders pay premiums monthly; a few pay annually, semi-annually, or quarterly. Renewal rates are not made part of the policy; instead, a letter or some other form of notice is used to calculate the initial premium. At renewal insurers commonly omit premium rates from the policy; instead, they use a letter or some other form of notice to tell the policyholder of the renewal rates. Most policies guarantee initial premium rates for 12 months unless the terms of the policy are changed.

Occasionally, however, rates are guaranteed for as little as three months or as long as two or three years.

After the initial guarantee period, rates may be changed only at certain times. Practices vary but typically rates may be changed:

- on any premium due date, provided the insurer notifies the policyholder at least 31 days before the premium due date; or
- when the terms of the policy are changed.

Grace Period

Group contracts provide for a grace period (commonly 31 days after the due date) during which the policyholder may pay overdue premiums without an interest penalty. During this time the coverage remains in force unless the policyholder has given the insurer written notice of contract termination. If by the end of the grace period the overdue premium has not been paid, the contract terminates. Because coverage is in force and the insurer is liable for claims incurred during the grace period, the policyholder is liable for the premium for this period.

Experience Refunds

A contract may have a specific provision for the return of premium to the policyholder in the form of an experience refund, determined as of the policy anniversary date if the contract is in force and premiums have been paid. Policyholders who have transferred their group plan to another insurer as of a date other than the policy anniversary also may be eligible for a refund from the former insurer. The experience refund may be in cash, applied to subsequent premiums, or left on deposit with the insurer.

Authority to Modify the Contract

Policy provisions are modified only by agreement between the policyholder and the insurance company. Brokers, agents, or other representatives of the insurer do not have the right to make changes in contract provisions. The contract specifically designates those who do have the authority to modify it. Usually, these authorized persons are the officers of the insurance company.

Right to Terminate

A policyholder may terminate its policy on any premium due date, giving 31 days' advance written notice to the insurer. The HIPAA of 1996 generally requires insurers to renew all group medical expense contracts. An insurer's right to terminate (nonrenew or discontinue) a contract for group coverage is limited to the following circumstances. Insurers are allowed to nonrenew in cases of nonpayment of premium, fraud or intentional misrepresentation, or violation of the insurer's minimum contribution or participation requirements. For the typical employer group, these participation requirements may be expressed in the contract as a percentage of all employees eligible to participate in the plan, such as 75 percent, or as a numerical minimum, such as ten employees—or both. For an association or union group plan, different participation requirements may apply. A minimum requirement of ten participants is not unusual. Network plans are allowed to nonrenew or discontinue a group if there is no longer any member of the group who lives or works in the plan's service area. In addition, insurers are allowed to terminate coverage, subject to certain requirements, if they are exiting the market entirely, or withdrawing a particular type of coverage.

Provisions Relating to Insureds

The group contract includes provisions that relate specifically to insureds.

Eligibility

The definition of *eligible persons* varies, depending on whether an employer group or some other entity is the policyholder. The date on which a person becomes eligible for coverage normally is the later of the effective date of the plan or the first day after completion of a probationary waiting period.

Effective Date of Coverage

The rules defining effective date of coverage vary, depending on whether the persons to be insured are contributing part of the premium. When the policyholder is paying the full cost of the group plan, a request for coverage is not necessary; nevertheless, the enrollees are asked to complete enrollment cards for record keeping purposes. Coverage automatically begins on an employee's eligibility date. When employees contribute, the eligible person applies for coverage by completing an enrollment card that includes authorization for payroll deductions—the usual method used by the policyholder to collect employee contributions.

Benefits

Contracts include benefit provisions that fully describe the conditions and level of benefits as well as limitations of coverage. The number and type of these provisions depend on the plan the policyholder buys.

Pre-Existing Conditions

Medical expense plans may contain a preexisting conditions provision. This excludes or limits the benefits for an injury or sickness that has existed during a specified period—such as three or six months—prior to a person's becoming insured. Group plans may cover pre-existing conditions on the same basis as any other condition once the individual has been insured for a certain period of time or meets other criteria.

Insurer practice determines the size of the groups and the types of coverage to which this provision applies. Many states have restricted the applicability of pre-existing condition provisions for small groups and individual coverage. In 1996 Congress passed the Health Insurance Portability and Accountability Act (HIPAA) to minimize the impact of the pre-existing conditions provision on insureds. Under the new law an exclusion of up to twelve months can be imposed only once; when insureds switch plans they are given credit for previous coverage toward any new pre-existing conditions exclusions.

Coordination of Benefits

In many families both husband and wife are employed. An increasing number of people also are insured under more than one health benefits plan. If claims are filed with two plans for the same medical incident, it is possible that total benefits received may exceed the expenses incurred. This situation permits an insured to make a profit, leading to overutilization of the benefit plan and to increased health insurance premium rates.

Inclusion of a coordination of benefits (COB) provision avoids such over-payment. This provision, common in group policies, takes into account total benefits paid to a person who has overlapping coverage under more than one plan. The total benefit payments will not exceed, and may be less than, the total expenses. For more information on coordination of benefits see Chapter 3: Claim Administration and Examination in *Fundamentals of Health Insurance: Part B.*

Insuring Clause

The insuring clause provides that the insurer agrees to pay the benefits described in the policy to each individual who is insured and who, according to the terms of the policy, is entitled to the benefits. The clause also specifies that proof of loss must be submitted to the insurer before the claim payment will be made.

Termination of an Individual's Insurance

The provisions for terminating an individual's insurance vary depending on the type of group and coverage. The most common termination provisions are those based on conditions pertaining to employment in plans that cover employees. These provisions terminate coverage at:

- the date the group policy terminates;
- the date the policy is amended to terminate the eligibility of the class of employees to which the employee belongs;
- at the end of the period for which the last premium has been paid for the employee;

- the date employment terminates; or

- the date the employee transfers out of a class eligible for coverage.

In a union or an association group, coverage terminates when membership terminates. Dependent health insurance terminates when the insured employee no longer has an eligible family member. Dependent coverage ends earlier if an employee's insurance terminates or for a particular dependent if that person no longer meets the definition of an eligible dependent in the policy.

Coverage Continuation

Under the Consolidated Omnibus Budget Reconciliation Act of 1985 (COBRA), employers of 20 or more employees are required to include in their medical benefit plans a right of continuation of coverage for 18 months for employees upon termination of employment for any reason (other than gross misconduct) or upon reduction of hours worked. The continued coverage is paid by the employee. The right of continuation applies to spouses and dependents upon divorce (or legal separation) from the employee, death of the employee, or the employee becoming eligible for Medicare. Dependent children also may continue coverage when their eligibility as a dependent otherwise terminates. Dependent continued coverage lasts up to 36 months.

The Federal Family and Medical Leave Act of 1993 entitles eligible employees to 12 work weeks of unpaid leave during a 12-month period for any of the following reasons:

- the birth of a child or placement of a child for adoption or foster care;

- the care of a child, spouse, or parent who has a serious health condition;

- the employee's own serious health condition that prevents performance of his or her job.

Employers are required to keep enrolled in the group plan any employee who is out on family or medical leave.

Conversion Privilege

The conversion privilege permits employees and dependents to continue their insurance protection with an individual policy or group certificate if coverage under a medical expense policy ceases when:

- the employee terminates employment in a class of employees insured under the group policy;
- the policy is amended to terminate coverage on the class to which the employee belongs;
- the group policy is terminated; or
- a dependent child reaches the limiting age.

The medical insurance conversion privilege is available to persons:

- who have been insured under a group medical expense contract for at least three months; and
- who terminate membership in the group and are not eligible for similar coverage under another group plan.

Although evidence of insurability is not required, the person usually must apply in writing and pay the first premium within 31 days of termination of the group coverage. Those who voluntarily discontinue their insurance coverage while still employed are not eligible to convert. Under various state laws, conversion rights are required only upon expiration of any applicable continuation of coverage.

Characteristics of Individual Health Insurance Policies

The National Association of Insurance Commissioners (NAIC) has developed four model laws that relate to individual health insurance policies. (See Appendix A for a more complete listing of NAIC model laws.) Model laws are established to guide individual states in crafting their own insurance law. They are not mandatory.

- The Official Guide for Filing and Approval of Accident and Health Contracts sets forth standards for policy language, type size, policy provisions, exclusions, and limitations.
- The Uniform Policy Provisions Law (UPPL) specifies mandatory and optional provisions for use in all health insurance forms.
- The Individual Accident and Sickness Insurance Minimum Standards Act designates several categories for basic forms of coverage, with required minimum benefit levels for each.
- The Model Life and Health Insurance Policy Language Simplification Act establishes standards regarding readability.

Even with these model laws there is substantial variation in the structure and wording of policy provisions used by individual health insurers.

Individual Medical Expense Insurance Contract Provisions

Individual medical expense insurance contracts contain a number of basic provisions. Although some are similar to group medical expense insurance provisions, they are repeated here in the approximate order in which they usually appear in a policy to give readers a better understanding of the full individual medical expense insurance contract.

Basic Provisions

Insuring Clause

The insuring clause expresses in general terms the insurer's promise to pay benefits. It identifies the insurer, expresses the promise to pay, and recites in very general terms the scope and limits of coverage.

Consideration Clause

In the consideration clause, the insurer states that it is issuing a policy in consideration of the application and that the payment of the first premium must occur on or before delivery of the policy.

Notice of Right of Examination

The notice of the right to examine the policy and return it must appear on the front page of the policy. It also is known as the ten-day "free-look" provision.

Renewal Provision

Traditionally, most medical expense policies have been renewable for additional terms under certain conditions. (In contrast, accident policies and other health insurance designed to cover short-term risk situations are issued for a single term and terminate at the end of that term.) Renewal arrangements varied according to whether the policy was issued as "noncancellable," "guaranteed renewable," "nonrenewable for stated reasons only," or "optionally renewable."

Beginning with policies issued on or after July 1, 1997, the Health Insurance Portability and Accountability Act of 1996 requires most individual medical expense policies to be guaranteed renewable, at the option of the individual policyholder. Nonrenewal is allowed only for specified circumstances such as nonpayment of premiums, fraud or misrepresentation, or an insurer's decision to exit the market. For policies not subject to the HIPAA, the traditional renewal arrangements are still available.

Noncancellable. A noncancellable policy gives the insured the right to continue it in force by the timely payment of premiums set forth in the policy until at least age 50 or, in the case of a policy issued after age 44, for at least five years from its date of issue. The insurer has no right to make unilaterally any change in any provisions of the policy while the policy is in force.

In other words, with a noncancellable policy the insurer cannot cancel, refuse to renew, or raise the premium rates higher than shown in the policy for a period of time, provided the insured continues timely payment of premiums.

Guaranteed renewable. The definition for guaranteed renewable is the same as for noncancellable policies, except that the insurer may

111

make changes in premium rates by classes. Class here means broad categories such as age or occupation, thus eliminating the possibility of any premium rate increases on an individual basis.

Nonrenewable for stated reasons only. These policies fall between guaranteed renewable and optionally renewable. The insurer is restricted in its right to nonrenew any particular individual's policy. It may nonrenew only under certain circumstances, such as:

- when the insured reaches a certain age;
- when the insured ceases to be employed; or
- when the insurer refuses to renew all policies bearing the same form number as the insured's policy.

This form of renewal provision does not protect the insured as well as a guaranteed renewable provision, but it is more protective than a policy that is renewable solely at the option of the insurer.

Optionally renewable. Optionally renewable insurance gives the insured the least security in terms of continuation of coverage. It is renewable only with the consent of the insurer, which has a unilateral right to refuse renewal at the end of any period for which premiums have been paid. In lieu of nonrenewal, the insurer may set conditions that must be fulfilled before it will agree to renewal of the policy. Such conditions could include a policy amendment eliminating coverage for certain types of losses, eliminating coverage for injuries to certain parts of the body, or limiting the extent of coverage for certain occurrences.

Cancellation vs. nonrenewal. Cancellation is distinct from nonrenewal. Nonrenewal may occur only on a premium due date; cancellation may occur any time during the term of coverage following a required period of advance notice. Cancellation also assumes the pro-rata return of any unearned premium. Some states prohibit cancellation provisions, which are seldom used anyway.

Eligibility of Family Members

The UPPL specifically provides for the writing of family insurance. It stipulates that coverage may be afforded to "all eligible members of the family including husband, wife, dependent children . . . and any other person dependent on the insured." It further provides that any child under a specified age (not to exceed 19 years) may be included without meeting a dependency test. Children over the age specified for assumed dependency must be established as dependents of the insured. Once a policy has been issued, newborn children are automatically covered.

The usual eligibility provision would include the spouse of the insured and the unmarried children of the insured and of the insured's spouse who are not more than 19 years of age, or age 23 if they are attending school on a full-time basis and remain dependent upon the insured. Handicapped children remain covered past age 23. The spouse remains eligible unless there is a divorce or until a stated age, usually 65, or eligibility for Medicare.

A dependent's coverage terminates when he or she reaches a certain age or ceases to be dependent on the insured. Medical expense coverage usually terminates when insureds become eligible for Medicare. Children whose coverage terminates, and spouses whose coverage terminates because of divorce or annulment, may convert to other similar coverage if offered by the insurer. All states, however, do not require insurers to include this conversion privilege.

Definitions

As with group medical expense insurance, individual medical expense insurance contracts include specific definitions of terms concerning the conditions and circumstances for coverage. The words *injury* and *sickness,* for example, are specifically defined. Not every insurer, of course, defines these and other terms in precisely the same way.

Benefit Provisions

The benefit provisions section is the essence of any insurance contract and sets forth the insurer's promises. Each benefit provided by the policy is explained in detail, indicating the conditions that establish the insurer's liability to make payment, the conditions under which payment will be made, the nature and extent of benefits payable, and the applicable benefit limitations.

113

Schedule of Benefits

The benefits provided by a policy must be clearly spelled out in a manner that affords the policyholder easy reference and understanding. This is customarily done on a separate schedule of benefits or policy specifications page, which shows the policy number and date of issue, the name of the insured, the various types and amounts of benefits, the initial annual premium, any maximum benefit periods, any elimination periods, and any other variables.

Exclusions and Limitations

The exclusions and limitations section of a contract limits an insurer's liability in cases that otherwise would be covered. An exclusion may protect the insurer against any of an insured's voluntary activities that are hazardous and either greatly increase the risk of a loss (such as attempted suicide) or actually result in loss. An exclusion also might protect the insurer against a very large number of losses in a short period of time, which could impair its ability to pay benefits.

Execution Clause

Just as the applicant must sign the application, the insurer must, through an authorized executive officer, sign the insurance policy. This signifies that the insurer has entered into the contract and will be bound by its terms. In modern policy issue systems, the signature is a facsimile printed on the policy.

Agent's Countersignature

Where it is required by law or by the terms of the policy, the agent's countersignature on the cover of the policy is the last act performed before delivery of the policy to the insured. Even where it may not be a legal requirement, an insurer may wish to require it as an additional control over the issuance of its policies. The signature evidences the identity of the agent and makes her or his participation a matter of record. Agents required to sign policies might be expected to exercise care in carrying out their responsibilities. This requirement also may help to ensure that business will be preserved for agents licensed to write business in the state.

Riders

A rider is a separate document that amends the policy to which it is attached. The three types of riders to individual health insurance contracts concern policy language, optional benefits, and exclusions. Insurers use the terms rider, endorsement, and amendment interchangeably.

UPPL Required Provisions

Entire Contract

Only those items actually included in the policy are part of the contract of insurance. Any changes may be made only by an executive officer of the insurer. Agents do not have the authority to change or waive policy provisions. Representations made in the application do not bind the insured unless a copy of the application is made part of the policy and the insured has the opportunity to review it.

Time Limit on Certain Defenses and the Incontestable Clause

The UPPL restricts to three years an individual health insurer's right to rescind or void a policy because of misstatements in the application. Misstatements refer to incorrect or omitted information from the applicant that was material to the risk. If the misstatements were fraudulent, the time limit does not apply, although fraud can be difficult to prove.

The incontestable clause is an alternative provision to the time limit provision that may be used in noncancellable or guaranteed renewable policies. This clause also limits an insurer's right to contest the policy to two years. It excludes from this time frame any period during which the insured is totally disabled.

The certain defenses provision and the incontestable clause place a limit of two years on an insurer's right to avoid coverage for pre-existing conditions, except for any that are specifically excluded by name. The

115

obvious advantage of these provisions for insureds is that they offer protection against loss of a policy or being deprived of benefits after the contract has been in force for a substantial period of time.

Grace Period

Insurers are required to give insureds a specified period of grace beyond the due date of each premium. During this grace period the premium can be paid and the policy maintained in force. Coverage remains in effect during the grace period.

Reinstatement

If a premium is not paid before the end of the grace period, coverage ceases. This provision sets forth the procedure for allowing the insured to apply for reinstatement of the policy and affording the insurer the opportunity to reevaluate risk. A reinstated medical expense policy limits coverage to sickness beginning more than ten days after the date of reinstatement. The ten-day delay for coverage is designed to avoid claims on illnesses in existence at the time of reinstatement.

Claim Provisions

The UPPL has five provisions that deal with the filing of claims:

- Notice must be given to the insurer within 20 days of loss or as soon as is reasonably possible.
- Forms must be supplied by the insurer within 15 days after the insured gives notice of claim.
- Proof of loss must be submitted within 90 days after the date of such loss, or as soon as is reasonably possible, but not later than one year from the end of the 90-day period, except in the absence of legal capacity.
- Claims must be paid promptly.
- Benefits must be paid to the insured, if living; otherwise, to the beneficiary or estate. There is an optional clause that insurers may include to

116

allow for payment of up to $1,000 to a relative of the insured in the event the insured has died or is incapable of accepting the benefits.

Legal Actions

The insured must wait at least 60 days after submitting proof of loss before starting legal action against the insurer. This provision protects the insurer against untimely lawsuits begun before it has had a reasonable opportunity to investigate the claim. Further, the insured is prohibited from bringing legal action more than three years after proof is required.

Optional Provisions

There are several other provisions that an insurer may or may not include. Some of the salient optional provisions include:

- premium adjustment if the insured changes to an occupation that is more or less hazardous than the occupation at the time the policy was issued;

- deduction of unpaid premium from claim payments; and

- in case of a misstatement of age, adjusting the benefit amount to what the premium paid would have purchased if the insured's correct age had been given.

■ Emerging Trends

With the current rate of mergers, acquisitions, joint ventures, and development of subsidiary companies, insurance companies are faced with the necessity of developing and filing contracts in the name of the new corporate entity. All of the requirements addressed in this chapter must be considered so that insurance companies create contracts that are in compliance with the insurance laws of the states in which they operate.

117

■ Summary

An insurance policy is an important document. It represents promises made by an insurer and, for the most part, is the document upon which the policyholder must rely as evidence of those promises. Although there are many variations in health insurance contracts issued by insurers, certain key elements are essential to all. Insurers are concerned with creating a contract that is both a clear, unambiguous, binding agreement under the law and in compliance with the insurance laws of the state in which the contract is issued. Requirements can vary substantially by state, although NAIC model laws and regulations have resulted in some uniformity in those states adopting the models.

■ Key Terms

Acceptance
Aleatory contract
Ambiguity
Application
Assignment of benefits
Benefit provision
Capacity to contract
Conditional contract
Conditional receipt
Consideration
Contract
Contract filing
Contract provision
Contracts of adhesion
Conversion privilege
Coordination of
    benefits (COB)
Dependents

Effective date
Eligibility
Entire contract
Exclusions
Experience refund
Extended benefits
Grace period
Incontestable clause
Insuring clause
Limitations
Meeting of the minds
Minimum Standards
    Model Law
Misstatement of age
National Association
    of Insurance
    Commissioners
    (NAIC)

Noncancellable
Nonrenewable
Offer
Optional provisions
Pre-existing conditions
    provision
Rescission
State insurance
    department
Termination
    provisions
Uniform Policy
    Provisions Law
    (UPPL)
Unilateral contract

Chapter 5

MARKETING AND SALES OF HEALTH INSURANCE PRODUCTS

■ Introduction

In the past, marketing was considered synonymous with selling. Many people thought that marketing was concerned only with the seller's actual sales plans and the methods used to convince the consumer to buy the product. The concept and understanding of marketing has been expanded and broadened in recent years. Insurers now realize that every facet of their business process ultimately affects the successful sale of their products. Currently marketing is defined as the sum total of all corporate functions and activities directly and indirectly involved in the effective selling of products to the consumer and the efficient fulfillment of the product's promises with the objective of earning reasonable profit.

Marketing group and individual health insurance products is a complex process. First, a market need must be identified. For example, when there were no hospitals, there was no need for hospital coverage. Marketing includes identifying and evaluating needs and selecting markets. Appropriate products must be developed, promoted, and distributed through a well-trained and professional sales force. Other insurance company functions—especially actuarial science, underwriting, policy service, and claims—affect product sales or the retention of a policyholder in some way.

This chapter discusses the components necessary for successful marketing and sales of group and individual health insurance.

■ Health Insurance Markets

The market for group and individual health insurance products is both large and diverse.

Group Health Insurance Markets

Insurers categorize group insurance markets primarily by size and types of group policyholders.

Size

Approximately 80 percent of all insured groups have fewer than 100 lives. Generally contracts for these smaller groups provide standardized benefit structures and are administered by the insurer. The primary purchasing considerations in this market are price, ability to buy the same kinds and quality of benefits that are available to larger groups, and simplified administration.

Groups of 100 to 500 lives account for about 10 percent of all group contracts in force. Greater flexibility in benefit design and administration characterizes plans in this market. Both individual sales insurance agents and brokers/consultants actively sell to this market. The insurer's group field sales representative frequently is involved directly in the sale and service to the policyholder. Purchasing considerations in this market are net cost, plan design flexibility, and quality of service.

Although they account for over half of the total premium dollars, groups of 500 or more lives make up only about 10 percent of all group insurance contracts in force. Insurers often tailor benefits to the specifications of the buyer and modify administrative procedures to suit policyholder needs. Insurers usually sell these contracts through brokers/consultants or directly. In either case, the insurer's group field sales representative or home office sales personnel are involved. The interests of the buyer are represented by an employee benefit consultant.

Types of Group Policyholders

To acquire and retain employees, an employer must provide not only a fair wage but also a package of insurance benefits to offset the expense and economic loss resulting from medical treatment, disability, or death. Employers purchasing group insurance on behalf of their employees usually are characterized as single employers. Unions and multiple-employer groups also are policyholders of group insurance for their members.

Single employers. A single employer may be a sole proprietor, a partnership, a corporation, or a number of entities (such as subsidiaries) insured through a common owner. Single employer contracts make up by far the largest share of the group market, accounting for about 90 percent of all group policies in force.

Employers may pay all premiums, or the employer and employee both contribute to the amount. In addition, state insurance laws and regulations may affect requirements regarding minimum group size, employee eligibility, life insurance maximums, and requirements pertaining to health insurance coverage of these groups. Unions also may influence which benefits are offered.

Labor unions. A national, regional, or local labor union may provide coverage for its members under a policy issued to the union. In these contracts the union pays premiums through its dues structure or member contributions. Only a small number of all group contracts in force are issued to unions. This market is diminishing in importance because unions prefer to obtain their benefits through collective bargaining.

121

The purchase of group insurance under a contract issued to a labor union can be an important membership benefit for unions unable to negotiate these benefits through an employer.

Multiple-employer groups. Multiple-employer groups involve union/management trusts, groups combining several employers, trade and professional organizations, and creditor arrangements.

- **Negotiated Trusteeships (Taft-Hartley Groups).** Negotiated trusteeships involve a trust established under the authority of the Labor Management Relations Act of 1947 (Taft-Hartley Act). Composed of one or more unions and one or more employers, the trust provides coverage for union members engaged in activities that affect interstate or foreign commerce under a group contract issued to the named trustees. These contracts, established as a result of a collective bargaining agreement between the union(s) and the employer(s), account for about 2 percent of all group insurance contracts in force.

- **Multiple-Employer Trusts (METS).** METS involve the participation of single employers, usually in the same or related industries, brought together by an insurer, agent, broker/consultant, or administrator. The purpose for uniting these employees is to provide insurance for their employees through a master contract issued to a trustee under a trust agreement. In this way small employers can provide lower cost benefits that are usually available only to big companies.

- **Trade Associations.** Single employers, bound together by membership in a trade association, may provide insurance for their employees under a contract issued to the association. This type of contract accounts for a small percentage of all group contracts in force.

- **Professional and Individual Membership Associations.** Individuals in various professions—law, medicine, engineering, and education, for example—can provide coverage for themselves and sometimes their employees through a contract issued to an association or to a trust formed to administer the insurance. The premium for insurance coverage in these groups ordinarily is paid by the association member. Like trade association contracts, professional and individual association programs compose a small part of all group contracts in force.

- **Creditor Groups.** A creditor institution, such as a bank or finance company, may contract to insure its debtors to provide for payment of a debt if a debtor dies or suffers a period or periods of disability.

Individual Health Insurance Markets

Insurers market individual health insurance policies to three specific consumer groups:

- A primary permanent market of people who depend solely on individual health policies for insurance protection.

- A primary interim market of people who need temporary coverage. These individuals, who usually will be covered by a group health plan within one to six months, typically are temporarily unemployed, just out of college, or recently discharged from military service. Newly employed workers who are ineligible for group coverage during an initial probationary period are also a market for interim individual health insurance.

- A supplemental market composed of households covered by a primary plan but needing additional coverage to cover deficiencies in their primary plan.

Product Research and Development

The potential for new products or improvements to existing products is limited only by imagination and creativity. To be effective, however, insurers undertake research and development (R&D) activities to ensure that new products support insurer goals. These activities are similar for group and individual health insurers.

Every insurance company writing group or individual health insurance is involved in product research and development efforts to some degree, but the organization of these efforts varies. The research and development responsibility is delegated either to an R&D department or to a specially appointed ad hoc committee. Experts from various insurer departments usually are consulted.

Most insurers prepare a carefully designed product development statement that targets specific customers and defines the degree of risk the company is willing to undertake and the financial objectives of product development efforts.

The product development process has seven basic stages.

Idea Generation

Idea generation usually starts with some specific input from the field, the home office staff, or senior management.

Market Research

Market research involves analysis of competition and market needs, market penetration studies, office location studies, and detailed analysis of sales results.

Product Outline

The product outline is a general statement of the target market (group size and type, geographic area, industry, socioeconomic group, and so forth), the essential distinguishing characteristics that differentiate the product from others, a preliminary estimate of the cost of developing the product, and a list of potential benefits to be derived from its development.

Market Analysis

A market analysis examines whether a product is compatible with the product development statement and if it relates to other products and services the insurer sells in the market it services. It assesses the expertise and ability required to support developing the product and considers whether its current distribution and administration systems can handle the product. Also important is the influence of external factors such as consumers, providers of health care, the government, and competitors.

Product Design and Development

Product design and development involves:

- creating and filing the contract with the state insurance departments;

- developing rates and commission schedules;

- setting underwriting limits, requirements, and guidelines;

- writing underwriting manuals, field releases, field training programs, and marketing brochures for policyholders and agents; and

- modification of data processing systems and administrative processes (proposing, rating, issuing, billing, accounting, benefits processing, and ongoing administrative maintenance).

Product Introduction

The product is introduced by the sales department. Brochures, sales presentations, competitive comparisons, sales manuals, mailers, flip charts, agent training materials, and, in the case of larger insurers, films, videotapes, or audio recordings are used to present the product to clients.

Sales Monitoring and Review

The final stage of the product development process—monitoring and review—involves analysis of sales results, analysis of a number of quotes, and direct input from the sales staff and agency force.

■ Methods of Distribution

Health insurance is sold through a number of distribution channels. These channels differ for group and individual insurance.

Group Health Insurance Distribution

Home office salespeople support the field sales office by product promotion and development, training, and administrative and national account services. In the group field sales offices are group representatives and a staff responsible for sales and service through agents and brokers within a defined geographic area. Each field sales office also has a manager who reports to a regional vice president or manager.

An insurer with a group operation too small to have a group field sales force usually delegates sales and service responsibilities to general agents and brokers. Regardless of the size and organization of the group sales operation, the sales and service activities generally are the same.

Most insurers conduct marketing activities involving policyholder contact through their group representatives and through group producers— insurance agents, brokers, and consultants. A few insurers, known as direct writers, solicit business directly from prospective policyholders. They employ salaried representatives to obtain group business rather than work through commissioned agents or brokers.

Group Representatives

Group representatives are insurance company employees trained in the techniques of selling and servicing group insurance plans. (Because of the different skills required, some companies break the job down into group sales representative and group service representative.) The responsibilities of group representatives are to:

- work with agents and brokers in developing group prospects;
- secure data and submit them to the insurer's home office with recommendations for a proposal;
- prepare field group proposals and present group proposals to prospects;
- assist in the closing of group sales;
- assist in the enrollment of employees under new group plans;
- set up administrative procedures for new policyholders;

126

- make regular service calls to assist in administration and plan modernization;

- "sell" rate increases and retain present policyholders; and

- keep the home office informed of competitive developments in the group field.

Insurers generally compensate group representatives by a salary or by salary plus an incentive bonus for exceeding goals or quotas. The importance of bonus compensation varies from insurer to insurer; a few provide no bonus, while others use a bonus as the principal form of compensation. (See the section on agent compensation later in this chapter.)

Agents

Agents of a group insurer usually are under contract to sell its full line of products. They are a primary source of small- and medium-sized group sales. On these smaller cases the agent may work without the assistance of a group representative, thus providing valuable personal service to clients.

In addition to receiving compensation for the sale and service of a group plan insurance, some agents are attracted to selling group health insurance because:

- it is an excellent source of prospects for other business insurance or personal lines;

- it enables agents to offer a complete range of products and service to business clients; and

- it allows agents to sell during the normal nine-to-five workday.

Brokers

Brokers are individuals or business firms that represent the policyholder in placing coverage with an insurer. They are the principal source of large group sales.

127

Although business written by individuals and small brokerage firms accounts for a significant portion of the market, the largest percentage in terms of premium is controlled by specialized group brokers and by the largest brokerage firms with specialized group departments. Their contacts with top management for general insurance lines (property, casualty, and fire) are helpful to them in handling group health insurance for larger accounts. These specialists are knowledgeable about the technical aspects of insurance as well as the policyholder's operations.

A broker also may act as a third-party administrator (TPA) handling the administration of one or more group plans, including premium accounting, maintainenance of employee-eligibility lists, and claims.

Employee Benefit Consultants

Employee benefit consultants are individuals or firms specializing in the design, sales, and service of employee benefit plans. Because they may deliver the same services as the large brokerage firms, it is difficult to distinguish between consultants and brokers. The consultant, however, is less likely to be involved in the placing of coverage with an insurer, but rather makes recommendations to the policyholder. Consultants usually are paid a fee by the policyholder rather than commissions by the insurance company.

Individual Health Insurance Distribution

Most individual policies are solicited through the efforts of brokers and agents who deal directly with the public, but many agents also use mass marketing to reach prospects.

Brokers

Brokers for individual health insurance are licensed independent salespersons who commonly place health insurance business with a number of insurers, selecting an insurer based on what the broker believes to be the proper coverage at the right price for his/her client. Many brokers sell a full line of property and liability coverages as well as life and health insurance.

Although most insurers writing health coverage currently accept broker-age business, some decline to do so. They feel that only well-trained, full-time agents who are specialists in health insurance can provide the proper service to the consumer and at the same time assist the insurer's underwriting staff in risk appraisal matters.

In recent years, though, many large independent property and liability brokerage firms have established life and health departments staffed by life and health insurance specialists. As a result many brokers have become just as sophisticated in health insurance underwriting as full-time, company-trained health insurance agents.

Brokers also can play an important role in representing prospects for large group insurance plans. When appointed by large corporations as insurance advisors for all lines of insurance, brokers are in a position to influence the selection of the insurer that will provide all insurance—life and health as well as property and casualty.

Agents

A hallmark of the insurance business is the agency system, in which peo-ple under contract to an insurance company act as agents for that com-pany. Agents for individual health insurance may work through a branch office, a general agency office, or a personal producing general agent's (PPGA) office.

The agent does the actual person-to-person selling to the consumer and serves the following vital functions:

- field underwriting—initial risk selection;
- policyholder service—answering questions and assisting in policy changes; and
- public relations—projecting the proper image of the insurer to the consumer.

Although most agents are independent contractors, they may be employ-ees of either the insurer or the agency for which they work. In return for selling policies, the agent receives desk space, clerical and backup

129

services, compensation (usually commissions), and fringe benefits. Prospective agents also receive training to prepare for state licensing examinations, as well as product and sales training.

Branch offices.   Under the branch office system the insurer has exclusive control over the sales office. The office is managed by a branch sales manager who is an employee of the insurance company. Agents assigned to a branch office may be either employees of the insurer or independent contractors.

The branch sales manager, who generally reports to a regional or divisional manager, is an employee of the insurer and exercises control over several branches. A branch sales manager's responsibilities include the following:

- recruiting and training new agents;
- supervising office employees and the activities of the field force assigned to the branch office;
- disseminating information from the insurer to the agent;
- handling service problems from policyholders; and
- ensuring that the office develops a certain quality and quantity of insurance sales.

Insurers compensate branch sales managers by direct salary, although the sales managers usually receive additional compensation based on the quality and quantity of sales, retention of business, and/or the amount of premiums that policyholders continue to pay year after year.

General agents.   General agents operate an agency under contract with an insurer. They provide their own office facilities and clerical and supervisory personnel. They recruit, train, and supervise their own agents and may share with the insurer many of the expenses of training and financing new agents for the general agency.

Personal producing general agents (PPGAs).   Personal producing general agents also work independently under a contract with an insurer. PPGAs usually have had a number of successful years in the business as personal producers and seek contractual relationships that

give them greater commission compensation than they received
as agents.

In general, personal producing agents absorb all their own expenses,
including office facilities, clerical staff, and any other overhead
expenses. They usually receive fringe benefits, such as group life
and health coverages and retirement benefits, under the insurer's
benefit plans.

Most PPGAs have the authority to hire or appoint their own agents and/
or use independent brokers.

Mass Marketing

Individual health insurance is sold through mass marketing as a way to
approach a large number of prospects simultaneously. The mass marketing techniques used are direct mail, franchise plans, third-party sponsorship, vending machines, and over-the-counter sales.

Direct mail. Insurers use direct-mail marketing to approach selected
groups of individuals. They send an offer by mail to individual households, including a proposal outlining the type of coverage offered and a
short-form application that requires answers to a minimum number of
health and occupation questions.

When marketing policies have limited benefits, mainly hospital indemnity or limited medical expense coverage, some insurers use newspaper
and magazine advertisements that contain a short-form application
that can be completed easily by the respondent and mailed directly to
the insurer.

In addition to printed media, insurers frequently advertise by radio and
television to obtain responses from consumers interested in the policy
offered. The insurer usually provides consumers with a toll-free telephone number to call for additional information or to apply for the coverage. The insurer then answers these consumer responses by a direct
mail approach or by arranging for an agent to call on the consumer.

Franchise plans. Franchise plans are designed to provide some of the advantages of group coverage to employees or individuals who do not qualify for true group insurance—that is, they do not meet the definition of an eligible group in the various state statutes. Franchise plans are written to cover hospital and surgical expense, major medical, disability income, and accidental death benefits. Dependents of the applicants usually are eligible for all these benefits except disability income. The chief advantage of getting insurance through a franchise plan is a reduction in the premium rate for individual insurance, which insurers can offer because of lower costs to them due to a volume processing discount and a lower commission schedule for such sales.

The insurer underwrites each application individually and may reject or issue on a substandard basis. The policy may be renewable at the option of the insurer or it may be a guaranteed renewable type. Employers or some designated person, acting on behalf of the employer or association, pay premiums to the insurer periodically.

Employers that want to make a franchise plan available to all employees may establish a payroll deduction or salary allotment plan. Under this arrangement an employer offers the employees the convenience of paying for individual insurance through a salary deduction.

The franchise method of marketing gives insurers another significant market for selling individual health insurance coverage to employees of smaller firms, members of associations, and members of partnerships and limited corporations. It has resulted in new individual health insurance products, billing procedures, and underwriting practices. Products specifically designed for this market typically do not provide for the policy to be continued when the insured leaves the organization, but they often include the privilege of converting the policy to a similar individual plan at that time.

Third-party sponsorship. Under this system the insurer joins with a third-party organization that is not an insurance company—such as a bank, a savings and loan association, or a corporation that uses credit cards or some other regular billing system—to approach customers. The customers of the third party are offered policies by direct mail. Insurers send advertisements with the third party's billing or correspondence, or place advertisements in the third party's place of business.

The third party usually bills the customer for insurance premiums. The insurer performs all other policy-related transactions for the insured customer.

Vending machines and over-the-counter sales. Most of these types of sales are travel accident policies, available from coin-operated vending machines. These policies offer coverage that provides benefits in case of death or dismemberment while the insured is a passenger on a common carrier such as an airplane. The protection is for a single trip, usually on a round-trip basis. The coverage may extend to death or dismemberment incurred on any common carrier used on the trip. Although vending machines appear to have reached their greatest level of use at airports, they also can be found in bus terminals and railroad stations. Large amounts of this limited type of coverage are available at low cost. There is never any contact with an agent or other insurance representative.

Travel agencies provide another outlet for travel accident coverage. Coverage can be purchased as an additional option or prepackaged into the traveler's tour plan. Various credit card companies also provide this type of coverage as an additional benefit.

■ Agent Compensation

Agent compensation for group and individual health insurance products is primarily through commissions. Other compensation methods differ.

Group Health Insurance Compensation

Group health insurance producers usually are compensated for group sales and services by commissions for business that they personally sell. Two types of commission schedules are in general use: the high-low

133

Table 5.1

High-Low and Level Commission Schedule

| Annual premium | High-low scale percentage commission | | Level scale percentage commission |
	1st year	2nd through 10th year	All 10 years
First $1,000	20.0%	5.0%	6.5 %
Next 4,000	20.0	3.0	4.7
Next 5,000	15.0	1.5	2.85
Next 10,000	12.5	1.5	2.6
Next 10,000	10.0	1.5	2.35
Next 20,000	5.0	1.5	1.85
Next 200,000	2.5	1.0	1.15
Next 250,000	1.0	.5	.55

commission schedule and the level commission schedule. Other compensation arrangements for selling group health insurance are override commissions, vesting, and direct fee payments from clients.

High-Low and Level Commission Schedule

The high-low commission schedule provides higher commissions the first year and lower commissions in renewal years. The level commission schedule provides the same total commission dollars each year (assuming the same premium each year) and is becoming the most common schedule. Over a ten-year period, either schedule usually will produce the same commissions (assuming that the premium is the same each year and that the group stays with the same insurer for those ten years). Persistency fees may be paid for business that continues beyond the tenth policy year. (Table 5.1)

Although insurance company practices vary, the agent or broker may sometimes choose either the higher first-year commission schedule or the level schedule. However, insurers or regulators in some states require a level schedule when cases are:

■ transferred from another insurer, a situation that occurs far more often than groups being insured for the first time;
■ reinstated;

134

Table 5.2

Override Commission Schedule

	High-low scale percentage commission		Level scale percentage commission
Annual premium	1st year	2nd through 10th year	All 10 years
First $1,000	4.0%	1.0 %	1.3 %
Next 4,000	4.0	.6	.94
Next 5,000	3.0	.3	.57
Next 10,000	2.5	.3	.52
Next 10,000	2.0	.3	.47
Next 20,000	1.0	.3	.37
Next 200,000	.3	.13	.15
Next 250,000	.2	.10	.55

- set up for participants to pay all the premium;
- judged by the insurer to have a high chance of lapse; or
- negotiated with unions.

Some insurers accelerate the payment of commissions to the agent by advancing substantially all the first-year commissions in one sum as soon after the sale as possible. Commissions for groups of less than 25 employees may be paid at a slightly higher scale in the first year and later years because the agent may be expected to do much of the work connected with selling, installing, and servicing the small group.

Override Commissions

Since a general agent or agency manager who is an experienced group producer can provide assistance to the writing agent that the insurer would otherwise expect to provide, insurers sometimes will agree to pay an override commission. This payment is in addition to the commission paid to the selling agent or broker, which is produced by the high-low schedule or level schedule. (Table 5.2)

Vesting

Vested commissions grant writing agents or their estates ownership of renewal commissions, whether or not the agent remains with the insurer. Vesting practices differ among insurers, but the trend in group insurance is away from this concept. Commissions generally are paid only when continuing service is provided to the policyholder by the writing agent who remains under contract with the insurer.

Other Compensation Arrangements

Sometimes group health insurance producers negotiate a fee arrangement directly with clients according to the services provided, based on some measure other than premium. For example, they may negotiate a flat monthly or annual fee or a per employee, per month charge. These arrangements are most common with producers who are either acting as third-party administrators or representing large clients.

Group representatives sometimes receive a bonus. Bonuses are a percentage of premium—first-year premiums or both first-year and renewal premiums. Bonus payments range between 10 and 50 percent of a group representative's salary, sometimes with a maximum payout limited to an amount equal to the salary. The bonus may count along with salary as total compensation and be used to determine the amount of company fringe benefits due to the group representative.

Individual Health Insurance Compensation

Insurers compensate agents who sell individual health insurance primarily through commissions, sometimes providing a training allowance for beginners and fringe benefits to established agents.

Commissions

The two basic types of commission arrangements for individual health insurance are high-low and level commissions, which operate much the same way as for group health insurance.

Many insurers provide their agents with special payment plans during their first few years in the business. This procedure helps agents to survive financially during that initial period when they have a small client base and no stream of renewal commissions to rely on. Many new-agent financing plans allow the new agent to draw current income from future commissions. The maximum drawable amounts and schedules of such financing plans differ from one organization to another.

Most insurers use different commission scales for hospital, surgical, and major medical coverages than for disability income coverage. A lower scale usually is applied to medical expense coverages because they have higher expense ratios and tend to be dropped/changed by the insured more often than does disability income insurance. Some insurers also justify higher commissions for disability income policies because the agent expends more sales effort to present the need for income protection and to propose the proper amount of coverage than he or she would for medical expense insurance.

Agents normally receive a commission that varies by:

- the amount of premiums to be paid for the coverage sold;
- the percentage amount called for by the terms of the commission plan in effect with the insurer or agency;
- the type of policy sold; and
- the length of time the policy has been in force.

Vesting

Vesting is the right of an agent to receive all or part of the commissions payable from an insurance sale, even after termination of his or her contract with the insurer. The agent's commission contract specifies these vesting rights.

Vesting may be unconditional or it may depend either on how long the agent has been with the insurer or on the amount of that agent's sales. Vesting also may vary depending on the agent's reason for termination—whether by death, disability, or voluntary or involuntary termination. If commissions are vested after the agent's death, they may be payable to the agent's estate or a person the agent has designated.

Other Compensation Arrangements

Individual health insurers use several other methods to compensate their producers, ranging from cash and fringe benefits to production rewards.

Training allowance. Some insurers give a training allowance to new agents. The agent is paid a salary but is required to produce a certain amount of premium or commission to validate the salary. The arrangement may last for a few months or a few years.

Development expense allowance. Many general agents operate under a supplemental agreement with the insurer that calls for payment of a development expense allowance. This payment usually is based on two factors: how much business is sold by the general agent and how long it stays in force. The purpose of such an allowance is to help pay the agency's overhead expenses.

Fringe benefits. Full-time agents who meet the minimum production requirement that most insurers have usually are covered under an insurer-sponsored group health and life insurance plan. They also often are covered under the insurer's pension plan, with the insurer and the agent both contributing to the agent's pension account.

Full-time agents who have coverage for fringe benefits usually are covered under the insurer's Social Security program. The employer pays half the Social Security tax and withholds the other half from the agent's commissions.

Conventions, sales campaigns, and recognition. Sales conventions open to those agents who meet or exceed set standards of performance provide a means of recognizing and encouraging excellence. Sales campaigns, with specified awards for increased levels of production, serve to motivate agents to perform at maximum levels.

■ The Sales Process

The sales processes for group and individual health insurance have a number of common elements. They both include steps ranging from prospecting to closing the sale to servicing the client after the sale. Each of these steps differs, however, for selling group and individual insurance.

Group Health Insurance Sales

Prospecting

Group health insurance representatives generally prospect for new group insurance clients through agents and brokers and devote considerable time and effort to developing them as sources of business. These representatives may take a comprehensive approach to developing group prospects among the full-time agents of the insurance company by participating periodically in agency meetings, conducting training sessions for groups of agents, and distributing sales and informational bulletins.

The most effective development of group prospects usually occurs when the group representative is able to establish a close working relationship with an agent and educate and motivate that agent to prospect regularly. General insurance brokers may be developed and cultivated in much the same way as individual insurance agents. One-on-one motivation and training of the individual broker are the keys to the successful development of group prospects.

Group representatives prospect somewhat differently in dealing with large, specialized brokers. Through establishing a close working relationship, group representatives attempt to demonstrate their own abilities to the broker and to motivate the broker to place group insurance with a particular insurer because of its products and capabilities. The development of group business through employee benefit consultants is similar to the methods used with large brokers. Group representatives also make direct contact with a large employer and attempt to secure its group business.

Regardless of the methods used in prospecting for group insurance, an essential element of a successful effort is securing information necessary for plan design and proposal preparation.

Plan Design and Proposal Preparation

To prepare a proposal an insurer must evaluate the prospect's needs, design the benefit plan, underwrite the plan, calculate the rates, and arrange all plan aspects into an attractive sales proposal. Preparing a proposal requires certain information regarding the prospect, including an employee census and descriptions of the present and proposed plans and of the claims and premium experience of the present plan. Other items of information that may be considered are the business of the prospect, any collective bargaining agreements affecting the coverage, trust agreements, objectives of the client, and a statement of financial condition.

The development of plan specifications varies according to the preferences of individual brokers or consultants. The main purpose of plan specifications is to give the client a basis for comparing apples to apples, and to establish, as objectively as possible, which insurer can best administer the program at a competitive net cost.

The local group representative's recommendation is always a strong factor in an insurer's decision to submit a quotation on a case. The representative must feel the prospect meets the insurer's underwriting standards and that there is a reasonably good chance of making the sale before the insurer proceeds with the proposal.

The proposal format for large group prospects usually includes the following information:

- brief description or outline of each coverage included in the benefit package;

- schedule of the rates and premiums quoted for each coverage;

- underwriting assumptions and requirements related to the proposed program of benefits;

- a cost illustration of the program usually covering a three- or five-year period; and

- information regarding the insurer's financial strength and accomplishments together with a list of well-known group policyholders.

140

Proposals for small groups usually include the above items, except the cost illustration. A cost illustration shows what portion of the premium is used to pay benefits, expenses, and so forth, and how much, if any, is returned to the policyholder in the form of a dividend. Cost illustrations usually are not made for smaller groups because the individual claim experience of such groups does not entitle them to an experience refund.

Proposal Presentation

Employee benefit consultants and large brokers usually want proposals submitted directly to them for analysis and recommendation to the client. This also is true of some smaller brokers. However, many smaller brokers and agents encourage direct participation by the group representative in presenting the proposal to the client.

General considerations in the final evaluation of the proposal are the insurer's capabilities, experience, and reputation. Specific considerations are the insurer's plan design, degree of compliance with plan specifications, and the competitive position of the insurer's rate quotation and cost illustration.

Closing the Sale

Whether the group is large or small, this part of the sales process is completed with a signed application and receipt for the first month's premium from the new policyholder.

Employee Enrollment and Plan Installation

The enrollment process differs between new and existing plans.

New plans. When a group plan is offered for the first time, or a line of insurance (such as dental insurance) is added to an existing plan, the next step after closing the sale is presenting the plan to the employees. After the insurance company prepares an announcement letter or booklet that explains the plan to the employees, the employer arranges for employee presentation meetings, distribution of employee enrollment cards, and key employees' follow-up to obtain the signed cards. The active support of the employer and the use of key personnel is essential to getting signed employee enrollment cards, particularly if employees are paying part of the cost of the plan.

Existing plans. If an existing plan is awarded to a new insurance company, re-enrollment may be conducted even though no new line of insurance is added and the existing lines remain unchanged. This re-enrollment might be done for a number of reasons, including:

- improving employee awareness of the plan;
- making the employees comfortable with the new insurer; or
- ensuring adequate participation when employee contributions are increased.

Upon completion of the enrollment process, the group or service representative sends the signed application, the enrollment cards, and the first month's premium to the insurance company's home office or group field office for final acceptance and issuance of the master policy, individual certificates, and administrative material. Thereafter, this material is sent to the representative for installation of the program.

The representative, usually accompanied by the agent or broker, delivers the material to the client and thoroughly reviews all aspects of the plan's administration, including premium billing and accounting, claim procedures, and benefits. For smaller groups the installation may be made by the agent alone.

Servicing the Policyholder

The group or service representative makes periodic service calls on the policyholder to assist in the proper administration of the plan. It is customary to use a check-off type form as a guide in making a thorough review of administrative practices and the status of various aspects of the case. This form generally is used as a service report to the home office of the insurer.

Retention of business is an important part of the service function. For example, a rate increase could lead to a lapse of policy or its transfer to another insurer. However, good relations with the group or service representative could lead to a better understanding by the policyholder or broker of why the rate increase was needed.

Good service contributes greatly to increased policyholder satisfaction and retention. Poorly serviced plans are prime targets for sales efforts by other insurance companies and brokers. One very important advantage for the group representative who gives regular and efficient service is the opportunity to sell expanded or additional group coverages to the client.

Individual Health Insurance Sales

Prospecting

All prospects for individual health insurance have names, but not all names are prospects. Names are only the beginning of the prospecting activity, and after securing them the agent starts the process of converting them into prospects. To be considered prospects for individual health insurance, the names on an agent's list must have a current need for health insurance and the ability to pay for it and to meet the insurer's underwriting requirements.

Health insurance agents develop a file of prospects from many different sources, such as present policyholders of the agent or insurer, friends and relatives of the agent, referrals from policyholders, or persons who can influence other persons favorably toward the purchase of insurance from a particular agent.

Other sources include city and county records, telephone directories, graduation lists, mortgage lists, and community activity lists. Announcements of marriages and births and specialized lists from listing companies that compile and sell them also can be useful.

There are a variety of approaches the agent may use to obtain an interview with a prospect. Some of the more common approaches are:

- *cold calls*—the agent makes an unannounced sales call on a prospect;
- *preapproach telephone calls*—the agent attempts to create interest in setting up a sales interview;

143

- *preapproach letters*—the agent sends a letter to a prospect stating why he or she wants to visit, followed by the agent's calling in person or by telephone to arrange an interview; and

- *policyholder referrals*—a mutual friend of the agent and prospect makes an appointment for the agent, or a preapproach letter is sent with a list of clients recommending the agent. These clients are known to the prospect.

The last point is very important to an agent's business—developing policyholders who act as centers of influence to support the agent's sales activity. A center of influence, such as an attorney, accountant, banker, or realtor, has extensive contact with persons who respect this individual's opinions.

Fact Finding

After a successful approach the agent begins the sales interview. Before an appropriate health insurance plan can be recommended to a prospect, the agent must obtain a clear picture of the prospect's needs. These needs are determined by the answers to two basic questions:

- What health insurance protection does the prospect already have?
- What gaps should be filled to ensure adequate protection?

When the agent determines the answers to these questions based on a needs analysis, the prospect's needs will fall into one of the major market categories mentioned earlier: primary permanent, primary interim, or supplemental.

If answers reveal that the agent has a primary permanent market prospect who has no group insurance and is not covered by any government health care program, the health plan offered should include basic or comprehensive hospital and surgical protection in line with hospital costs in the community and also major medical expense coverage and disability income coverage at a level of protection adequate for the prospect's living expenses.

The prospect may need coverage on a temporary or interim basis. Many group coverages require 30, 60, or 90 days of employment before the group insurance covers the new employee. If this is the situation, the prospect would need coverage only until the group insurance coverage begins. The prospect's answers also may indicate a need for supplemental coverage, even if the prospect is covered by group insurance.

Presenting the Sales Materials

After determining the nature and extent of the prospect's needs, the agent recommends the product or coverages best suited to meet those needs. Agents generally present coverages using sales material from the insurer. This material includes brochures, pamphlets, and visual presentations that list the benefits and limitations of the particular plan presented. Through proper use of the sales material and a clear explanation of how the recommended product will meet the identified needs, the agent provides the prospect with the information needed to make the decision to buy.

Closing the Sale

To close the sale the agent completes an application for the plan agreed upon and obtains a prepayment of the first premium, although the latter is not always a requirement.

Servicing the Policyholder

After the coverage is issued, the agent can deliver the policy personally to the new policyholder and review the benefits it provides. The agent should explain the procedure for submitting a claim and give the policyholder a claim form.

Efficient and timely service should continue throughout the lifetime of the contract. In many instances after helping a policyholder make changes in the policy or answering questions, the agent gets referrals for new prospects and/or has the opportunity to sell additional coverage to the policyholder as changes in need develop.

145

■ Emerging Trends

Health care delivery systems are evolving and changing, and health insurers also must evolve and change or risk having their products become obsolete. Insurers will have to continue to increase their marketing research, develop innovative products to fit specific needs, improve agent training, explore new markets, and develop new or modify existing distribution systems. The success of group and individual health insurance marketing and sales systems will depend on how well insurers service and satisfy consumers' needs.

The disability income insurance marketplace is changing rapidly because claims and morbidity experience on both the group and the individual side have deteriorated badly since the late 1980s. A number of insurers have withdrawn from this market, and those that remain committed to the disability insurance product have had to make drastic changes in product definitions and features, underwriting requirements and standards, claim administration techniques, product pricing, and commission structures to bring their product lines back into a profitable position. Insurers must be prepared to move quickly and be innovative if they intend to remain in the health insurance product arena.

■ Summary

The marketing function plays a vital role in group and individual health insurance. It represents the area most closely linked with the generation of new insurance premiums—the lifeblood of any insurance company. To keep and find new customers in today's competitive environment, the marketing department needs to work closely with other areas of the company such as underwriting, actuarial, claims, and policyholder services.

■ Key Terms

Agency system	Commission	Employee benefit
Agent	Development expense	consultant
Broker	allowance	Franchise plan
Cold call	Direct mail	General agent

Group representative
High-low commission
Level commission
Market analysis
Market research
Marketing
Mass marketing
Multiple-employer
  group
Needs evaluation
Override commission
Personal producing
  general agent
  (PPGA)

Plan specifications
Policyholder referral
Policyholder service
Preapproach letters
Preapproach
  telephone calls
Primary interim
  market
Primary permanent
  market
Product design
Proposal
Prospect

Prospecting
Research and
  development (R&D)
Sales monitoring and
  review
Third-party
  sponsorship
Training allowance
Underwriter
Vending machine
Vesting

Chapter 6

UNDERWRITING OF HEALTH INSURANCE RISKS

■ Introduction

The term *underwriting* identifies that process by which an insurer determines if it will accept an application for insurance. Insurers that underwrite group health insurance operate on the premise that any large group of individuals will have only a few persons who, because of severe and frequent medical problems, either are not insurable risks or are not insurable on a standard basis.

Except in very small groups, individual health conditions usually are not of concern to the group underwriter. What is important is a wide spread of risk—a high percentage of eligible employees and their dependents participating in the plan. This spread creates a good chance that persons in the group are generally healthy.

Insurers that underwrite individual health insurance do not have the luxury of a wide spread of risk. Instead, they must evaluate each applicant's medical history to determine whether that applicant is an acceptable risk. If they do not, they subject themselves to possible anti-selection and potentially higher claim costs than they have priced for in their product.

This chapter discusses the basic functions of underwriters, the factors they must consider for determining risk selection, and sources of information that help them evaluate whether a group or an individual is an acceptable risk for health insurance. Most of the examples used relate to medical expense and disability income insurance.

■ Underwriters at Work

An underwriter may be an insurance agent working in the field dealing directly with the customer, or a home office underwriter whose primary responsibility is the evaluation of risks. This chapter discusses underwriting from the perspective of a home office group or individual health insurance underwriter.

Group Health Insurance Underwriter

The group health insurance underwriter's primary responsibilities apply to:

- new plans, renewal of existing plans, and plan modifications;
- smaller plans that are rated according to a rating formula; and
- larger plans that have rates based entirely or in part on their own experience.

The group health insurance underwriter examines the characteristics of a group's plan, weighs the variables, determines if a plan is acceptable as submitted or as modified to conform to the insurer's standards, and decides what to charge.

Other functions of the group health insurance underwriter are:

- identifying exceptions to standard underwriting rules;
- analyzing past experience;
- projecting claims;
- calculating claim reserves;
- determining administrative costs;

150

- underwriting new and existing groups; and

- reviewing policy revisions and evidence of insurability applications and modifying where appropriate.

Selection Process

Groups have many similarities, but the group underwriter is concerned mainly with analysis of the characteristics that distinguish a particular group. The underwriter determines if a group falls within the parameters set by the insurer for acceptable groups. Problem characteristics of a group often are not immediately obvious, but show up as potential problems as the underwriter examines the prospective group.

The selection process involves a number of steps, including:

- analyzing each group's characteristics, such as type of group, industry, size, eligible lives, participation, and financial considerations;

- evaluating the characteristics of the eligible individuals, such as sex, age, occupation, geographic location, income, employee turnover, administrative facilities, and employee contributions;

- determining that the contract applied for can be issued in the jurisdiction where it will be written;

- ascertaining that the prospective plan can be administered satisfactorily by both the policyholder and the insurer;

- determining the credibility of past claims experience or health history reported by a small group policyholder; and

- establishing premium rates that can be expected to produce a reasonable contribution to surplus or profit.

Many states in the early 1990s enacted a number of "small group market reforms," including a requirement that insurers serving the small group market accept (guarantee-issue) any small group that applies. The Health Insurance Portability and Accountability Act of 1996 enacts this requirement federally for small groups with two to fifty employees. The legislation does not limit the rates an insurer can charge small groups, but rating is governed by state insurance laws and regulations.

For groups not affected by state or federal guarantee-issue requirements, both the group and the benefits plan need to be acceptable to the insurer. If the group is acceptable, the underwriter determines the cost of the plan of benefits to be written and the services to be provided, including the methods for funding claims, reserves, and administrative expenses. If the group and plan are not compatible with the insurer's standards, the insurer declines the group.

Special underwriting conditions arise. For example, a group underwriter asked to duplicate a benefit plan that a large group has with another insurer may find that the plan does not conform to the requirements of the underwriter's insurance company. The underwriter may suggest alternative benefits, provisions, or methods of funding as a solution to a problem in underwriting a particular group. For example, if an analysis of outpatient claims shows an abnormally high incidence of questionable claims in a group, the underwriter might suggest contractual limitations on this coverage to avoid overutilization of benefits.

Rating

When rating a small group plan, an insurer's basic rate manual is applied to the group's composition (sex, age, earnings, and so forth). For larger risks, insurers typically use an experience rating formula to adjust their manual rates for prior claims experience. On very large accounts, insurers give full credibility to actual claims experience.

Certain types of industries also produce losses so materially in excess of those anticipated by the manual rates that insurers establish substandard or unacceptable risk classes and will not accept them under standard rating procedures. For more information on pricing see Chapter 4: Pricing Health Insurance Products in *Fundamentals of Health Insurance: Part B.*

Individual Health Insurance Underwriter

The individual health insurance underwriter is concerned primarily with morbidity—the frequency, duration, and severity of accident or sickness within a particular class of insured individuals. Because morbidity deals with many intangibles, it is difficult to establish a sound basis for evaluating risks.

The principal functions of the individual health insurance underwriter are:

- appraising and selecting health insurance applicants;
- determining whether an application should be approved and, if approved, the basis of that approval; and
- maintaining adequate communications with the field force.

Field communications are vital to the individual health insurance underwriter. The agent needs prompt advice about the status of pending applications. Proper communication, by contributing to the timely processing of applications and the agent's ability to deal effectively with clients, is an essential aspect of maintaining good field force morale.

The Health Insurance Portability and Accountability Act of 1996 places certain restrictions on individual insurers' underwriting practices. All insurers serving the individual market must accept any "eligible" individual who applies for coverage. Eligibility is defined by the act to mean an individual who has been covered for 18 months, most recently under a group health plan, who is not eligible for insurance from another source. Furthermore, insurers may not apply any pre-existing condition limitations on coverage issued to an "eligible" individual.

■ Risk Selection Factors

Risk selection factors in underwriting new business vary considerably between group health insurance and individual health insurance.

Group Health Insurance Selection Factors

When evaluating a new group (often a case transferred from another insurer), the underwriter assimilates and considers all relevant information. Of particular importance are the following factors:

153

- size of the group;

- industry;

- composition of the group;

- location of the group;

- plan of insurance;

- cost sharing;

- policyholder's administrative facilities;

- previous coverage and experience, including changes in benefits or rates during period;

- commission arrangements;

- expected persistency; and

- ability to meet financial obligations (particularly true on larger accounts).

Size of the Group

Underwriting considerations differ by group size.

Large groups. The larger the number of individuals insured, the more accurately the level of claims can be predicted. In a comprehensive medical care plan, a large group will by itself produce a relatively credible (statistically reliable) claim experience pattern year-to-year. (An exception is when there are extremely large claims due to the catastrophic illness of one or more individuals in the group.)

A principle concern in underwriting larger groups is the availability and accuracy of prior experience patterns for establishing initial premium rates. A small group with a 10 to 20 percent increase in claim experience from that anticipated in the rates would have no significant effect on the insurer's overall operation, since results could be averaged out by another small group with a similar percentage decrease in claims. The same deviation in a very large group could produce a loss to the insurer running into hundreds of thousands of dollars—a significant amount for even the largest of insurers. Also, with small groups such a deviation often arises from simple chance. With large groups it is more likely to be intrinsic to the group and to be repeated unless some action is taken.

To safeguard against such deviations, most insurers will not underwrite a very large group based on the standard rate tables. Instead, they will require information on prior experience and establish premium rates adjusted for prior experience deviations. A large plan's own experience is the best predictor of future claims. If actual claim experience shows that the initial rates were too high, they can be adjusted by an experience refund formula or prospective rate reductions.

Small groups. Groups with under 50 lives pose different underwriting problems. Many insurers issue policies to groups with as few as two lives. Because expenses in small groups are high in relation to the premium charged, insurers usually limit available benefit variations to keep administrative costs down. Additionally, because of the limited spread of risk in each small group, claim experience generally fluctuates widely.

These claim loss fluctuations lead most insurers to pool the experience of their small groups. The total premiums and total claims for such groups are combined into categories, with all groups in each category treated as a single risk for rating purposes. Many states have enacted small group rating regulations that require such pooling.

A specific hazard in underwriting small groups is the possibility that some employees in a small firm might purchase or substantially increase group insurance benefits because they or a family member have a physical impairment that will result in an immediate or substantial claim. This, together with the normal claims of the entire group, would place the insurer in a precarious loss position if it did not apply more restrictive underwriting requirements to small groups.

Most insurers attempt to control hazards inherent in small groups by using special underwriting rules, such as:

■ limiting the benefits available to standard plans; or

■ applying pre-existing condition limitations or exclusions that restrict coverage during some period, usually one year, for a condition treated immediately prior to coverage being effective.

155

Note that the use of pre-existing condition limitations and evidence of insurability have been limited by the Health Insurance Portability and Accountability Act (HIPAA) of 1996, as well as by many state small-group reform laws.

The HIPAA requires group insurers to credit prior insurance coverage toward any new pre-existing period, as long as there has not been more than a 63-day gap in coverage. Group insurers also may not exclude individual employees from coverage based on their health status.

In addition, pre-existing exclusions are limited to 12 months, with a six-month look-back (how far back you go to see if the condition existed before coverage began).

Industry

Health insurance generally provides benefits on a nonoccupational basis (not arising out of a person's employment), because occupational hazards usually are covered by workers' compensation law. Persons employed in certain industries, however, may develop health problems that are not considered occupational in origin. Group plans usually cover secondary health conditions that result from the physical environment in which the employees work. Employees working in a very hot area (e.g., a foundry) are more susceptible to respiratory ailments than those working in normal temperatures and may have more than average claims for these conditions. Occupations that require too much sitting can result in back problems that are not directly attributable to the job itself.

Other businesses, such as restaurants and parking garages, present a different underwriting problem. Health costs are related to education, income level, and a number of other socio-demographic factors. A substantial number of employees in these types of occupations receive low pay and need little or no training. Individuals who cannot meet the health standards of more selective employers might be forced to find employment in these marginal occupations, and their physical conditions would result in a much higher-than-expected health claim ratio. High rates of turnover mean that the composition of the group can change rapidly, making it difficult to predict costs. In addition, turnover in these occupations can result in sporadic coverage and health care, meaning high utilization when coverage is available. For these reasons certain industries either are not acceptable for health insurance or are classified as substandard and written at higher rates.

Composition of the Group

Certain characteristics of employees can affect the claim experience of a group. These characteristics usually are compensated for by specific adjustment factors in the rate structure.

Classes of employees. Generally, an underwriter desires to cover all full-time employees who are actively at work, since a large spread of risk can reduce selection against the insurer and lower the expense rate per insured employee. Part-time, seasonal, and temporary employees often are not covered or are covered in a way different from full-time employees. Their occupations may show frequent turnover, and administrative expense may be high.

Hourly employees also are excluded sometimes because many of them are insured for benefits under a separate collective bargaining agreement. Exclusion of hourly workers generally does not create an underwriting problem, provided the remaining eligible employee group is sufficiently large to meet the insurer's minimum requirements.

However, the underwriter must use caution if the employer elects to extend coverage only to executives and key personnel. Duplicate coverage or selection against the insurer is a possibility in this situation, since the insurer may find itself covering mainly a specific health condition of one of the executives or a member of the executive's family.

Age distribution. Most insurance companies have an automatic adjustment for age in their rate structure. Older individuals have a higher morbidity rate and larger disability income and medical care claims than younger employees. Even though this adjustment factor automatically will modify rates, the age distribution will be analyzed for deviations from norms. For example, an older group not only would have much

157

higher mortality and morbidity rates, but also might indicate, because of few young entrants into the group, financial difficulties in the employer's business.

If a group is losing its younger members continuously, initial rates based on the ages of the original members of the group soon will become inaccurate. Also, a younger group possibly could indicate high turnover, which would entail high administrative costs.

Sex distribution. Health insurance rates (except for accidental death and dismemberment insurance) show that at most ages women generally have a higher incidence of health claims than men. Women also have 25 percent more disabilities than men and are more likely to have frequent, short-duration disabilities in their younger years, with the frequency decreasing but duration increasing as they reach the 40- to 50-year-old range.

These sex differences are reflected in group rates as follows:

- Gender differences are not evident in the rate-setting process for large groups, since the rates are based on an evaluation of the claims experience of the entire group. However, gender-related claims are included as a part of the group's total claims experience used to establish the rate to be charged.

- Small group rates take gender differences into consideration in the actual rate calculation. This affects the total premium charged the employer. Individual employee contributions are established on a sex-neutral basis.

Dependent distribution. Where there is a high percentage of married women in a group, the percentage of employees carrying dependent coverage may be well below the 75 percent enrollment participation required because their husbands often have coverage with their own employers. However, when a spouse has an existing health condition, the employee usually elects duplicate coverage because of the high probability of a claim. The underwriter is faced with the possibility of selection against the insurer if only a few employees choose to insure their spouses.

Where there is low dependent participation, insurers may make inquiries into the dependent status of all employees, both men and women, to determine if other coverage is in effect. The risk generally will be accepted if there is adequate enrollment participation—that is, 75 percent of those with dependents who do not have other coverage.

In recent years, traditional dependent distributions have changed because of the increase in the number of single-parent households and the decrease in the number of children in most families.

Earning distribution. The earnings of employees in a group may affect the underwriting of the risk in several ways. Individuals with higher-than-average incomes generally seek more frequent and higher-priced medical care. This results in higher utilization of medical care services and expenditure of more claim dollars available under the program. (This effect is particularly evident with dental benefits.) A group consisting of primarily low-income employees may have significant underwriting implications, such as undesirable type of work or working conditions or a substandard risk because of work location. These situations might lead to difficulty in obtaining the proper participation required under the plan if the employees pay part or all of the premium cost.

Location of the Group

Charges for medical and dental care can vary widely by geographic area. Hospitals in the Southeast United States on average charge less than those in the Northeast, and charges in urban areas generally are higher than in rural areas. Since rate manuals adjust for these differences by use of area factors, geographic location is not a problem in rating.

Location is a concern for underwriters in terms of the insurer's service facilities. Many employers insist on local insurer representation to assist in day-to-day problems. Solicitation, installation of the group, and handling policyholder questions make it desirable for the insurer to have service facilities within a reasonable distance of the policyholder, especially when the agent or broker expects local support. The underwriter may be reluctant to accept a group that has a substantial number of employees at a location where the insurance company has no service facility.

159

Location is also an issue for network-based medical/dental plans. The network service area must meet the access needs of the employees.

Insurance Plan

The basic elements of an insurance plan are eligibility and benefit structure. Eligibility for insurance determines who will be insured; the benefit structure determines the coverage that will be provided.

Eligibility.   Employee eligibility for group insurance is based on conditions pertaining to employment. Eligibility cannot be determined by age, race, or sex, since these are not conditions of employment. The Health Insurance Portability and Accountability Act prohibits making any health status–related factor of individual employees a condition for eligibility. For more information on requirements see Chapter 5: Government Regulation in *Fundamentals of Health Insurance: Part B.*

In addition to the insured employee or member, the group insurance plan usually will cover dependents for medical care benefits. Dependents are the spouse of the employee and the unmarried children under 19 years of age. Many policies provide coverage for children who are beyond age 19 if they are unmarried full-time students, with a maximum age limit between age 23 and age 26. Many insurers continue medical coverage of handicapped children beyond the normal termination age if they are incapable of self-support.

A probationary or waiting period of one to three months may be included in the plan. This feature is designed to eliminate the cost of maintaining records for employees who may terminate quickly. The probationary period must be long enough to cover the usual period of time when quick turnover may occur, but not so long as to prevent a continuing flow of new entrants into the group.

Benefit structure.   Although insurance company underwriting rules usually establish standards for minimum and maximum benefit structures, the underwriter takes special note of any prospective plan in which the benefits are either minimal or overly liberal.

160

Minimal benefits can be indicative of policyholder financial problems. Also, if a program is inadequate many employees will secure additional coverage by purchasing individual policies and thus present a problem of overinsurance. This kind of overinsurance is difficult to prevent or even detect, since the coordination of benefits (COB) provision in most group plans does not coordinate benefits with individual policies. For more information about coordination of benefits see Chapter 3: Claim Administration in *Fundamentals of Health Insurance: Part B.*

An overly liberal program, on the other hand, can indicate selection against the insurer, especially where the choice of such a plan may be prompted by the need to provide broad benefits for an existing disability of a key employee. In addition, a liberal plan that requires heavy employee contributions may lose continued employee participation because of its high cost.

Cost Sharing

Premium payment may be contributory, with the insureds paying some or all of the cost, or noncontributory, with the employer paying all of the premium. From an underwriting perspective the noncontributory plan is preferable.

First, it ensures full participation in the program and simplifies administration by eliminating the requirement that late entrants submit evidence of insurability.

Second, insurance companies sometimes require that certain groups— for example, very small groups with fewer than ten lives—be written on a noncontributory basis as a condition of issuing the policy.

Third, if the policyholder's employees are distributed at a number of locations, the noncontributory approach may help simplify administration where local administrative facilities are not adequate.

The underwriting rules of most insurance companies prohibit fully contributory health insurance programs except in certain circumstances and only in locations where they are legally permitted. There are reasons for this, including the following:

- Requiring full contribution could indicate a lack of employer interest in the program, resulting in poor administration and lack of cooperation with the insurer.

- The full cost of an adequate medical expense insurance program may be more than the average employee can afford.

- Requiring employees to pay the total premium will cause a lack of initial participation.

- Problems may occur in resolicitation and maintaining participation because a required rate increase will be passed on entirely to the employees.

Because of these negative factors, insurers offer fully contributory plans only as an opportunity for the insureds to purchase additional benefits to meet their needs under special circumstances, such as long-term care insurance and voluntary accidental death and dismemberment insurance. The benefits generally have lower and more stable premiums than medical expense benefits. Even in these circumstances insurers have some minimum participation requirements.

Policyholder's Administrative Facilities

Responsibility for administering the group health program lies with an employee or staff of people employed by the group policyholder. Administrative responsibilities may consist of:

- preparing premium statements;
- processing enrollments and terminations;
- issuing certificates of insurance;
- certifying eligibility for coverage when there is a claim; and
- processing claims for medical care benefits in some cases.

If an employer has several locations, an administrator of the group plan at each location is responsible for enrolling new employees and reporting terminations and additions. Most group plans cover employees automatically if they join the plan within 31 days of their eligible date. Without proper policyholder administration, employee additions may not be made on time and new employees would be required to furnish evidence of insurability because they were enrolled as late entrants. In

162

addition, terminations may not be properly recorded and premium billings would have to be adjusted continually for debits and credits because of poor reporting by the policyholder. Not enrolling newly hired and usually healthy employees also can result in selection against the plan and, consequently, higher loss ratios (claims to premiums).

Previous Coverage and Experience

It is not unusual for employers to transfer their benefit plans from one insurer to another. A growing number of groups are transferring to obtain greater managed care opportunities, such as increased employee access to health maintenance organizations (HMOs) and preferred provider organizations (PPOs). In some cases the transfer is for administrative reasons—poor service, unsatisfactory claims handling, or difficult administration. Increasingly, employers, particularly those with multistate locations, are changing insurers to gain optimum managed care opportunities. Most transfers are because of cost, especially when the present insurer requires an increase in rates or administrative services only fees. An insurer asked to quote on a group being transferred from another insurer reviews rating, claims history, the prior benefit structure, and the history of changes in insurers.

Rating. The rate-determination process involves the underwriter evaluating the risk and establishing the proper premium rates. This is important for large groups because past claims experience indicates future results. With small group claims, experience may be high due purely to random claim fluctuations, and the insurer's underwriting policy may be to ignore the prior claims experience entirely.

If a small group case has large losses, the underwriter usually will examine individual claims. This examination determines the nature of the claims: Are they for accidents that probably will not recur? Or do they indicate a chronic condition that automatically will present a continuing claim under the risk, causing high loss ratios?

In groups with rates based on their own prior experience, insurers may require special underwriting consideration for the larger individual claims. For example, if a dependent had a very large major medical claim and subsequently died, the underwriter may eliminate a substantial part of that particular loss in evaluating the acceptance of risk, considering it is nonrepetitive. However, if the dependent is still insured and the condition is chronic, the underwriter may assume that the claim for this particular condition will continue, and will not eliminate part of it.

In addition, when evaluating a group's past claims experience, insurers need premium and claim information by line of coverage for the past three years. In this case the competing insurer determines what its renewal rate would be if it had the same claims experience on the same plan of benefits. For larger risks, insurers use a formula similar to their renewal formula in determining the rates to be charged, based on the group's prior experience.

The new insurer also may recommend a HMO or PPO. In such a case the insurer adjusts projected claims to reflect lower anticipated claims, with an appropriate adjustment in the proposed premium or fee level.

Finally, the new insurer carefully reviews the benefit structure of the previous group plan, since it may reveal areas of possible abuse that might have led to unfavorable loss ratios. In such cases the insurer would take corrective action by suggesting benefit modifications.

Previous group insurance plan.   To do a complete underwriting analysis, the underwriter secures as much information as possible about the previous group insurance plan. As a general rule, the underwriter prefers to review the contract, but a copy of the employee booklet or certificate of insurance usually will suffice. There are a number of reasons why an insurer needs information about the present plan of benefits.

First, the underwriter uses it to determine if there are any provisions in the previous plan that are not essentially the same as or equal to the insurer's standard contract. If there are, the underwriter must make sure the policyholder understands that the new insurer's group contract contains different provisions for some coverages. Also, if the group is large enough to warrant special plan design, the insurer can consider the inclusion of broader benefits in the rate-making process—after the underwriter has determined that the insurer can handle these benefits from both an administrative and claims standpoint.

Second, the underwriter is concerned with the effect on existing claims if the policy is transferred. If the group is located in a state that has adopted some form of group insurance no loss–no gain regulation, the new insurer may have to assume substantial existing liabilities. These regulations stipulate that no employee shall suffer a benefit loss in the event of a policy transfer. They usually prohibit pre-existing condition limitation clauses for individuals insured under the employer's prior group plans as the basis for denying or reducing a claim that is otherwise payable under the policy.

Even if not legally required, the employer may ask the new insurer to pick up existing health conditions and to waive policy requirements limiting pre-existing conditions for the initial group. This is typical with larger employers. In these cases, to eliminate possible duplicate coverage, the underwriter must review the present policy to determine what benefits the policy provides on termination of the contract—for example, the continuation of coverage for some period of time for an existing total disability.

Third, the underwriter wants to identify any benefit provisions in the present plan that could have caused the problems that motivated the policyholder to change insurers. If any are found, the underwriter can require certain plan changes for acceptance of the risk.

Prior claim experience. The new insurer uses the group's past claim experience to determine whether the group is accepted and often to establish the premium rates to be charged. Although reliable past claim loss experience is not always available, an underwriter would be unwise to ignore the possibility that the transfer is being sought because the group's present insurer has or is about to raise rates as a result of an unsatisfactory claims record.

Also, renewal action of the present insurer may have involved plan changes, such as increased deductibles or additional contract limitations, that attempted to solve specific claim problems. The new insurer analyzes these suggested revisions to determine if they are needed in its contract.

Managed care has made underwriting for transferred business and renewals particularly complex. Careful attention must be paid to projecting claims. Projections are particularly tricky on transferred business when the new insurer replaces the prior insurer's HMOs and PPOs. The new insurer must:

- estimate savings under the prior carrier's networks;
- determine anticipated savings under its own networks; and
- compare those figures.

To accurately project claims under this or similar scenarios, insurers need the following information:

- HMO and/or PPO penetration under the prior plan;
- HMO and/or PPO discounts under the prior plan;
- trends such as growth in migration to HMOs;
- portion of claims attributable to each network;
- level of savings under the prior plan; and
- the degree of effectiveness of medical management on point-of-service quotes (i.e., savings generated by the prior plan's gatekeeper).

Reliability of prior claim experience. Whether prior claims experience may be considered reliable depends on many factors, including the following:

- Is the length of time covered by the statistical data sufficiently long to reduce chance fluctuations and reflect a true loss trend?
- Is the unfavorable experience the result of many claims of minor severity (to which the underwriter usually gives heavy credibility), or is it the result of only a few claims of major proportion that are not likely to recur and that might be discounted in the rating process?
- Is the group so large (e.g., 1,000 lives) that its loss experience is statistically credible, or is it so small (e.g., 10 lives) that its past losses may reflect chance fluctuations and are not fully statistically credible?
- Is more than one year of experience available to determine if the most recent year's experience is typical, abnormally high, or abnormally low?

There are no exact answers to the problems that arise in establishing the credibility of claims experience. Each underwriter makes decisions based on his or her own degree of experience and the insurer's standards for writing quality business at adequate rates.

Premium rates to be charged. An insurer carefully determines the rates to use for a transferred group. It may include all risks of a certain size (e.g., under 50 lives) in a general rating pool. The underwriter may not be permitted to adjust rates to reflect prior experience for these risks, but only to decline or accept them at current standard rates. If a rate adjustment can be made, underwriters usually develop initial rates using the same approach they would use in developing renewal rates.

Possible administrative problems. As the last general underwriting consideration in transferred business, the underwriter determines if the policyholder has or expects special administrative handling. When transferring a risk, a policyholder usually expects that both its administrative work and the services of the new insurer will be comparable with those of the former insurer.

The policyholder may expect the new insurer to continue using the special enrollment and administrative procedures of the former administrator. For example, the new insurer may be asked to use all existing records and beneficiary designations, where appropriate. The policyholder also may expect to make greater use of the insurer's administrative facilities than the insurer is prepared to provide.

If the policyholder has various locations throughout the country, the new insurer must determine whether special administrative facilities have been established.

- Are separate billings required for each location?
- Will the new insurer be expected to maintain separate records at each of the policyholder's locations and to have local service offices deal directly with these locations?
- In handling claims, will the new insurer be expected to provide local claim service for each of the branch locations, or will the branches process all claims through the policyholder's home office?
- Will billing procedures cause a problem?
- If the policyholder presently gets a list billing that names each employee and shows each employee's amount of coverage and premium, will it accept self-billing, which requires the policyholder to keep all records and report only totals each month?

The underwriting of transferred business requires more extensive and detailed consideration than does the underwriting of new risks because of the need to analyze the past experience. To perform the essential analysis properly, group representatives and underwriters must work closely together and have sufficient time prior to the contemplated date of transfer to examine all pertinent data.

Commission Arrangements

Many insurance companies use a level commission scale on both transferred business and new business, thus spreading the usually high first-year commission over a period of time. The underwriter may make the level scale compulsory as a condition for accepting the risk, particularly in situations where there is some uncertainty about the rates and the underwriter wants to add some additional cost margins to the plan. The level scale helps keep the policyholder's first-year cost low.

Expected Persistency

There are substantial costs incurred by an insurer when underwriting a new group. These are referred to as acquisition expenses. Such costs include field sales, new business underwriting costs, and issue expenses. The underwriter looks for some assurance that, barring special circumstances, the new business will remain on the books for a reasonable period (certainly not less than three years) so that these expenses can be recovered in the renewal rates. Toward this end the underwriter tries to avoid businesses that:

- may be temporary in nature (e.g., for a specific project);
- have a history of frequently changing insurers; or
- are in financial difficulties.

Any one of these conditions may cause the insurer to decline the business.

Individual Health Insurance Selection Factors

Basic risk selection for individual health insurance falls into four broad categories: medical, age, financial, and occupational.

168

Medical Factors

Medical underwriting of an applicant for individual health insurance requires consideration of both medical history and current physical condition to determine on what basis insurance can be offered or if it should be refused. Underwriters evaluate a risk primarily by estimating the probable influence of current impairments and previous medical histories on future claims.

From an underwriting perspective, applicants are considered impaired risks if they have or have had a medical condition or history that could either contribute to future injuries or sicknesses or create complications that prolong a disability. Underwriters classify applicants according to the extent that their health history and current physical condition differs from that of unimpaired lives.

As noted earlier, the Health Insurance Portability and Accountability Act of 1996 guarantees availability of individual health insurance coverage without pre-existing condition limitations to certain individuals who have lost group coverage.

Medical history. Medical evaluation begins with a review of statements on the application. For example, if the applicant reports receiving treatment for elevated blood pressure, an attending physician's statement usually will be required. In addition to obtaining general medical information, the underwriter will ask the attending physician about blood pressure readings recorded, medication prescribed, and the degree of control achieved.

Insurers review histories of previous conditions to determine the:

- possibility of recurrence;
- effect of a medical history on the applicant's general health;
- complications that may develop at a later date;
- normal progression of any impairment; and
- possible interaction of this normal progression with a future disability from an unrelated cause.

169

Some diseases have a tendency to recur. An applicant with a recent history of peptic ulcer, for example, is more likely to become disabled or hospitalized from ulcers in the future than someone who has never had an ulcer. Disabilities resulting from other diseases of the digestive system also may be more frequent or prolonged than would be anticipated without such a history. Many acute disorders such as bone fractures or appendectomy can be disregarded if recovery has been prompt and complete and without evidence of any residual impairment.

Latent complications, or the progression of an existing impairment to the point of hospitalization or disability, are possible with many conditions. For example, overweight and elevated blood pressure, while normally not disabling of themselves, are considered indicators of a higher future incidence of cardiovascular impairment.

Current physical condition. Applicants' statements on an application and medical examination results are the first indicators of present physical condition. Additional tests and studies, such as urinalysis, blood studies, and electrocardiograms, may be required routinely, depending on age and amount of coverage applied for.

Underwriters may add requirements to evaluate further a given history or impairment. For example, they may require a blood sugar tolerance test if a urinalysis finds sugar or request an analysis of a blood sample for various chemicals to evaluate a history of liver or kidney disease.

Age Factors

Medical problems tend to increase with age. The underwriting guidelines of most insurers, therefore, call for more frequent use of medical examinations and attending physician's statements on older applicants. Also, the underwriter reviewing individual applications is inclined to investigate medical histories of older applicants more thoroughly than younger applicants because of the increased possibility of related problems that may not be included on the form.

Disability income insurers often reduce their maximum indemnity limits for applicants aged 50 or over because of poor experience with applicants who buy insurance at older ages.

Financial Factors

An applicant's financial status is of less importance in the underwriting of medical expense insurance than it is for disability income insurance. Generally, an insurer will issue the maximum amount of coverage it decides an insured should have to cover hospital and medical expenses.

The financial status of the applicant is a prime consideration in underwriting disability income coverage. Insurance companies have always had guidelines defining the maximum amount of disability income coverage they will provide. Many insurers establish a minimum income at which they will sell disability income coverage. The minimum income tends to screen out those people who may find premium payments unduly burdensome, resulting in unprofitable early lapses. Although some insurers do not have minimum income requirements, many will not insure individuals with earned incomes of less than $18,000 per year.

Issue and participation limits. Disability insurers have guidelines about the percentage of an applicant's income they are willing to insure. This percentage may range from 30 to 80 percent of the applicant's earned income. Because applicants at lower income levels may have little discretionary income, a greater percentage of their earned income can be covered. At the higher levels the percentage of earned income that will be covered decreases because of the larger amount of discretionary income available to them. Many insurers publish a table showing amounts of coverage available at various incomes rather than stating a fixed percentage rate.

In addition to an amount limit based on percentage of income, most insurance companies establish a maximum amount of disability coverage they will participate in writing on any one risk regardless of income. The limit usually varies by the occupational class of the insured. Some insurers set their maximum limit at $15,000 per month or higher on insureds under age 50 in the most risk-free environment.

Certification of annual income. Most insurers writing disability income insurance require that applicants certify their annual income by a statement on the application or a separate statement affixed to the application. They also may request a copy of the applicant's latest income tax return.

Because the insured's financial incentive to return to work after disability is an important consideration, the underwriter also must be concerned with an applicant's net worth and unearned income. A high net worth is significant even though it may not be generating any unearned income (e.g., investment income, dividends, interest, and so forth) at the time of underwriting. If the person becomes disabled, this net worth may be converted into income-producing assets. The resulting income combined with disability insurance payments may lessen an insured's incentive to return to work.

Occupational Factors

As with group health insurance, occupational considerations are relatively unimportant in underwriting medical expense coverages. The premium charged usually does not vary by occupational class because of the workers' compensation exclusion in most policies. For individual health insurance underwriters, the major concern is extremely hazardous occupations, such as professional rodeo riding or deep-sea diving. Most insurers either will refuse to issue coverage to people in those occupations or will exclude any expenses incurred because of occupational injuries.

Insurers classify risks by occupation primarily for disability income and accidental death and dismemberment insurance. Traditionally, occupational classifications are based on the hazard of accidental injury or occupational disease. Since industrial safety programs have reduced greatly the hazards in many occupations, social and environmental factors that influence claim experience are becoming increasingly important in determining occupational classes.

Occupational classifications in disability income insurance help to determine premiums and the type and the amount of coverage to be offered. Lower premiums, higher limits, and more liberal policies are made available to the more favorable classes. Statistics show that, as a group, persons in professional occupations, such as engineers, architects, and accountants, and those with relatively high incomes have fewer periods

172

of disability and disabilities of shorter duration than persons in other occupations. Class 1 represents the least hazardous occupations, including persons with primarily executive, administrative, or clerical duties, while Class 4 represents occupations that require heavy manual duties or where there are accidental hazards.

■ Sources of Underwriting Information

Underwriters use a variety of information sources to evaluate whether a group or an individual is an acceptable risk. These sources are different for group and individual insurance.

Group Health Insurance Information Sources

For underwriting group insurance, the following factors are used for gathering information:

- request for proposal;
- enrollment cards;
- inspection reports;
- financial statements and credit reports;
- federal disclosure information;
- agent or broker information; and
- group representatives.

Request for Proposal (RFP)

The request for proposal and accompanying forms provide underwriting information, including employee data and claim history. For example, they give the number of employees who are eligible, which is useful for determining if there is adequate participation in the plan. Identifying excluded classes also helps to determine if there is adverse selection against the plan.

The request for proposal also usually provides prior insurance history, which helps the underwriter determine the stability for the risk. Because of high first-year expense in the sale and issue of a group, insurers look for groups that can be expected to remain insured for a number of years. A request for proposal that shows the group has changed insurers several times in recent years indicates a lack of stability, or perhaps a tendency to change insurers when a rate increase is requested.

Enrollment Cards

These cards usually provide underwriting information about age, sex, earnings, dependent status, and occupation.

Inspection Reports

On smaller groups, insurers sometimes use commercial investigating companies that supply underwriting information about the applicant. Representatives of these companies visit the employer's business, report on any adverse working conditions, and help verify the eligibility information supplied by the employer in the request for proposal.

Financial Statements and Credit Reports

The financial stability of an employer is an important factor to consider when evaluating the likelihood of keeping the group for several years. In addition, premium grace periods and other financing features often result in the insurer, in essence, loaning money to the policyholder. The credit risk must be understood.

Federal Disclosure Information

Employers with 100 or more insured employees are required under the Employee Retirement Income Security Act (ERISA) to distribute annual plan experience reports to their employees and file similar information with the U.S. Department of Labor. Underwriters often secure copies of these reports to verify experience information supplied by the applicant.

Agent or Broker Information

For new groups, insurers usually require the agent or broker to get information from the policyholder about past experience, benefits, and rates.

174

This detailed information is given to the group representative or home office of the insurer.

Group Representatives

The sale of a group plan often involves a visit to the employer's premises by the insurer's group representative to discuss the plan of benefits. The group representative can give the underwriter first-hand information about the employer and the employees.

Individual Health Insurance Information Sources

In the process of selecting and classifying risk, the individual health insurance underwriter uses many sources of information. For medical expense and disability income insurance, these include:

- application;
- agent's statement;
- medical or paramedical examinations;
- attending physician statements (APS);
- inspection reports;
- MIB, Inc. (Medical Information Bureau); and
- DIRS (Disability Income Record System).

Application

The primary part of the application for individual insurance is the basic tool used by the underwriter. (Exhibit 6.1) It is the basis for the underwriter's decision to provide the requested coverage, to modify it, to try to obtain more information, or to reject the application entirely.

Although the agent usually asks the questions and fills in the answers on the application, the applicant must sign it. The application includes a statement to the effect that the applicant has answered the questions truthfully and completely to the best of his or her knowledge and belief. An authorization form, signed by the applicant, also accompanies the application. This form authorizes the underwriter to obtain required information from outside sources.

175

Exhibit 6.1
Sample Application for Individual Life and Medical Expense Insurance

A. Applicant Information

Applicant's Name (Please Print)			Birthdate			Sex	Social Security Number
(First)	(Middle)	(Last)	Mo.	Day	Year	☐ Male ☐ Female	

Street Address or P.O. Box	County you live in:	Are you a U.S. Citizen? ☐ Yes ☐ No

City	State	Zip Code	Telephone no. where we can reach you during the day Area Code( )

Applicant's Occupation/Nature of Business (if retired, nature of former business)

Are you currently covered by an employer sponsored group medical plan?   ☐ Yes   ☐ No

If yes, please indicate:
Plan Number _____   Date Coverage to Cease _____

Carrier _____   Reason for Termination _____

B. Plan Information

Effective Date:

☐ I request insurance effective the 1st of the month following Home Office approval

OR

☐ I request insurance effective the 1st day of (month) _____ , 19 _____ . *

* I understand I will be liable for premium from this date and the date cannot be changed even if notice of approval is not received by rhe until a later date.

Applicant's Initials _____

Plan Options:	Optional Benefits:
Deductible $ _____	
☐ 80/20 ▇▇▇ ☐ 80/20 PPO	☐ Yes ☐ No Premium Saver
☐ 50/50 ▇▇▇ PPO Name _____	☐ Yes ☐ No Freedom Option
☐ _____ PPO Number _____	☐ Yes ☐ No Supplemental Life

Beneficiary Name:	Maternity:
(First) (Middle) (Last) (Relationship)	☐ No If no, complications only will be covered.
	☐ Yes If yes, I realize this plan includes a six month waiting period that begins the date the female becomes insured or elects full maternity coverage, whichever is later. Benefits may vary by state.
Beneficiary changes are not effective until recorded in the Home Office. Unless written otherwise, if more than one beneficiary is named, proceeds will be payable in equal shares to surviving beneficiaries. If more space is needed, use a "Request for Change of Beneficiary" form.	Applicant's Initials _____

Special Instructions:

C. Dependent Information - *Complete this section only if applying for Dependent Coverage. If so, list full names of all dependents.*

Marital Status: ☐ Single ☐ Married	Names	Sex M / F	Birthdate			F- Time Student	Foster Child	Step Child	Lives in Your Home?
			Mo.	Day	Yr.				
If any dependent is not approved, do you still want coverage for those who are approved? ☐ Yes ☐ No	Spouse					(X)	(X)	(X)	Yes?	No?
	Children								
Special Notes:	1.								
Foster and stepchildren eligibility is subject to Home Office approval. If applying for coverage for foster children, complete Foster Child Questionnaire. ▇▇▇	2.								
	3.								
Dependents age 19 or older, must meet student eligibility requirements.	4.								
	5.								

To be completed by Soliciting Agent ▶	Signature of Soliciting Agent			Agent's Group Code	Agent's Social Security No.	
	Agent Name (Please Print)	Street	City	State		Zip

To be completed by Regional Office ▶	Regional Office Signature	Date Signed	Regional Office Signature (For Affiliate Program)	Date Signed	Rep Code Off Code

To be completed by Home Office ▶	Effective Date of Coverage

Exhibit 6.1 (*continued*)

D. Medical History for Applicant and Dependents - *Give full details to any questions answered* "yes."

	Yes	No
1. Applicant's Height ____ ft. ____ in. Weight ____ lbs. Gain or loss of 10 lbs. in the last year? If "yes," explain.	☐	☐
2. Applicant's tobacco use: ☐ current ☐ past ☐ never		
Date last used _____ (If "never," skip to question 3)		
Type/Frequency:		
☐ cigarettes ____ pks/day ☐ cigars ____ day		
☐ pipes ____ full/day		
3. Spouse's Height ____ ft. ____ in. Weight ____ lbs. Gain or loss of 10 lbs. in the last year? If "yes," explain.	☐	☐
4. Spouse's tobacco use: ☐ current ☐ past ☐ never		
Date last used _____ (If "never," skip to question 5)		
Type/Frequency:		
☐ cigarettes ____ pks/day ☐ cigars ____ day		
☐ pipes ____ full/day		
5. Is anyone now planning, scheduled for, getting or thinking about getting medical treatment, psychotherapy, counseling, having surgery, or taking any medicine, drugs, pills, shots etc?	☐	☐
6. Has anyone been told of a need to schedule any tests, treatment, surgery, biopsy, hospitalization, or specialist consultation?	☐	☐
7. Is anyone pregnant, or has anyone (male or female) been evaluated for infertility in the last 5 years?	☐	☐
8. Does anyone have any physical or mental birth defects, a developmental or learning disability, a behavior disorder or a physical or mental impairment?	☐	☐
9. Has anyone had persistent, lingering or prolonged fevers, night sweats, fatigue/tiredness or weakness in the last 2 years?	☐	☐
10. Has anyone been told by a doctor, counselor, therapist or other medical specialist of the need to reduce or discontinue the use of alcohol or drugs in the last 5 years?	☐	☐

IN THE LAST 10 YEARS HAS ANYONE:	Yes	No
11. had surgery?	☐	☐
12. been hospitalized?	☐	☐
13. been to or consulted a doctor, chiropractor, counselor, therapist or any medical, dental, or eye specialist or had blood tests other than for HIV infection, other medical tests or been referred to a medical specialist?	☐	☐
14. been treated for the use of alcohol or drugs?	☐	☐
15. had any back, neck or spinal problems, a joint or muscle disorder?	☐	☐
16. had gallbladder problems, ulcers, chronic diarrhea, colitis, other digestive problems, hepatitis, cirrhosis or liver problems?	☐	☐
17. had urinary problems, a disorder of the reproductive system, menstrual disorder, breast disorders, venereal disease or other infectious disease?	☐	☐
18. had shortness of breath, chronic cough, bronchitis, tuberculosis, asthma, pneumonia, or other respiratory problems?	☐	☐
19. been unconscious, or had epilepsy, seizures, convulsions or other neurological disorder?	☐	☐
20. had depression, stress, anxiety or received any counseling, psychotherapy, or had a mental or nervous disorder?	☐	☐
21. had cancer, tumors, cysts or growths of any kind or a skin disorder? Benign? ☐ Malignant? ☐	☐	☐
22. had diabetes, gout, arthritis, thyroid disorder, or a disorder of the lymph nodes or lymph system?	☐	☐
23. had any chest pain, heart trouble, heart attack, heart murmur, rapid, slow or irregular heart beat, high blood pressure, stroke or other circulatory problems?	☐	☐
24. had an EKG or stress test (exercise EKG)?	☐	☐
If "yes," describe the reason for the test and the results.		
25. been treated for or diagnosed as having HIV infection, AIDS, AIDS-related Complex (ARC), or any disease or disorder of the immune system?	☐	☐

NOTE: If more space is needed below, please attach a sheet of paper with additional information with your signature and date.
If either question 10 or 14 was answered yes, describe the frequency, amount and type of alcohol or drug used now or in the past.

Question No. From Above	Name of Person	Nature of Illness / Injury, Symptoms, Treatment, Testing, Medical Attention, Diagnosis	Date of onset mo-day-yr	Duration	Results, Findings, Remaining Symptoms / Problems	Names and Addresses of Physicians or Hospitals

E. Statement of Understanding and Authorization

- ██ ████████████████████

- I authorize any medical practitioner, medically-related facility, insurance company or any other organization, institution or person to give ████████ ████████████████████ representatives any information about me or any named dependents, including physical or mental history and drug or alcohol use.

- I represent all information, statements and answers recorded on this ████████████████ as well as any attachments to this enrollment form are full, correct, and true to the best of my knowledge. I agree that a photostat of this form is as valid as the original. I understand that omissions and/or misstatements regarding age or medical history, could cause an otherwise valid claim to be denied and/or cause the insurance, if issued, to be cancelled as if never effective.

- Applicants will be informed whether or not application has been approved within 60 days or be given the reason for delay.

- I understand no insurance will become effective (a) unless medical history is evaluated and satisfactory to ████████ and (b) for anyone while home or hospital confined on the effective date.

- I understand the Effective Date will be the date I selected subject to approval by the home office ████████ The effective date cannot be on or before the date the application is signed.

- I understand I will be liable for all premium due from the effective date I selected in Section B even if notice of approval is received by me after that date.

- I authorize premiums to be drawn from my account at a financial institution.

- I understand the premium charged and coverage issued will be those offered on the Effective Date.

- I understand an agent cannot guarantee coverage or revise rates, benefits or plan provisions without the written approval by an officer of

Signature of Applicant	Date Signed

The format of the application and the depth and direction of its questions vary by insurer and by its intended use. If it is to be used with only one type of insurance, then the questions on the application will elicit only information the insurer considers pertinent to underwriting that particular insurance. However, if the application is intended for use in applying for a variety of types of coverage, then the questions will be designed to elicit information required for the underwriting of those various coverages.

Disability insurers also obtain copies of an applicant's most recent tax returns. With this information insurers can be confident that the amount of disability coverage an applicant applies for is the amount that he or she qualifies for under the insurer's issue and participation rules.

Agent's Statement

Most insurers provide space on the back of their applications for remarks by agents, such as how long and how well they have known the applicant. The agent may also be asked to indicate:

- knowledge of any information regarding the applicant that is not included on the application but that might have a bearing on risk selection; and
- the applicant's approximate net worth, annual earned income, and income from sources other than employment.

An agent who lets the underwriter know of special circumstances of the sale or a special problem not otherwise identified will gain the underwriter's confidence. Often the agent's remarks will clarify a situation that is questionable or unclear based on information from other sources.

Medical and Paramedical Examinations

Insurers sometimes require medical personnel to submit forms detailing an applicant's current health and medical history.

Medical examinations. Insurers may require a medical examination because of the amount of coverage applied for, the age of the applicant, or the need for more specific details of medical history. (Exhibit 6.2) A

Exhibit 6.2
Sample Application for Group Life and Health Insurance

A. Employee Information

| Your name (last, first, middle initial) | | | | | Social security number | | | |

| Address (street) | | City | | State | ZIP code | County | Phone number |

| Date of birth (mo/day/yr) | ☐ male ☐ female | ☐ single ☐ widowed | ☐ married ☐ divorced | ☐ legally separated |

Is your spouse employed by this school? ☐ yes ☐ no If yes, please give spouse name and social security number

B. Dependent Information: List your spouse and all eligible Dependent children.

| Name of eligible Dependents | Social security number | Date of birth | | | Full-Time Student | Foster Child | Step Child | Handi-capped | Adopted |
		mo	day	yr					
1									
2									
3									
4									

- Foster child and stepchild eligibility is subject to approval ▇▇▇▇▇▇▇▇▇▇▇ Complete a Foster Child/Stepchild Questionnaire form.
- If you have Developmentally Disabled/Physically Handicapped children, complete an Application to Continue Handicapped Child form.

C. Beneficary Designation: Complete only if your coverages include group term life insurance.

Beneficiary for employee group term life insurance (Print as "Doe, Mary A.", not "Mrs. John Doe".)

| last name | first name | middle initial | relationship |

Unless otherwise provided herein, if two or more beneficiaries are named, the proceeds shall be paid in equal shares to the named beneficiaries surviving the insured. If no beneficiary has been designated, any proceeds will be payable as provided by the group policy.

D. Benefit Election: Ask your employer what coverages the plan has. Check your election option below.

If eligible for Medical, I elect coverage for   ☐ Myself   ☐ Dependents   If applicable, indicate which plan you choose.
If eligible for Dental, I elect coverage for   ☐ Myself   ☐ Dependents
If eligible for Dependent Life, I elect coverage for my Dependents   ☐ yes   ☐ no   Medical _____
If eligible for Supplemental Life, I elect coverage for Myself   ☐ yes   ☐ no   (i.e. HSM, Comp 100, PPO)
If eligible for Life, I elect coverage for Myself   ☐ yes   ☐ no   Dental _____
If eligible for LTD, I elect coverage for Myself   ☐ yes   ☐ no

E. Acceptance

I declare I am eligible to enroll in this plan and request to be covered. If the group plan provides that contributions be made by me, I authorize my employer to deduct them from my pay. I hereby declare that, to the best of my knowledge and belief, the information given on this enrollment form is correctly recorded, complete and true. I understand that a broker or agent cannot guarantee coverage or revise rates, benefits or plan provisions without prior written approval ▇▇▇▇▇

Please be sure form is complete so enrollment is not delayed.

| Signature of employee (Please do not print) | Date signed |

F. Refusal of Coverage Section

I hereby acknowledge that I have been given an opportunity to apply for all insurance coverages for which I may be eligible under the policy issued by ▇▇▇▇▇▇▇▇▇ If I am not applying for all coverages for which I am eligible, I understand the benefits available under the plan and I DECLINE to enroll

myself for   ☐ medical*   ☐ dental   ☐ Life   ☐ LTD   ☐ all coverages provided by the plan
my Dependents for   ☐ medical*   ☐ dental   ☐ Dep Life   ☐ all coverages provided by the plan
because _____

I UNDERSTAND if I refuse any coverage under the plan
  (a) my Dependent(s) are not eligible for any coverage for which I am not covered.
  (b) I (and/or my Dependents) will not be able to enroll in the plan later unless satisfactory proof of good health is provided. Any medical information will be provided at my own expense and coverage will not become effective until approved by ▇▇▇▇▇▇▇▇▇▇▇ subject also to Actively-at-Work and Period of Limited Activity provisions.
  (c) that any health conditions which have already been diagnosed, are being treated now or develop later may prevent me (and/or my Dependents) from ever being approved for coverage.
  (d) I cannot, under any conditions, reenter the plan as a retired person.
*If you waive medical coverage and your plan provides prescription drugs and/or vision coverage(s) you will not be enrolled for them.

| Signature of employee (Please do not print) | Date signed |

G. Employer to Complete this Section

▇▇▇▇▇ to Complete

| Company name as it appears on your billing | Location | Employee effective date |

| Date employed | Occupation | Hours worked per week | Earnings $ | ☐ yr ☐ mo ☐ wk ☐ hr | Dependent effective date |

physician usually completes the examination and records the answers to the medical questions. The applicant must then sign the medical application.

The examination also provides information regarding height and weight, pulse, blood pressure, and other findings. Many times an applicant will discuss previous medical history with a physician more readily than with an agent, but the underwriter must not be lulled into a sense of security because of a completely satisfactory medical examination. Some people who are totally uninsurable because of a previous medical history may pass a medical examination. For example, a past history of heart attack may not be readily detected by an examiner.

Paramedical examinations.   Several organizations now offer paramedical services. While they may have different methods of operation, they usually are centrally located, have convenient office hours with a medical technician on duty at all times, and have a group of physicians who are on call to conduct medical examinations and supervise the operation of the service. The basic service provides for the completion of a medical form that includes the applicant's medical history, height, weight, pulse rate, and blood pressure and the results of urinalysis.

For an additional fee a vital capacity test and electrocardiogram may be obtained. The service usually provides facilities for other tests, such as blood profiles, glucose tests, and X-rays, if they should be needed. Much of the information obtained, especially from blood profiles, lends itself to important statistical studies.

The use of a medical technician has the advantage of lowering the cost of obtaining medical information and freeing physicians from the time-consuming job of performing routine physical examinations for insurers. A blood chemistry analysis has been shown to be rather effective in detecting or confirming diabetes and disorders of the kidneys and liver, although it does not indicate hypertension or heart disease. Blood pressure readings and electrocardiogram tracings, however, provide information regarding these conditions.

180

The completion of the medical history form, a blood chemistry analysis, electrocardiogram, and blood pressure readings provide a considerable amount of medical information for the home-office underwriter at a modest cost. Unfavorable results of the paramedical examination will prompt a request for a regular medical examination by a physician.

Blood and Other Lab Tests.   Particularly with the outbreak of the acquired immune deficiency syndrome (AIDS), blood testing has become much more common for medical expense and disability income insurance. In addition to testing for the presence of the human immuno-deficiency virus (HIV), blood and urine tests have proven to be invaluable tools in the detection of other conditions that can affect morbidity. For example, blood tests can show elevated cholesterol and lipids, which often lead to strokes or heart attacks.

Liver abnormalities are another common condition detected through blood studies and may indicate the presence of alcohol addiction. Drug use also can be detected in blood studies so applicants can be weeded out before they obtain coverage. Nicotine is readily traceable through urine tests and can indicate if the applicant is a user of tobacco products.

Attending Physician Statements

If the application or medical examiner's report discloses any serious or questionable medical history, the underwriter will ask for a report from the attending physician or a hospital. This is commonly referred to as an attending physician statement (APS). This type of report is the best source of information for an accurate description of medical history. The underwriter must know exactly what the applicant was treated for, dates of treatment, the length of treatments, consulting physicians, if any, and whether there was a complete recovery. Most medical conditions for which applicants were treated do not present any problems. Some conditions, however, are likely to cause additional claims because of an unrelated accident or sickness. Epilepsy, for example, increases the chances of an injury, and hypertension or obesity could cause or prolong a disability.

Inspection Reports

An inspection report is a report of an investigation of an applicant conducted by an independent agency that specializes in insurance investigations. The report, which usually is written, covers pertinent factors such as occupation, financial status, and health history.

Inspection companies are nearly as old as the insurance industry itself, and inspection reports are valuable underwriting tools. Both the inspection companies and the insurers have always been aware of the confidential nature of the information gathered and have established procedures to protect the individuals involved.

MIB, Inc.

MIB, Inc. (formerly the Medical Information Bureau) is a system for the exchange of underwriting information among insurers writing life and health insurance. It is an association with more than 700 members in the United States and Canada. To qualify for full membership in the association, an insurance company must have a medical director and sell life insurance. Because of this membership requirement, some insurers specializing in health insurance cannot qualify for membership.

One of the primary purposes of MIB is to detect or deter fraud in the procurement of insurance by those who may omit or try to conceal facts essential to accurate, proper, and reasonable determination of insurance risks. MIB is responsible for maintaining a list of medical and nonmedical impairments that are of underwriting significance. The list is continually reviewed to ensure its relevance to the underwriting process.

MIB's information does not indicate what action may have been taken by a reporting member company or the type or amount of insurance applied for or issued. Only a member company may submit a report to MIB, and then only in connection with information found while underwriting an application for insurance. MIB does not employ investigators, nor does it obtain copies of records from agents, doctors, hospitals, and other providers. Its sole function is to record accurately the information that is submitted in coded form and to disseminate this information to its members pursuant to the rules.

Disability Income Record System (DIRS)

A service provided by MIB is the Disability Income Record System (DIRS). This system provides insurers with information about applications for disability income insurance and assists them in recognizing situations involving potential overinsurance.

The DIRS employs a central file that records certain nonmedical information about disability applications processed by the subscribing companies. When a member receives an application for disability income insurance involving a monthly disability income benefit of $300 or more with a benefit period of at least up to 12 months, it sends this information to the DIRS file. This information is retained for five years and is made available to any other member company to which an individual may apply for disability income insurance.

Membership in the DIRS is available to any insurer that writes disability income insurance. Since some subscribers to DIRS are not eligible for MIB membership, MIB has established an associate membership for those insurers that wish to participate in DIRS. This associate membership permits them to receive both DIRS and MIB information in connection with a disability application, subject to the requirements previously described.

■ Emerging Trends

Health insurance profit margins are continually being squeezed on both medical and disability insurance product lines. Morbidity continues to climb relative to mortality. Health care costs still increase at higher than the consumer price index. And insurers' disability claim experience has been poor since the mid-1980s.

One of the ways that health insurers hope to turn these trends around is by focusing on and maintaining higher standards in underwriting health insurance products. Other efforts include continued growth of managed care and its ability to help control claim costs, aggressive management of expenses, and improvement in efficiency and productivity by, for example, expanding computer applications related to products and administration. Only time will tell if these actions will result in improved profitability for these insurers.

On the other hand, both state and federal laws are restricting an insurer's ability to underwrite. In many cases, insurers are required to accept all applicants from certain defined classes. The Health Insurance Portability and Accountability Act of 1996 requires carriers serving the small group market (defined as groups with two to fifty employees) to accept any small employer that applies for coverage. Carriers serving the individual market must accept (with no pre-existing health condition limitations) any applicant who is losing group coverage and has 18 months of prior coverage. These rules apply to medical expense coverage.

■ Summary

Underwriting is one of the most crucial functions of an insurance company because it determines risk selection and the basis on which applicants will be offered insurance coverage. Health insurance risk selection is a vital and primary function of any insurer for group and individual health insurance. The insurance underwriter, using various methods and informational sources, performs this essential task. The underwriting of group and individual health insurance requires investigative and analytical skills, careful attention to detail, and a thorough knowledge of the insurer's business philosophy.

■ Key Terms

Acceptable group	Age	Attending physician
Adverse selection	Application	statement (APS)

Benefit structure
Contributory plan
Coordination of
    benefits (COB)
Credibility
Dependent
    distribution
Disability Income
    Record System
    (DIRS)
Duplicate coverage
Earning distribution
Eligibility
Eligible group
Enrollment card
Evidence of
    insurability
Experience

Geographic
    distribution
Industry
Inspection report
Late entrants
Loss ratio
Medical Information
    Bureau (MIB, Inc.)
Medical underwriting
Minimum
    participation
Morbidity
Mortality
Noncontributory plan
Occupational class
Overinsurance
Paramedical
    examination

Persistency
Plan design
Pre-existing condition
Previous coverage
Prior claim
    experience
Rating
Request for proposal
    (RFP)
Risk
Risk selection factors
Sex
Sex distribution
Turnover
Underwriter
Underwriting
Workers'
    compensation

Appendix A
UNIFORM INDIVIDUAL ACCIDENT AND SICKNESS POLICY PROVISION LAW

(Model Regulation Service—January 1993)

From the NAIC *Model Laws, Regulations and Guidelines.* Reprinted with the permission of the National Association of Insurance Commissioners.

Table of Contents

Section 1.   Definition of Accident and Sickness Insurance Policy

The term "policy of accident and sickness insurance" as used herein includes any policy or contract covering the kind or kinds of insurance described in [insert here the section of law authorizing accident and sickness insurance].

Note: If the insurance law of the state in which this draft is proposed for enactment does not have a section specifically authorizing the various types of insurance which may be written, this section should be modified to define accident and sickness insurance as "insurance against loss resulting from sickness or from bodily injury or death by accident, or both."

Section 2.   Form of Policy

A.   No policy of accident and sickness insurance shall be delivered or issued for delivery to any person in this state unless:

   (1)   The entire money and other considerations therefor are expressed therein; and

   (2)   The time at which the insurance takes effect and terminates is expressed therein; and

(3)   It purports to insure only one person, except that a policy may insure, originally or by subsequent amendment, upon the application of an adult member of a family who shall be deemed the policyholder, any two (2) or more eligible members of that family, including husband, wife, dependent children or any children under a specified age which shall not exceed nineteen (19) years and any other person dependent upon the policyholder; and

Note: In states having community property systems derived from the civil law it is suggested that in the foregoing subparagraph the words "an adult member" be replaced with "the head."

(4)   The style, arrangement and over-all appearance of the policy give no undue prominence to any portion of the text, and unless every printed portion of the text of the policy and of any endorsements or attached papers is plainly printed in light-faced type of a style in general use, the size of which shall be uniform and not less than ten point with a lower-case unspaced alphabet length not less than one hundred and twenty point (the "text" shall include all printed matter except the name and address of the insurer, name or title of the policy, the brief description if any, and captions and subcaptions); and

(5)   The exceptions and reductions of indemnity are set forth in the policy and, except those which are set forth in Section 3 of this Act, are printed, at the insurer's option, either included with the benefit provision to which they apply, or under an appropriate caption such as "Exceptions," or "Exceptions and Reductions," provided that if an exception or reduction specifically applies only to a particular benefit of the policy, a statement of such exception or reduction shall be included with the benefit provision to which it applies; and

(6)   Each form, including riders and endorsements, shall be identified by a form number in the lower left-hand corner of the first page; and

(7)   It contains no provision purporting to make any portion of the charter, rules, constitution, or bylaws of the insurer a part of the policy unless the portion is set forth in full in the policy, except in the case of the incorporation of, or reference to, a statement of rates or classification of risks, or short-rate table filed with the Commissioner.

Editor's Note: Insert the title of the chief insurance regulatory official wherever the term "commissioner" appears.

B.   If any policy is issued by an insurer domiciled in this state for delivery to a person residing in another state, and if the official having responsibility for the administration of the insurance laws of the other state shall have advised the Commissioner that the policy is not subject to approval or disapproval by the official, the Commissioner may by ruling require that the policy meet the standards set forth in Subsection A of this section and in Section 3.

Section 3.   Accident and Sickness Policy Provisions

A.   Required Provisions.

Except as provided in Subsection C, each policy delivered or issued for delivery to any person in this state shall contain the provisions specified in this subsection in the words in which the same appear in this section; provided, however, that the insurer may, at its option, substitute for one or more such provisions corresponding provisions of different wording approved by the Commissioner which are in each instance not less favorable in any respect to the insured or the beneficiary. Such provisions shall be preceded individually by the caption appearing in this subsection or, at the option of the insurer, by such appropriate individual or group captions or subcaptions as the Commissioner may approve.

(1)   A provision as follows:

Entire Contract; Changes: This policy, including the endorsements and the attached papers, if any, constitutes the entire contract of insurance. No change in this policy shall be valid until approved by an executive officer of the insurer and unless such approval be endorsed hereon or attached hereto. No agent has authority to change this policy or to waive any of its provisions.

Note: When enacted in states which prohibit amendment of a policy form by means other than attached printed rider upon a separate piece of paper the new law should contain (but not as a required policy provision) an added section defining "endorsement" in such a manner as to make the new law consistent with current statutes.

(2)   A provision as follows:

Time Limit on Certain Defenses:

(a)   After three (3) years from the date of issue of this policy no misstatements, except fraudulent misstatements, made by the applicant in the application for the policy shall be used to void the policy or to deny a claim for loss incurred or disability (as defined in the policy) commencing after the expiration of the three-year period.

Note: The foregoing policy provision shall not be so construed as to affect any legal requirement for avoidance of a policy or denial of a claim during the initial three-year period, nor to limit the application of Sections 3B(1), (2), (3), (4) and (5) in the event of misstatement with respect to age or occupation or other insurance.

Note: A policy which the insured has the right to continue in force subject to its terms by the timely payment of premium until at least age 50 or, in the case of a policy issued after age 44, for at least five years from its date of issue, may contain in lieu of the foregoing the following provision (from which the clause in parentheses may be omitted at the insurer's option) under the caption "Incontestable:"

After this policy has been in force for a period of three (3) years during the lifetime of the insured (excluding any period during which the insured is disabled), it shall become incontestable as to the statements contained in the application.

(b)   No claim for loss incurred or disability (as defined in the policy) commencing after three (3) years from the date of issue of this policy shall be reduced or denied on the ground that a disease or physical condition not excluded from coverage by name or specific description effective on the date of loss had existed prior to the effective date of coverage of this policy.

(3)   A provision as follows:

Grace Period: A grace period of [insert a number not less than 7 for weekly premium policies, 10 for monthly premium policies and 31 for all other policies] days will be granted for the payment of each premium falling due after the first premium, during which grace period the policy shall continue in force.

Note: A policy in which the insurer reserves the right to refuse renewal shall have, at the beginning of the above provision:

Unless not less than thirty (30) days prior to the premium due date the insurer has delivered to the insured or has mailed to his last address, as shown by the records of the insurer written notice of its intention not to renew this policy beyond the period for which the premium has been accepted;

(4)   A provision as follows:

Renewal: Each policy in which the insurer reserves the right to refuse renewal on an individual basis shall provide, in substance, in a provision thereof or in an endorsement thereon or in a rider attached thereto, that subject to the right to terminate the policy upon non-payment of premium when due, the right to refuse renewal shall not be exercised before the renewal date occurring on, or after and nearest each anniversary, or in the case of lapse and reinstatement at the renewal date occurring on, or after and nearest each anniversary of the last reinstatement, and that any refusal of renewal shall be without prejudice to any claim originating while the policy is in force. The preceding sentence shall not apply to accident insurance only policies.

(5)   A provision as follows:

Reinstatement: If any renewal premium be not paid within the time granted the insured for payment, a subsequent acceptance of premium by the insurer or by any agent duly authorized by the insurer to accept such premium, without requiring in connection therewith an application for reinstatement, shall reinstate the policy; provided, however that if the insurer or such agent requires an application for reinstatement and issues a conditional receipt for the premium tendered, the policy will be reinstated upon approval of the application by the insurer or, lacking such approval, upon the forty-fifth day following the date of the conditional receipt unless the insurer has previously notified the insured in writing of its disapproval of the application. The reinstated policy shall cover only loss resulting from such accidental injury as may be sustained after the date of reinstatement and loss due to such sickness as may begin more than ten (10) days after that date. In all other respects the insured and insurer shall have the same rights as they had under the policy immediately before the due date of the defaulted premium, subject to the provisions of any rider which may be attached in connection with the reinstatement. Any premium accepted in connection with a reinstatement shall be applied to a period for which premium has not been previously paid, but not to any period more than sixty (60) days prior to the date of reinstatement.

Note: The last sentence of the above provision may be omitted from any policy which the insured has the right to continue in force subject to its terms by the timely payment of premiums until at least age 50 or, in the case of a policy issued after age 44, for at least five years from its date of issue.

Editor's Note: For a statement of interpretation of this provision. See 1963 NAIC Proceedings II 514-517.

(6)   A provision as follows:

Notice of Claim: Written notice of claim must be given to the insurer within twenty (20) days after the occurrence or commencement of any loss covered by the policy, or as soon thereafter as is reasonably possible. Notice given by or on behalf of the insured or the beneficiary to the insurer at [insert the location of such office as the insurer may designate for the purpose], or to any authorized agent of the insurer, with information sufficient to identify the insured, shall be deemed notice to the insurer.

Note: In a policy providing a loss-of-time benefit which may be payable for at least two years, an insurer may at its option insert the following between the first and second sentences of the above provision:

Subject to the qualifications set forth below, if the insured suffers loss of time on account of disability for which indemnity may be payable for at least two (2) years, he shall, at least once in every six (6) months after having given notice of claim, give to the insurer notice of continuance of said disability, except in the event of legal incapacity. The period of six (6) months following any filing of proof by the insured or any payment by the insurer on account of such claim or any denial of liability in whole or in part by the insurer shall be excluded in applying this provision. Delay in the giving of notice shall not impair the insured's right to any indemnity which would otherwise have accrued during the period of six (6) months preceding the date on which notice is actually given.

(7)   A provision as follows:

Claim Forms: The insurer, upon receipt of a notice of claim, will furnish to the claimant such forms as are usually furnished by it for filing proof of loss. If forms are not furnished within fifteen (15) days after the giving of notice the claimant shall be deemed to have complied with the requirements of this policy as to proof of loss upon submitting, within the time fixed in the policy for filing proofs of loss, written proof covering the occurrence, the character and the extent of the loss for which claim is made.

(8)   A provision as follows:

Proofs of Loss: Written proof of loss must be furnished to the insurer at its office in case of claim for loss for which this policy provides any periodic payment contingent upon continuing loss within ninety (90) days after the termination of the period for which the insurer is liable and in case of claim for any other loss within ninety (90) days after the date of the loss. Failure to furnish proof within the time required shall not invalidate nor reduce any claim if it was not reasonably possible to give proof within that time, provided such proof is furnished as soon as reasonably possible and in no event, except in the absence of legal capacity, later than one year from the time proof is otherwise required.

(9)   A provision as follows:

Time of Payment of Claims: Indemnities payable under this policy for any loss other than loss for which this policy provides any periodic payment will be paid immediately upon receipt of due written proof of loss. Subject to due written proof of loss, all accrued indemnities for loss for which this policy provides periodic payment will be paid [insert period for payment which must not be less frequently than monthly] and any balance remaining unpaid upon the termination of liability will be paid immediately upon receipt of due written proof.

(10)   A provision as follows:

Payment of Claims: Indemnity for loss of life will be payable in accordance with the beneficiary designation and the provisions respecting such payment which may be prescribed herein and effective at the time of payment. If no such designation or provision is then effective, the indemnity shall be payable to the estate of the insured. Any other accrued indemnities unpaid at the insured's death may, at the option of the insurer, be paid either to the beneficiary or to the estate. All other indemnities will be payable to the insured.

Note: The following provisions, or either of them, may be included with the foregoing provision at the option of the insurer:

If any indemnity of this policy shall be payable to the estate of the insured, or to an insured or beneficiary who is a minor or otherwise not competent to give a valid release; the insurer may pay such indemnity, up to an amount not exceeding $[insert an amount which shall not exceed $1000], to any relative by blood or connection by marriage of the insured or beneficiary who is deemed by the insurer to be equitably entitled thereto. Any payment made by the insurer in good faith pursuant to this provision shall fully discharge the insurer to the extent of the payment.

191

Subject to any written direction of the insured in the application or otherwise, all or a portion of any indemnities provided by this policy on account of hospital, nursing, medical or surgical services may, at the insurer's option and unless the insured requests otherwise in writing not later than the time of filing proofs of loss, be paid directly to the hospital or person rendering such services; but it is not required that the service be rendered by a particular hospital or person.

(11) A provision as follows:

Physical Examinations and Autopsy: The insurer at its own expense shall have the right and opportunity to examine the person of the insured when and as often as it may reasonably require during the pendency of a claim hereunder and to make an autopsy in case of death where it is not forbidden by law.

(12) A provision as follows:

Legal Actions: No action at law or in equity shall be brought to recover on this policy prior to the expiration of sixty (60) days after written proof of loss has been furnished in accordance with the requirements of this policy. No such action shall be brought after the expiration of three (3) years after the time written proof of loss is required to be furnished.

(13) A provision as follows:

Change of Beneficiary: Unless the insured makes an irrevocable designation of beneficiary, the right to change of beneficiary is reserved to the insured and the consent of the beneficiary or beneficiaries shall not be requisite to surrender or assignment of this policy or to any change of beneficiary or beneficiaries, or to any other changes in this policy.

Note: The first clause of this provision, relating to the irrevocable designation of beneficiary, may be omitted at the insurer's option.

B.   Other Provisions

Except as provided in Subsection C, no policy delivered or issued for delivery to any person in this state shall contain provisions respecting the matters set forth below unless such provisions are in the words in which the same appear in this section; provided, however, that the insurer may, at its option, use in lieu of any such provision a corresponding provision of different wording approved by the Commissioner which is not less favorable in any respect to the insured or the beneficiary. Any such provision contained in the policy shall be preceded individually by the appropriate caption appearing in this subsection or, at the option of the insurer, by such appropriate individual or group captions or subcaptions as the Commissioner may approve.

(1) A provision as follows:

Change of Occupation: If the insured is injured or contract sickness after having changed his occupation to one classified by the insurer as more hazardous than that stated in this policy or while doing for compensation anything pertaining to an occupation so classified, the insurer will pay only such portion of the indemnities provided in this policy as the premium paid would have purchased at the rates and within the limits fixed by the insurer for the more hazardous occupation. If the insured changes his occupation to one classified by the insurer as less hazardous than that stated in this policy, the insurer, upon receipt of proof of change of occupation, will reduce the premium rate accordingly, and will return the excess pro-rata unearned premium from the date of change of occupation or from the policy anniversary date immediately preceding receipt of proof, whichever is the more recent. In applying this provision, the classification of occupational risk and the premium rates shall be such as have been last filed by the insurer prior to the occurrence of the loss for which the insurer is liable or prior to date of proof of change in occupation with the state official having supervision of insurance in the state where the insured resided at the time this policy was issued; but if such filing was not required, then the classification of occupational risk and the premium rates shall be those last made effective by the insurer in such state prior to the occurrence of the loss or prior to the date of proof of change in occupation.

(2)   A provision as follows:

Misstatement of Age: If the age of the insured has been misstated, all amounts payable under this policy shall be such as the premium paid would have purchased at the correct age.

(3)   A provision as follows:

Overinsurance: If an accident or sickness or accident and sickness policy or policies previously issued by the insurer to the insured be in force concurrently herewith, making the aggregate indemnity for [insert type of coverage or coverages] in excess of $[insert maximum limit of indemnity or indemnities] the excess shall be void and all premiums paid for such excess shall be returned to the insured or to his estate.

or, in lieu thereof:

Insurance effective at any one time on the insured under this policy and a like policy or policies in this insurer is limited to the one policy elected by the insured, his beneficiary or his estate, as the case may be, and the insurer will return all premiums paid for all other such policies.

(4)   A provision as follows:

Overinsurance: If, with respect to a person covered under this policy, benefits for allowable expense incurred during a claim determination period under this policy together with benefits for allowable expense during such period under all other valid coverage (without giving effect to this provision or to any "overinsurance provision" applying to such other valid coverage), exceed the total of the person's allowable expense during the period, this insurer shall be liable only for the proportionate amount of the benefits for allowable expense under this policy during the period as the total allowable expense during such period bears to the total amount of benefits payable during the period for expense under this policy and all other valid coverage (without giving effect to this provision or to any overinsurance provision applying to the other valid coverage) less any amount of benefits for allowable expense payable under other valid coverage which does not contain an overinsurance provision. In no event shall this provision operate to increase the amount of benefits for allowable expense payable under this policy with respect to a person covered under this policy above the amount which would have been paid in the absence of this provision. This insurer may pay benefits to any insurer providing other valid coverage in the event of overpayment by such insurer. Any such payment shall discharge the liability of this insurer as fully as if the payment had been made directly to the insured, his assignee or his beneficiary. In the event that this insurer pays benefits to the insured, his assignee or his beneficiary, in excess of the amount which would have been payable if the existence of other valid coverage had been disclosed, this insurer shall have a right of action against the insured, his assignee or his beneficiary, to recover the amount which would not have been paid had there been a disclosure of the existence of the other valid coverage. The amount of other valid coverage which is on a provision of service basis shall be computed as the amount the services rendered would have cost in the absence of such coverage.

For purposes of this provision:

(a)   "Allowable expense" means 110 percent of any necessary, reasonable and customary item of expense which is covered, in whole or in part, as a hospital, surgical, medical or major medical expense under this policy or under any other valid coverage.

(b)   "Claim determination period" with respect to any covered person means the initial period of [insert period of not less than 30 days] and each successive period of a like number of days, during which allowable expense covered under this policy is incurred on account of such person. The first period begins on the date when the first expense is incurred, and successive periods shall begin when expense is incurred after expiration of a prior period.

or, in lieu thereof:

"Claim determination period" with respect to any covered person means each [insert calendar or policy period of not less than a month] during which allowable expense covered under this policy is incurred on account of such person.

(c)   "Overinsurance provision" means this provision and any other provision which may reduce an insurer's liability because of the existence of benefits under other valid coverage.

Note: The foregoing policy provision may be inserted in all (guaranteed renewable and non-cancellable as well as guaranteed renewable) policies providing hospital, surgical, medical or major medical benefits. The insurer may make this provision applicable to either or both (a) other valid coverage with other insurers and, (b) except for individual policies individually underwritten, other valid coverage with the same insurer. The insurer shall include in this provision a definition of "other valid coverage" approved as to form by the Commissioner. The term may include hospital, surgical, medical or major medical benefits provided by group, blanket or franchise coverage, individual and family-type coverage, Blue Cross-Blue Shield coverage and other prepayment plans, group practice and individual practice plans, uninsured benefits provided by labor-management trusteed plans, or union welfare plans, or by employer or employee benefit organizations, benefits provided under governmental programs, workmen's compensation insurance or any coverage required or provided by any other statute, and medical payments under automobile liability and personal liability policies. Other valid coverage shall not include payments made under third party liability coverage as a result of a determination of negligence, but an insurer may at its option include a subrogation clause in its policy. The insurer may require, as part of the proof of claim, the information necessary to administer this provision.

(5)   A provision as follows:

Overinsurance: After the loss-of-time benefit of this policy has been payable for ninety (90) days, the benefit will be adjusted, as provided below, if the total amount of unadjusted loss-of-time benefits provided in all valid loss-of-time coverage upon the insured should exceed [insert amount] percent of the insured's earned income; provided, however, that if the information contained in the application discloses that the total amount of loss-of-time benefits under this policy and under all other valid loss-of-time coverage expected to be effective upon the insured in accordance with the application for this policy exceeded [insert amount] percent of the insured's earned income at the time of such application, the higher percentage will be used in

place of [insert amount] percent. The adjusted loss-of-time benefit under this policy for any month shall be only such proportion of the loss-of-time benefit otherwise payable under this policy as (i) the product of the insured's earned income and [insert amount] percent (or, if higher, the alternative percentage described at the end of the first sentence of this provision) bears to (ii) the total amount of loss-of-time benefits payable for such month under this policy and all other valid loss-of-time coverage on the insured (without giving effect to the overinsurance provision in this or any other coverage) less in both (i) and (ii) any amount of loss-of-time benefits payable under other valid loss-of-time coverage which does not contain an overinsurance provision. In making the computation, all benefits and earnings shall be converted to a consistent [insert "weekly" if the loss-of-time benefit of this policy is payable weekly, "monthly" if the benefit is payable monthly, etc.] basis. If the numerator of the foregoing ratio is zero or is negative, no benefit shall be payable under this policy. In no event shall this provision operate to reduce the total combined amount of loss-of-time
benefits for such month payable under this policy and all other valid loss-of-time coverage below the less of $300 and the total combined amount of loss-of-time benefits determined without giving effect to any overinsurance provision, or operate to increase the amount of benefits payable under this policy above the amount which would have been paid in the absence of this provision, or take into account or operate to reduce any benefit other than the loss-of-time benefit.

For purposes of this provision:

(a)   "Earned income," except where otherwise specified, means the greater of the monthly earnings of the insured at the time disability commences and his average monthly earnings for a period of two (2) years immediately preceding the commencement of disability, and shall not include any investment income or any other income not derived from the insured's vocational activities.

(b)   "Overinsurance provision" shall include this provision and any other provision with respect to any loss-of-time coverage which may have the effect of reducing an insurer's liability if the total amount of loss-of-time benefits under all coverage exceeds a stated relationship to the insured's earnings.

Note: The foregoing provision may be included only in a policy which provides a loss-of-time benefit which may be payable for at least fifty-two weeks, which is issued on the basis of selective underwriting of each individual application, and for which the application includes a question designed to elicit information necessary either to determine the ratio of the total loss-of-time benefits or the insured to the insured's earned income or to determine that such ratio does not exceed the percentage of earnings, not less than sixty percent, selected by the insurer and inserted in lieu of the blank factor above. The insurer may require, as part of the proof of claim, the information necessary to administer this provision. If the application indicates that other loss-of-time coverage is to be discontinued, the amount of such other coverage shall be excluded in computing the alternative percentage in the first sentence of the overinsurance provision. The policy shall include a definition of "valid loss-of-time coverage," approved as to form by the Commissioner, which definition may include coverage provided by governmental agencies and by organizations subject to regulation by insurance law and by insurance authorities of this or any other state of the United States or of any other country or subdivision thereof, coverage provided for such insured pursuant to any disability benefits statute or any workmen's compensation or employer's liability statute, benefits provided by labor-management trusteed plans or union welfare plans by employer or employee benefit organizations, or by salary continuance or pension programs, and any other coverage the inclusion of which may be approved by the Commissioner.

(7)   A provision as follows:

Unpaid Premium: Upon the payment of a claim under this policy, any premium then due and unpaid or covered by any note or written order may be deducted therefrom.

(8)   A provision as follows:

Conformity with State Statutes: Any provision of this policy which, on its effective date, is in conflict with the statutes of the state in which the insured resides on such date is hereby amended to conform to the minimum requirements of such statutes.

(9)   A provision as follows:

Illegal Occupation: The insurer shall not be liable for any loss to which a contributing cause was the insured's commission of or attempt to commit a felony or to which a contributing cause was the insured's being engaged in an illegal occupation.

(10)   A provision as follows:

Intoxicants and Narcotics: The insurer shall not be liable for any loss sustained or contracted in consequence of the insured's being intoxicated or under the influence of any narcotic unless administered on the advice of a physician.

Note: Paragraphs (9) and (10) are suggested for states which desire such provisions.

C.   Inapplicable or Inconsistent Provisions

If any provision of this section is in whole or in part inapplicable to or inconsistent with the coverage provided by a particular form of policy the insurer, with the approval of the Commissioner, shall omit from such policy any inapplicable provision or part of a provision, and shall modify any inconsistent provision or part of the provision in such manner as to make the provision as contained in the policy consistent with the coverage provided by the policy.

D.   Order of Certain Policy Provisions

The provisions which are the subject of Subsections A and B of this section, or any corresponding provisions which are used in lieu thereof in accordance with such subsections, shall be printed in the provisions in the consecutive order of the provisions in such subsections or, at the option of the insurer, any such provisions may appear as a unit in any part of the policy, with other provisions to which it may be logically related, provided the resulting policy shall not be in whole or in part unintelligible, uncertain, ambiguous, abstruse, or likely to mislead a person to whom the policy is offered, delivered or issued.

E.   Third Party Ownership

The word "insured," as used in this Act, shall not be construed as preventing a person other than the insured with a proper insurable interest from making application for and owning a policy covering the insured or from being entitled under such a policy to any indemnities, benefits and rights provided therein.

F.   Requirements of Other Jurisdictions

(1)   Any policy of a foreign or alien insurer, when delivered or issued for delivery to any person in this state, may contain any provision which is not less favorable to the insured or the beneficiary than the provisions of this Act and which is prescribed or required by the law of the state under which the insurer is organized.

(2)   Any policy of a domestic insurer may, when issued for delivery in any other state or country, contain any provision permitted or required by the laws of such other state or country.

G.   Filing Procedure

The Commissioner may make such reasonable rules and regulations concerning the procedure for the filing or submission of policies subject to this Act as are necessary, proper or advisable to the administration of this Act. This provision shall not abridge any other authority granted the Commissioner by law.

Section 4.   Conforming to Statute

A.   Other Policy Provisions

No policy which is not subject to Section 3 of this Act shall make a policy, or any portion thereof, less favorable in any respect to the insured or the beneficiary than the provisions thereof which are subject to this Act.

B.   Policy Conflicting with this Act

A policy delivered or issued for delivery to any person in this state in violation of this Act shall be held valid but shall be construed as provided in this Act. When any provision in a policy subject to this Act is in conflict with any provision of this Act, the rights, duties and obligations of the insurer, the insured and the beneficiary shall be governed by the provisions of this Act.

Section 5.   Application

A.   The insured shall not be bound by any statement made in an application for a policy unless a copy of the application is attached to or endorsed on the policy when issued as a part thereof. If any such policy delivered or issued for delivery to any person in this state shall be reinstated or renewed, and the insured or the beneficiary or assignee of the policy shall make written request to the insurer for a copy of the application, if any, for such reinstatement or renewal, the insurer shall within fifteen (15) days after the receipt of the request at its home office or any branch office of the insurer, deliver or mail to the person making the request, a copy of the application. If the copy shall not be so delivered or mailed, the insurer shall be precluded from introducing the application as evidence in any action or proceeding based upon or involving the policy or its reinstatement or renewal.

B.   No alteration of any written application for any such policy shall be made by any person other than the applicant without his written consent, except that insertions may be made by the insurer, for administrative purposes only, in such manner as to indicate clearly that such insertions are not to be ascribed to the applicant.

C.   The falsity of any statement in the application for any policy covered by this Act may not bar the right to recovery thereunder unless such false statement materially affected either the acceptance of the risk or the hazard assumed by the insurer.

Note: Section 5, or any subsection thereof, is suggested for use in states which have no comparable statutes relating to the application.

Section 6.   Notice, Waiver

The acknowledgment by any insurer of the receipt of notice given under any policy covered by this Act, or the furnishing of forms for filing proofs of loss, or the acceptance of such proofs, or the investigation of any claim thereunder shall not operate as a waiver of any of the rights of the insurer in defense of any claim arising under such policy.

197

Section 7.   Age Limit

If any policy contains a provision establishing, as an age limit or otherwise, a date after which the coverage provided by the policy will not be effective, and if such date falls within a period for which premium is accepted by the insurer or if the insurer accepts a premium after such date, the coverage provided by the policy will continue in force subject to any right of cancellation until the end of the period for which premium has been accepted. In the event the age of the insured has been misstated and if, according to the correct age of the insured, the coverage provided by the policy would not have become effective, or would have ceased prior to the acceptance of such premium or premiums, then the liability of the insurer shall be limited to the refund, upon request, of all premiums paid for the period not covered by the policy.

Section 8.   Non-Application to Certain Policies

Nothing in this Act shall apply to or affect:

A.   Any policy of workmen's compensation insurance or any policy of liability insurance with or without supplementary expense coverage therein; or

B.   Any policy or contract of reinsurance; or

C.   Any blanket or group policy of insurance; or

D.   Life insurance, endowment or annuity contracts, or contracts supplemental thereto which contain only such provisions relating to accident and sickness insurance as:

(a)   Provide additional benefits in case of death or dismemberment or loss of sight by accident, or as

(b   Operate to safeguard such contracts against lapse, or to give a special surrender value or special benefit or an annuity in the event that the insured or annuitant shall become totally and permanently disabled, as defined by the contract or supplemental contract.

Note: This provision may, if desired, be modified in individual states so as to be consistent with current statutes of such states.

Section 9.   Violation

Any person, partnership or corporation willfully violating any provision of this Act or order of the Commissioner made in accordance with this Act, shall forfeit to the people of the state a sum not to exceed $[insert amount] for each violation, which may be recovered by a civil action.   The Commissioner may also suspend or revoke the license of an insurer or agent for any willful violation.

Note: This provision is to be used only in those states which do not have similar legislation now in effect.

Section 10.   Judicial Review

Any order or decision of the Commissioner under this Act shall be subject to review by appeal (writ of certiorari) to the [insert title] Court at the instance of any party in interest. The filing of the appeal (petition for such writ) shall operate as a stay of any such order or decision until the Court directs otherwise. The Court may review all the facts and, in disposing of the issue before it, may modify, affirm or reverse the order or decision of the Commissioner in whole or in part.

Note: This provision is to be used only in those states which do not have similar legislation now in effect.

Section 11.   Repeal of Inconsistent Acts

Note: This section should contain suitable language to repeal acts or parts of acts presently enacted and inconsistent with this Act. The repealing section should contain an appropriate exception with regard to Section 12 of this Act.

Section 12.   Effective Date of Act

This Act shall take effect on the [insert day] of [insert month], 19 [insert year]. A policy, rider or endorsement which could have been lawfully used or delivered or issued for delivery to any person in this state immediately before the effective date of this Act may be used or delivered or issued for delivery to any such person during five (5) years after the effective date of this Act.

APPENDIX A

PROPOSED REGULATION REGARDING OVERINSURANCE PROVISIONS

Each individual health insurance policy, delivered or issued for delivery in this State on or after [insert effective date], which contains the overinsurance provisions authorized in [insert reference to statutory section which contains Section 3B(4) of the Uniform Individual Accident and Sickness Policy Provisions Law] or [insert reference to statutory section which contains Section 3B(5) of the Uniform Individual Accident and Sickness Policy Provisions Law] or, at the option of the insurer, the application for such policy, shall contain, or have attached to or be stamped or endorsed to add, a statement to the effect that benefits under the policy are subject to reduction if the insured has benefits under any other coverage of the type described in the overinsurance provision causing overinsurance as defined in such provision. If the insurer elects to include such statement in the policy, rather than in the application, the policy shall also contain, or have attached to or be stamped or endorsed to add, an additional statement to the effect that during a period of ten (10) days from the date the policy is delivered to the policyholder, it may be surrendered to the insurer together with a written request for cancellation of the policy and in such event the insurer will refund any premium paid therefor including any policy fees or other charges.

Legislative History (all references are to the Proceedings of the NAIC).

1950 Proc. 398, 399-413, 414 (adopted).
1956 Proc. II 289-290, 315 (amended).
1964 Proc. I 91, 95, 98-101, 115 (amended).

See Also:
1979 Proc. I 375 (UPPL restated in simplified language) (P. 185-1).

Appendix B
GROUP HEALTH INSURANCE DEFINITION AND GROUP HEALTH INSURANCE STANDARD PROVISIONS MODEL ACT

(Model Regulation Service—July 1989)

From the NAIC *Model Laws, Regulations and Guidelines.* Reprinted with the permission of the National Association of Insurance Commissioners.

Table of Contents

Section 1.   Group Health Insurance Definition

Except as provided in Section 2, no policy of group health insurance shall be delivered in this state unless it conforms to one of the following descriptions:

A. A policy issued to an employer, or to the trustees of a fund established by an employer, which employer or trustees shall be deemed the policyholder, to insure employees of the employer for the benefit of persons other than the employer, subject to the following requirements:

   (1) The employees eligible for insurance under the policy shall be all of the employees of the employer, or all of any class or classes thereof. The policy may provide that the term "employees" shall include the employees of one or more subsidiary corporations, and the employees, individual proprietors, and partners of one or more affiliated corporations, proprietorships or partnerships if the business of the employer and of such affiliated corporations, proprietorships or partnerships is under common control. The policy may provide that the term "employees" shall include retired employees, former employees and directors of a corporate employer. A policy issued to insure the employees of a public body may provide that the term "employees" shall include elected or appointed officials.

NOTE: Last sentence may be deleted if its content is covered.

   (2) The premium for the policy shall be paid either from the employer's fund or from funds contributed by the insured employees, or from both. Except as provided in Paragraph (3), a policy on which no part of the premium is to be derived from funds contributed by the insured employees must insure all eligible employees, except those who reject such coverage in writing.

(3) An insurer may exclude or limit the coverage on any person as to whom evidence of individual insurability is not satisfactory to the insurer.

B. A policy issued to a creditor or its parent holding company or to a trustee or trustees or agent designated by two or more creditors, which creditor, holding company, affiliate, trustee, trustees or agent shall be deemed the policyholder, to insure debtors of the creditor or creditors with respect to their indebtedness, subject to the following requirements:

(1) The debtors eligible for insurance under the policy shall be all of the debtors of the creditor or creditors, or all of any class or classes thereof. The policy may provide that the term "debtors" shall include (i) borrowers of money or purchasers or lessees of goods, services, or property for which payment is arranged through a credit transaction; (ii) the debtors of one or more subsidiary corporations; and (iii) the debtors of one or more affiliated corporations, proprietorships or partnerships if the business of the policyholder and of such affiliated corporations, proprietorships or partnerships is under common control.

(2) The premium for the policy shall be paid either from the creditor's funds, or from charges collected from the insured debtors, or from both. Except as provided in Paragraph (3), a policy on which no part of the premium is to be derived from funds contributed by insured debtors specifically for their insurance must insure all eligible debtors.

(3) An insurer may exclude any debtors as to whom evidence of individual insurability is not satisfactory to the insurer.

(4) The total amount of insurance payable with respect to an indebtedness shall not exceed the greater of the scheduled or actual amount of unpaid indebtedness to the creditor. The insurer may exclude any payments which are delinquent on the date the debtor becomes disabled as defined in the policy.

(5) The insurance may be payable to the creditor or any successor to the right, title, and interest of the creditor. Such payment or payments shall reduce or extinguish the unpaid indebtedness of the debtor to the extent of each such payment and any excess of the insurance shall be payable to the insured or the estate of the insured.

(6) Not withstanding the preceding provisions of this section, insurance on agricultural credit transaction commitments may be written up to the amount of the loan commitment. Insurance on educational credit transaction commitments may be written up to the amount of the loan commitment less the amount of any repayments made on the loan.

C. A policy issued to a labor union, or similar employee organization, which shall be deemed to be the policyholder, to insure members of such union or organization for the benefit of persons other than the union or organization or any of its officials, representatives, or agents, subject to the following requirements:

(1) The members eligible for insurance under the policy shall be all of the members of the union or organization, or all of any class or classes thereof.

(2) The premium for the policy shall be paid either from funds of the union or organization, or from funds contributed by the insured members specifically for their insurance, or from both. Except as provided in Paragraph (3), a policy on which no part of the premium is to be derived from funds contributed by the insured members specifically for their insurance must insure all eligible members, except those who reject such coverage in writing.

(3) An insurer may exclude or limit the coverage on any person as to whom evidence of individual insurability is not satisfactory to the insurer.

D. A policy issued to a trust, or to the trustee(s) of a fund, established or adopted by two or more employers, or by one or more labor unions of similar employee organizations, or by one or more employers and one or more labor unions or similar employee organizations, which trust or trustee(s) shall be deemed the policyholder, to insure employees of the employers or members of the unions or organizations for the benefit of persons other than the employers or the unions or organizations, subject to the following requirements:

(1) The persons eligible for insurance shall be all of the employees of the employers or all of the members of the unions or organizations, or all of any class or classes thereof. The policy may provide that the term "employee" shall include the employees of one or more subsidiary corporations, and the employees, individual proprietors, and partners of one or more affiliated corporations, proprietorships or partnerships if the business of the employer and of such affiliated corporations, proprietorships or partnerships is under common control. The policy may provide that the term "employees" shall include retired employees, former employees and directors of a corporate employer. The policy may provide that the term "employees" shall include the trustees or their employees, or both, if their duties are principally connected with such trusteeship.

(2) The premium for the policy shall be paid from funds contributed by the employer or employers of the insured persons, or by the union or unions or similar employee organizations, or by both, or from funds contributed by the insured persons or from both the insured persons and the employer(s) or union(s) or similar employee organization(s). Except as provided in Paragraph (3), a policy on which no part of the premium is to be derived from funds contributed by the insured persons specifically for their insurance must insure all eligible persons, except those who reject such coverage in writing.

(3) An insurer may exclude or limit the coverage on any person as to whom evidence of individual insurability is not satisfactory to the insurer.

E. A policy issued to an association or to a trust or to the trustee(s) of a fund established, created, or maintained for the benefit of members of one or more associations. The association or associations shall have at the outset a minimum of 100 persons and have been organized and maintained in good faith for purposes other than that of obtaining insurance; shall have been in active existence for at least one year; and shall have a constitution and by-laws which provide that (i) the association or associations hold regular meetings not less than annually to further purposes of the members, (ii) except for credit unions, the association or associations collect dues or solicit contributions from members, and (iii) the members have voting privileges and representation on the governing board and committees. The policy shall be subject to the following requirements:

(1) The policy may insure members of such association or associations, employees thereof or employees of members, or one or more of the preceding or all of any class or classes thereof for the benefit of persons other than the employee's employer.

(2) The premium for the policy shall be paid from funds contributed by the association or associations, or by employer members, or by both, or from funds contributed by the covered persons or from both the covered persons and the association, associations, or employer members.

(3) Except as provided in Paragraph (4), a policy on which no part of the premium is to be derived from funds contributed by the covered persons specifically for their insurance must insure all eligible persons, except those who reject such coverage in writing.

(4) An insurer may exclude or limit the coverage on any person as to whom evidence of individual insurability is not satisfactory to the insurer.

F. A policy issued to a credit union or to a trustee or trustees or agent designated by two or more credit unions, which credit union, trustee, trustees, or agent shall be deemed the policyholder, to insure members of such credit union or credit unions for the benefit of persons other than the credit union or credit unions, trustee or trustees, or agent or any of their officials, subject to the following requirements:

   (1) The members eligible for insurance shall be all of the members of the credit union or credit unions, or all of any class or classes thereof.

   (2) The premium for the policy shall be paid by the policyholder from the credit union's funds and, except as provided in Paragraph (3), must insure all eligible members.

   (3) An insurer may exclude or limit the coverage on any member as to whom evidence of individual insurability is not satisfactory to the insurer.

G. A policy issued to cover persons in a group where that group is specifically described by a law of this state as one which may be covered for group life insurance. The provisions of such law relating to eligibility and evidence of insurability shall apply.

Section 2.   Limits of Group Health Insurance

Group health insurance offered to a resident of this state under a group health insurance policy issued to a group other than one described in Section 1 shall be subject to the following requirements:

A. No such group health insurance policy shall be delivered in this state unless the Commissioner finds that:

NOTE: Substitute the appropriate title, if "Commissioner" is not correct in the enacting state.

   (1) The issuance of such group policy is not contrary to the best interest of the public;

   (2) The issuance of the group policy would result in economies of acquisition or administration; and

   (3) The benefits are reasonable in relation to the premiums charged.

B. No such group health insurance coverage may be offered in this state by an insurer under a policy issued in another state unless this state or the state in which the group policy is issued, having requirements substantially similar to those contained in Subsections (A)(1), (2) and (3), has made a determination that such requirements have been met.

DRAFTING NOTE: Alternative language to Section 2B:

Alternative 1. (Add this language to Section 2B above):

   A company shall file for information purposes

    (1) A copy of the group master contract;

    (2) A copy of the statute of the state where the group policy is issued, authorizing the issuance of the group policy under the same or similar statute;

    (3) Evidence of approval in the state where the group policy is issued; and

    (4) Copies of all supportive material used by the company to secure approval of the group in that state including the documentation required in Subsections A(1), (2), and (3)

Alternative 2. (Add this language to Section 2B and Alternative 1 above)

   The Commissioner, at any time subsequent to receipt of such information, after finding that the standards of Subsections A(1), (2) and (3) have not been met, may order the insurer to stop marketing such coverage in this state.

Alternative 3. The following language could be substituted for Section 2B:

> No such group health insurance coverage may be offered in this state by an insurer under a policy issued in another state unless this state has determined that the requirements of Subsections A(1), (2) and (3) have been met.
>
> The insurer shall file:
>
> (1) A copy of the group master contract;
>
> (2) A copy of the statute of the state where the group policy is issued, authorizing the issuance of the group policy under the same or similar statute;
>
> (3) Evidence of approval in the state where the group policy is issued; and
>
> (4) Copies of all supportive material used by the company to secure approval of the group in that state including the documentation required in Subsections A(1), (2), and (3).
>
> If the Commissioner has not made such determination within thirty days of filing by the company, the requirements shall be deemed to have been met.

C. The premium for the policy shall be paid either from the policyholder's funds or from funds contributed by the covered persons, or from both.

D. An insurer may exclude or limit the coverage on any person as to whom evidence of individual insurability is not satisfactory to the insurer.

Section 3.   Notice of Compensation

A. With respect to a program of insurance which if issued on a group basis, would not qualify under Subsections A, B, C, D and F of Section 1 of the Act, if compensation of any kind will or may be paid to;

   (1) A policyholder or sponsoring or endorsing entity in the case of group policy, or

   (2) A sponsoring or endorsing entity in the case of individual, blanket or franchise policies marketed by means of direct response solicitation,

   the insurer shall cause to be distributed to prospective insureds a written notice that compensation will or may be paid.

B. Such notice shall be distributed

   (1) whether compensation is direct or indirect, and

   (2) whether such compensation is paid to or retained by the policyholder or sponsoring or endorsing entity, or paid to or retained by a third party at the direction of the policyholder or sponsoring or endorsing entity, or an entity affiliated therewith by way of ownership, contract or employment.

C. The notice required by this section shall be placed on or accompany any application or enrollment form provided prospective insureds.

D. The following terms shall have the meanings indicated:

   (1) "Direct response solicitation" means a solicitation through a sponsoring or endorsing entity through the mails, telephone, or other mass communications media;

   (2) "Sponsoring or endorsing entity" means an organization which has arranged for the offering of a program of insurance in a manner which communicates that eligibility for participation in the program is dependent upon affiliation with such organization or that it encourages participation in the program.

205

Section 4. Dependent Group Health Insurance

Except for a policy issued under Section 1B, a group health insurance policy may be extended to insure the employees or members with respect to their family members or dependents, or any class or classes thereof, subject to the following:

A. The premium for the insurance shall be paid either from funds contributed by the employer, union, association or other person to whom the policy has been issued, or from funds contributed by the covered persons, or from both. Except as provided in Subsection B, a policy on which no part of the premium for the family members or dependents coverage is to be derived from funds contributed by the covered persons must insure all eligible employees or members with respect to their family members or dependents, or any class or classes thereof.

B. An insurer may exclude or limit the coverage on any family member or dependent as to whom evidence of individual insurability is not satisfactory to the insurer.

Section 5. Group Health Insurance Standard Provisions

No policy of group health insurance shall be delivered in this state unless it contains in substance the following provisions, or provisions which in the opinion of the Commissioner are more favorable to the persons insured, or at least as favorable to the persons insured and more favorable to the policyholder, provided, however, (a) that provisions E, G and L shall not apply to policies insuring debtors; (b) that the standard provisions required for individual health insurance policies shall not apply to group health insurance policies; and (c) that if any provision of this section is in whole or in part inapplicable to or inconsistent with the coverage provided by a particular form of policy, the insurer, with the approval of the Commissioner, shall omit from such policy any inapplicable provision or part of a provision, and shall modify any inconsistent provision or part of the provision in such manner as to make the provision as contained in the policy consistent with the coverage provided by the policy:

A. A provision that the policyholder is entitled to a grace period of thirty-one days for the payment of any premium due except the first, during which grace period the policy shall continue in force, unless the policyholder shall have given the insurer written notice of discontinuance in advance of the date of discontinuance and in accordance with the terms of the policy. The policy may provide that the policyholder shall be liable to the insurer for the payment of a pro rata premium for the time the policy was in force during such grace period.

B. A provision that the validity of the policy shall not be contested except for nonpayment of premiums, after it has been in force for two years from its date of issue; and that no statement made by any person covered under the policy relating to insurability shall be used in contesting the validity of the insurance with respect to which such statement was made after such insurance has been in force prior to the contest for a period of two years during such person's lifetime nor unless it is contained in a written instrument signed by the person making such statement; provided however, that no such provision shall preclude the assertion at any time of defenses based upon the person's ineligibility for coverage under the policy or upon other provisions in the policy.

C. A provision that a copy of the application, if any, of the policyholder shall be attached to the policy when issued, that all statements made by the policyholder or by the persons insured shall be deemed representations and not warranties, and that no statement made by any person insured shall be used in any contest unless a copy of the instrument containing the statement is or has been furnished to such person or, in the event of the death or incapacity of the insured person, to the individual's beneficiary or personal representative.

D. A provision setting forth the conditions, if any, under which the insurer reserves the right to require a person eligible for insurance to furnish evidence of individual insurability satisfactory to the insurer as a condition to part or all of the individual's coverage.

E. A provision specifying the additional exclusions or limitations, if any, applicable under the policy with respect to a disease or physical condition of a person, not otherwise excluded from the person's coverage by name or specific description effective on the date of the person's loss, which existed prior to the effective date of the person's coverage under the policy. Any such exclusion or limitation may only apply to a disease or physical condition for which medical advice or treatment was received by the person during the twelve months prior to the effective date of the person's coverage. In no event shall such exclusion or limitation apply to loss incurred or disability commencing after the earlier of (a) the end of a continuous period of twelve months commencing on or after the effective date of the person's coverage during all of which the person has received no medical advice or treatment in connection with such disease or physical condition; and (b) the end of the two-year period commencing on the effective date of the person's coverage.

F. If the premiums or benefits vary by age, there shall be a provision specifying an equitable adjustment of premiums or of benefits, or both, to be made in the event the age of a covered person has been misstated, such provision to contain a clear statement of the method of adjustment to be used.

G. A provision that the insurer will issue to the policyholder for delivery to each person insured a certificate setting forth a statement as to the insurance protection to which that person is entitled, to whom the insurance benefits are payable, and a statement as to any family member's or dependent's coverage.

H. A provision that written notice of claim must be given to the insurer within twenty days after the occurrence or commencement of any loss covered by the policy. Failure to give notice within such time shall not invalidate nor reduce any claim if it can be shown not to have been reasonably possible to give such notice and that notice was given as soon as was reasonably possible.

I. A provision that the insurer will furnish to the person making claim, or to the policyholder for delivery to such person, such forms as are usually furnished by it for filing proof of loss. If such forms are not furnished before the expiration of fifteen days after the insurer received notice of any claim under the policy, the person making such claim shall be deemed to have complied with the requirements of the policy as to proof of loss upon submitting within the time fixed in the policy for filing proof of loss, written proof covering the occurrence, character, and extent of the loss for which claim is made.

J. A provision that in the case of claim for loss of time for disability, written proof of such loss must be furnished to the insurer within ninety days after the commencement of the period for which the insurer is liable, and that subsequent written proofs of the continuance of such disability must be furnished to the insurer at such intervals as the insurer may reasonably require, and that in the case of claim for any other loss, written proof of such loss must be furnished to the insurer within ninety days after the date of such loss. Failure to furnish such proof within such time shall not invalidate nor reduce any claim if it was not reasonably possible to furnish such proof within such time, provided such proof is furnished as soon as reasonably possible and in no event, except in the absence of legal capacity of the claimant, later than one year from the time proof is otherwise required.

K. A provision that all benefits payable under the policy other than benefits for loss of time will be payable not more than sixty days after receipt of proof, and that, subject to due proof of loss, all accrued benefits payable under the policy for loss of time will be paid not less frequently than monthly during the continuance of the period for which the insurer is liable, and that any balance remaining unpaid at the termination of such period will be paid as soon as possible after receipt of such proof.

L. A provision that benefits for loss of life of the person insured shall be payable to the beneficiary designated by the person insured. However, if the policy contains conditions pertaining to family status, the beneficiary may be the family member specified by the policy terms. In either case, payment of these benefits is subject to the provisions of the policy in the event no such designated or specified beneficiary is living at the death of the person insured. All other benefits of the policy shall be payable to the person insured. The policy may also provide that if any benefit is payable to the estate of a person, or to a person who is a minor or otherwise not competent to give a valid release, the insurer may pay such benefit, up to an amount not exceeding $[5,000], to any relative by blood or connection by marriage of such person who is deemed by the insurer to be equitably entitled thereto.

M. A provision that the insurer shall have the right and opportunity to examine the person of the individual for whom claim is made when and so often as it may reasonably require during the pendency of claim under the policy and also the right and opportunity to make an autopsy in case of death where it is not prohibited by law.

N. A provision that no action at law or in equity shall be brought to recover on the policy prior to the expiration of sixty days after proof of loss has been filed in accordance with the requirement of the policy and that no such action shall be brought at all unless brought within three years from the expiration of the time within which proof of loss is required by the policy.

O. In the case of a policy insuring debtors, a provision that the insurer will furnish the policyholder for delivery to each debtor insured under the policy a certificate of insurance describing the coverage and specifying that the benefits payable shall first be applied to reduce or extinguish the indebtedness.

Legislative History (all references are to the Proceedings of the NAIC).

1983 Proc. I 6, 35, 447, 667, 670-676 (adopted).
1984 Proc. I 6, 32, 528, 529 (amended).
1985 Proc. I 19, 38, 571, 599-604 (amended and reprinted).
1989 Proc. I 9, 24-25, 704, 839, 842-843 (amended).

SUGGESTED READING

Bluhm, W. F., principal editor. 1992. *Group Insurance.* Winstead, CT: ACTEX Publishers.

Brunner, Thomas W., and Kirk J. Nahra. 1993. *Fighting Health Care Fraud: A Guide to the Benefits and Risks of Fraud Investigations.* Washington, DC: National Health Care Anti-Fraud Association.

Carlstrom, Charles T. 1994. "The Government's Role in the Health Care Industry: Past, Present, and Future." *Economic Commentary* (1 June): 1–6.

Driving Down Health Care Costs: Strategies and Solutions, 1996. New York: Panel Publishers. Published annually.

Fyffe, Kathleen, et al. 1994. *Health Insurers' Anti-Fraud Programs.* Washington, DC: Health Insurance Association of America.

Health Insurance Association of America. 1995. *Source Book of Health Insurance Data.* Washington, DC: Health Insurance Association of America.

Jones, Harriett E., and Dani L. Long. 1996. *Principles of Insurance: Life, Health, and Annuities.* Atlanta, GA: Life Management Institute LOMA.

Meyer, William F. 1990. *Life and Health Insurance Law.* Cincinnati, OH: International Claim Association.

O'Grady, Francis T. 1988. *Individual Health Insurance.* Shaumburg, IL: Society of Actuaries.

Rosenbloom, Jerry S. 1996. *The Handbook of Employee Benefits Design, Funding and Administration.* 4th ed. Burr Ridge, IL: Irwin Professional Publishing.

Sadler, Jeff. 1994. *Disability Income: The Sale, The Product, The Market.* Cincinnati, OH: National Underwriter.

Sadler, Jeff. 1992. *Understanding Long-Term Care Insurance.* Amherst, MA: HRD Press, Inc.

Society of Actuaries. *Records of the Society of Actuaries.* Shaumburg, IL: Society of Actuaries. Published four times a year.

Society of Actuaries. *Transactions of the Society of Actuaries.* Shaumburg, IL: Society of Actuaries. Published annually.

Zwanziger, Jack, and Glenn Melnick. 1996. "Can Managed Care Plans Control Health Care Costs?" *Health Affairs* (Summer): 185–199.

GLOSSARY

A

ABUSE   Stretching the truth or exaggerating the treatment of services involved in health insurance claims. May not involve false misrepresentation or intention to defraud.

ACCEPTANCE   The decision made by a potential insured to enter into an insurance contract at the terms offered.

ACCIDENT   An unforeseen, unexpected, and unintended event.

ACCIDENT INSURANCE   A type of health insurance that insures against loss by accidental bodily injury.

ACCIDENTAL BODILY INJURY   An injury sustained as the result of an accident.

ACCIDENTAL DEATH AND DISMEMBERMENT INSURANCE (AD&D)   A form of health and accident insurance that provides payment to an insured's beneficiary in the event of death or the insured in the event of specific bodily losses resulting from an accident.

ACCOUNTING   The process of recording, summarizing, and allocating all items of income and expense of the company and analyzing, verifying, and reporting the results.

ACCRUED INCOME   Income earned on a stated sum that continues to increase until payout.

ACTIVELY AT WORK   A requirement (a form of individual evidence of insurability) that an insured be at his or her usual place of employment on the date insurance takes effect. Since this definition is impractical for dependents, plans usually require that, if a dependent is hospital confined on the date the insurance would become effective, the effective date of insurance will be deferred until release from the hospital.

ACTIVITIES OF DAILY LIVING (ADL)   Usual activities of an insured in the nonoccupational environment, such as mobility, personal hygiene, dressing, sleeping, and eating. Skills required for community or social living also are included.

ACTUARY   An accredited insurance mathematician who calculates premium rates, dividends, and reserves and prepares statistical studies and reports.

ADMINISTRATION   The handling of all functions related to the operation of the group insurance plan once it becomes effective. The claim function may or may not be included.

ADMINISTRATION MANUAL   A book of instructions provided the policyholder by the insurer that outlines and explains the duties of the plan administrator.

ADMINISTRATIVE SERVICES ONLY (ASO) AGREEMENT   A contract for the provision of certain services to a group employer, eligible group, trustee, and so forth by an insurer or its subsidiary. Such services often include actuarial activities, benefit plan design, claim processing, data recovery and analysis, employee benefits communication, financial advice, medical care conversions, preparation of data for reports to governmental units, and stop-loss coverage.

ADMINISTRATOR   The individual or third-party firm responsible for the administration of a group insurance program. Accounting, certificate issuance, and claims settlement may be included activities.

ADVERSE SELECTION   The tendency of those who are poorer-than-average health risks to apply for or maintain insurance coverage. Also called antiselection.

AGENCY SYSTEM   A method of selling insurance that uses persons under contract to an insurance company to act as agents for that company.

AGENT   An insurance company representative licensed by the state who solicits, negotiates, or effects contracts of insurance and services the policyholder for the insurer.

ALEATORY CONTRACT   A contract in which one of the parties may recover a substantially larger value than the value lost, depending on the happening of a future contingency.

ALL CAUSE DEDUCTIBLE   A policy provision under which the deductible amount is met by the accumulation of all eligible expenses for any variety of covered claims.

ALLOCATED BENEFITS   Benefits for which the maximum amount payable for specific services is itemized in the contract.

ALTERED BILLS   Bills for medical services that have been changed or modified in some way, forged, or are false in their entirety.

AMBULATORY CARE   Medical services provided on an outpatient (nonhospitalized) basis. Services may include diagnosis, treatment, surgery, and rehabilitation.

AMBULATORY SURGICAL CENTER   A place where certain medical services can be performed on a same day, outpatient basis.

AMENDMENT   A formal document changing the provisions of an insurance policy.

ANNOUNCEMENT MATERIAL   Written communications used to solicit, enroll, and explain a group insurance program.

ANNUAL STATEMENT   The end-of-year report, as of December 31, of an insurer to a state insurance department showing assets and liabilities, receipts and disbursements, and other financial data.

APPLICATION   Statement of relevant facts signed by an individual who is seeking insurance or by a prospective group policyholder; the application is the basis for the insurer's decision to issue a policy. The application usually is incorporated into the policy.

APPROPRIATENESS OF CARE   The term used to describe the proper setting—an acute care hospital, an extended care facility, and so forth—for delivery of medical care that best corresponds to a patient's diagnosis.

APPROVAL   (a) When used in connection with the filing of policy and certificate forms and rates with a state insurance department, approval signifies the legal acceptance of the forms by the state's representative; (b) when used in connection with underwriting, approval signifies the insurer's acceptance of the risk as set forth in the application (as originally made or as modified by the insurer); (c) approval also signifies the acceptance of an offer from an applicant or policyholder in the form of a contract for new insurance, reinstatement of a terminated policy, request for a policy loan, or other event, by an officer of the company.

ASSIGNMENT OF BENEFITS   A provision in a health benefits claim form by which the insured directs the insurance company to pay any benefits directly to the provider of care on whose charge the claim is based.

ASSURANCE   Term synonymous with *insurance;* more commonly used in Canada and Great Britain.

AUTOMATIC REINSURANCE   An agreement between a ceding insurer and a reinsurer that the insurer must cede and the reinsurer must accept all risks within certain explicitly defined limits.

B

BASE PLAN   Any basic medical care plan that provides limited first-dollar hospital, surgical, or medical benefits, as contrasted with major medical benefit plans that provide comprehensive hospital, surgical, and medical benefits.

BASIC COVERAGE   Refers to base plan benefits over which major medical benefits may be superimposed.

BENEFICIARY   The person or persons designated by a policyholder to receive insurance policy proceeds.

BENEFIT   The amount payable by the insurer to a claimant, assignee, or beneficiary when the insured suffers a loss covered by the policy.

BENEFIT PERIOD   The period of time for which benefits are payable under an insurance contract.

BENEFIT PROVISION   The promises made by the insurer, explained in detail in the contract.

BENEFIT WAITING PERIOD   The period of time that must elapse before benefits are payable under a group insurance contract.

BILLING SCHEMES   The manipulation of medical bills and charges to reflect amounts not justified by treatment or services rendered.

BLUE CROSS   A nonprofit membership corporation providing protection against the costs of hospital care in a limited geographic area.

BLUE SHIELD   A nonprofit membership corporation providing protection against the costs of surgery and other items of medical care in a limited geographic area.

BROKER   A state-licensed person who places business with several insurers and who represents the insurance buyer rather than the insurance company, even though paid commissions by the insurer.

BUSINESS INTEREST INSURANCE   Coverage that provides the cash for the purchase of the business interest of a partner or stockholder who becomes disabled. Also called a disability buyout.

C

CAFETERIA PLAN   Another term used for a flexible benefit plan that allows employees to choose benefits from a number of different options.

CANCELLABLE CONTRACT   A contract of health insurance that may be canceled during the policy term by the insurer.

CAPACITY TO CONTRACT   To form a valid contract, both parties must have the ability to understand its terms. Without this ability there can be no meeting of the minds.

CAPITATION   A method of payment for health services in which a physician or hospital is paid a fixed amount for each person served regardless of the actual number or nature of services provided to each person.

CARRIER   A term sometimes used to identify the party (insurer) to the group contract that agrees to underwrite (carry the risk) and provide certain types of coverage and service.

CARVE-OUT   The term used to describe certain services offered by a managed care organization but singled out for individual management, usually with a capitation arrangement. Examples of carve-out service are management of chronic diseases, mental health services, and prescription drugs. Also called a specialty managed care arrangement.

215

CASE   The term used to refer to the entire group plan of a policyholder.

CASE MANAGEMENT   Planned approach to manage service or treatment to an individual with a serious medical problem. Its dual goal is to contain costs and promote more effective intervention to meet patient needs. Also called large case management.

CASE SUMMARY CARD   A form distributed by an insurer's home office summarizing vital information concerning a new case or a change in an existing case.

CEDE   Activity of an insurer under a reinsurance treaty.

CEDING INSURER   The insurer that insures part of a financial risk with another insurer, called the reinsurer.

CENTER OF EXCELLENCE   A term referring to selected health care facilities that specialize and have demonstrated success in the performance of certain highly complex medical procedures.

CERTIFICATE HOLDER   The insured person under a group plan who has been issued a certificate of insurance.

CERTIFICATE OF INSURANCE   The document delivered to an individual that summarizes the benefits and principal provisions of a group insurance contract. May be distributed in booklet form.

CHECK DEPOSIT BILLING   A system, commonly referred to as preauthorized check, that allows the insurer to draw checks on the policyholder's bank account for premiums due.

CLAIM   A demand to the insurer by, or on behalf of, the insured person for the payment of benefits under a policy.

CLAIMANT   The insured or beneficiary exercising the right to receive benefits.

CLAIM COST CONTROL   Efforts made by an insurer both inside and outside its own organization to contain and direct claim payments so that health insurance premium dollars are used as efficiently as possible.

CLAIM RESERVES   Funds retained by an insurer to settle incurred but unpaid claims that may also include reserves for potential claim fluctuation.

CLASS The category into which insureds are placed to determine the amount of coverage for which they are eligible under the policy.

COINSURANCE The arrangement by which the insurer and the insured share a percentage of covered losses after the deductible is met.

COMMISSION The part of an insurance premium an insurer pays an agent or broker for services in procuring and servicing insurance.

COMPLAINT REGISTER A state insurance department list that includes the identification, handling, and disposition of consumer complaints. It may be used by states for enforcing unfair trade practices statutes.

COMPLIANCE In insurance, the act of conforming to or observing regulatory requirements.

COMPREHENSIVE MEDICAL EXPENSE INSURANCE A form of health insurance that provides, in one policy, protection for both basic hospital expense and major medical expense coverage.

CONDITIONAL CONTRACT A binding agreement under which the insured's acceptance is considered conditional throughout an initial set time period, and during which the insured may nullify the contract and receive a refund of the premiums.

CONDITIONAL RECEIPT A receipt given for the premium submitted with an application for insurance. Terms regarding the effective date of coverage usually are defined in the receipt.

CONSUMERISM A movement for protection of the consumer against inferior products or misleading advertising.

CONTESTABILITY The insurer's ability to investigate possible misrepresentation in an insurance application and challenge the policy's validity.

CONTESTABLE PERIOD That time allowed an insurer after a policy is issued to investigate possible misrepresentation in the application and contest the policy's validity. (See "Rescission".)

CONTRACT A binding agreement between two or more parties. A contract of insurance is a written document called the policy.

CONTRACT OF ADHESION A contract drafted by one party and accepted or rejected by the other, with no opportunity to negotiate its terms.

CONTRACT RATE The premium rate for a group insurance coverage that is specified in a master policy.

CONTRIBUTION That part of the insurance premium paid by either the policyholder or the insured or both.

CONVERSION PRIVILEGE The right given to an insured person under a group insurance contract to change coverage, without evidence of medical insurability, to an individual policy upon termination of the group coverage.

COORDINATION OF BENEFITS (COB) A method of integrating benefits payable under more than one group health insurance plan so that the insured's benefits from all sources do not exceed 100 percent of allowable medical expenses.

CORRIDOR DEDUCTIBLE A fixed out-of-pocket amount (e.g., $100) that the insured must pay above covered benefits of a basic plan before supplemental major medical plan benefits are payable.

COST CONTAINMENT Efforts by medical providers, insurance companies, insureds, or other interested groups to control health care costs.

COST-OF-LIVING ADJUSTMENT (COLA) A policy provision that periodically increases benefit payouts to compensate for the effects of inflation during a lengthy disability.

COST SHARING (COINSURANCE) Policy provisions that require insureds to pay, through deductibles and coinsurance, a portion of their health insurance expenses.

COST SHIFTING Transfer of health care provider costs that are not reimbursed by one payer to other payers. Many of these costs are shifted to and absorbed by private health insurance.

COVERAGE A major classification of benefits provided by a policy (i.e., short-term disability, major medical), or the amount of insurance or benefit stated in the policy for which an insured is eligible.

COVERED CHARGES   Charges for medical care or supplies, which, if incurred by an insured or other covered person, create a liability for the insurer under the terms of a group policy.

COVERED EXPENSES   Those specified health care expenses that an insurer will consider for payment under the terms of a health insurance policy.

COVERED PERSON   Any person entitled to benefits under a policy (insured or covered dependent).

CREDIBILITY   The weight assigned to a group's past claim experience in order to determine future expected claims for premium setting purposes, or to determine claim charges for experience refund purposes for that group. Usually expressed as a percentage between 0 percent and 100 percent.

CREDIT HEALTH INSURANCE   A form of health insurance on a borrower, usually under an installment purchase agreement. The benefits cover the obligations of the borrower and are payable to the creditor. This insurance is commonly used with automobile loans.

D

DAILY BENEFIT   A specified daily maximum amount payable for room and board charges under a hospital or major medical benefits policy.

DECREASE IN COVERAGE   Any type of change that reduces the risk assumed by the insurer.

DEDUCTIBLE   The amount of covered expenses that must be incurred and paid by the insured before benefits become payable by the insurer.

DEEMER CLAUSE   A statute that allows a policy form, filed with an insurance department, to be "deemed approved" after a certain length of time unless the commissioner has given notice of disapproval.

DEFENSIVE MEDICINE   Physician use of extensive laboratory tests, increased hospital admissions, and extended hospital stays for the principal purpose of reducing the possibility of malpractice suits by patients or providing a good legal defense in the event of such lawsuits.

DELINQUENT PREMIUM Premium due the insurer that has not been paid by the end of the grace period.

DEPENDENT An insured's spouse (wife or husband), not legally separated from the insured, and unmarried child(ren) who meet certain eligibility requirements and who are not otherwise insured under the same group policy. The precise definition of a dependent varies by insurer.

DEPOSIT PREMIUM The premium deposit paid by a prospective policyholder when an application is made for an insurance policy. It is usually at least equal to the first month's estimated premium and is applied toward the actual premium when billed.

DIAGNOSIS-RELATED GROUP (DRG) A system of categorizing inpatient medical services and assigning specific reimbursement fees to each category.

DIRECT BILLING The type of billing that involves sending a premium statement to the insured as advance notification that the premium is due.

DIRECT CLAIM PAYMENT A method of paying claims whereby the insured individuals deal directly with the insurance company.

DIRECT WRITER An insurer that deals directly with prospective policyholders without the participation of agents or brokers.

DISABILITY A physical or mental condition that makes an insured incapable of performing one or more duties of his or her own occupation or, for total disability, of any occupation.

DISABILITY BENEFIT A payment that arises because of the total and/or permanent disability of an insured; a provision added to a policy that provides for a waiver of premium in case of total and permanent disability.

DISABILITY INCOME INSURANCE A form of health insurance that provides periodic payments when the insured is unable to work as a result of illness, disease, or injury.

DISCHARGE PLANNING A managed health care process directed at limiting the duration of inpatient care to that which is medically necessary and systematically facilitating transfer of a patient to a more cost-effective care facility.

DISMEMBERMENT   The accidental loss of limb or sight.

DISTRIBUTION   The separation of all insureds (prospective or in force) under a group insurance plan by age, sex, location, income, dependency status, and benefit class for the purpose of computing gross premium rates.

DOMESTIC COMPANY   An insurer doing business in the state in which it is incorporated.

DOMICILE   The legal residence of an individual or the jurisdiction in which a corporation maintains its center of corporate affairs.

DRAFT BOOK CLAIM PAYMENT   A method of claim settlement whereby the insurer authorizes the policyholder to settle claims and to issue payment on behalf of the insurer.

DUPLICATE COVERAGE   Coverage of an insured under two or more policies for the same potential loss.

E

EFFECTIVE DATE   The date that insurance coverage goes into effect.

ELIGIBILITY   The provisions of the group policy that state the requirements that members of the group and/or their dependents must satisfy to become insured.

ELIGIBILITY DATE   The date on which a member of an insured group may apply for insurance.

ELIGIBILITY PERIOD   The time following the eligibility date (usually 31 days) during which a member of an insured group may apply for insurance without evidence of insurability.

ELIGIBILITY REQUIREMENTS   Underwriting requirements that the applicant must satisfy in order to become insured.

ELIGIBLE EMPLOYEES   Those employees who have met the eligibility requirements for insurance set forth in the group policy.

ELIGIBLE GROUP   A group of persons permitted, under state insurance laws and insurer underwriting practices, to be insured under a group policy; usually includes individual employer groups, multiple employer groups, labor union groups, and certain association groups.

ELIGIBLE MEDICAL EXPENSE   A term describing the various types of expense the policy covers. The provision that describes these expenses commonly contains limitations applicable to certain of these expenses.

ELIMINATION PERIOD   A specified number of days at the beginning of each period of disability during which no disability income benefits are paid.

EMPLOYEE BENEFITS CONSULTANT   A person or firm specializing in the design, sale, and service of employee benefit plans, usually representing the policyholder in placing insurance coverage with an insurer or assisting the employer in changing or enhancing a benefit program. Compensation is provided either by commissions from the insurer or by the policyholder on a fee-for-service basis.

ENROLLMENT (SOLICITATION)   The process of explaining the proposed group insurance plan to eligible persons and assisting them in the proper completion of their enrollment cards.

ENROLLMENT CARD   A document signed by an eligible person as notice of desire to participate in the group insurance plan. For a contributory plan, this card also provides an employer with authorization to deduct contributions from an employee's pay. If group life and accidental death and dismemberment coverage are involved, the card usually includes the beneficiary's name and relationship.

EQUITY   The value of an individual or business in excess of liabilities.

EVIDENCE OF INSURABILITY   Any statement or proof of a person's physical condition and/or other factual information affecting acceptability for insurance.

EXCESSIVE DIAGNOSTIC TESTING   The ordering of medical tests beyond that considered reasonable to diagnose or treat a condition.

EXCLUSIONS (EXCEPTIONS)   Specified conditions or circumstances, listed in the policy, for which the policy will not provide benefits.

EXCLUSIVE PROVIDER ORGANIZATION (EPO)   Form of managed care in which participants are reimbursed for care received only from affiliated providers.

EXECUTION CLAUSE   The signature of the insurer on the insurance policy signifying that the insurer has entered into the contract and will be bound by its terms.

EXPENSE LOADING   That portion of a group insurance premium required to cover acquisition and administration costs.

EXPENSE RATIO   A percentage showing the relationship of expenses to earned premiums.

EXPERIENCE RATING   The process of determining the premium rate for a group risk based wholly or partially on that risk's experience.

EXPERIENCE REFUND   The amount of premium returned by an insurer to a group policyholder when the financial experience of the particular group (or the experience refund class to which the group belongs) has been more favorable than anticipated in the premiums collected from the group.

EXPERIMENTAL TREATMENT   A method or mode of treatment not approved by medical regulatory authorities.

F

FACILITY OF PAYMENT   A contractual provision that the insurer may, under stated conditions, pay insurance benefits to persons other than the insured, the designated beneficiary, or the estate of the insured.

FACULTATIVE REINSURANCE   A type of reinsurance in which the reinsurer can accept or reject any risk presented by an insurance company seeking reinsurance.

FEE-FOR-SERVICE   A method of charging whereby a physician or other practitioner bills for each visit or service rendered.

FEE SCHEDULE   Maximum dollar or unit allowances for health services that apply under a specific contract.

FILING   The submission of a proposed policy form for approval to the insurance department of the jurisdiction where it will be issued.

FIRST-DOLLAR COVERAGE   A hospital or surgical policy with no deductible amount.

FLEXIBLE BENEFITS   Employee benefit coverage offered by an employer that allows employees to select type and amount of benefits from among a menu of benefits the employer offers. Also called cafeteria plans.

FOREIGN INSURER   The term a state uses to identify an insurer operating in a state other than the one in which it is incorporated.

FRANCHISE INSURANCE   Individual insurance contracts issued to members of a specific group (such as employees of a common employer or members of an association) under a group-like arrangement in which the employer or association collects and remits premiums and the insurer waives its right to cancel or modify any policy unless done for all persons in the group.

FRATERNAL INSURANCE   A cooperative type of insurance provided by social organizations for their members. The social group may pay premiums into a fund and withdraw monies to pay claims upon the death of one of its members.

FRAUD   An intentional act or misrepresentation that results in some type of loss to another.

FUND ACCOUNT   An accounting method that uses a specific formula for determining premium rates.

FUTURE INCREASE OPTION   A provision found in some policies that allows an insured to purchase additional disability income insurance at specified future dates regardless of the insured's physical condition.

G

GENERAL AGENTS   Agents under contract to an insurer who provide their own office facilities and clerical and supervisory personnel, and who are compensated primarily by an overriding commission.

GENERALLY ACCEPTED ACCOUNTING PRINCIPLES (GAAP)   Principles of accounting and business results reporting developed by the American Institute of Public Accountants.

GRACE PERIOD   A specified time (usually 31 days) following the premium due date during which the insurance remains in force and a policyholder may pay the premium without penalty.

GROSS PREMIUM   The contracted premium before applying any discounts.

GROUP CASE   Expression used to refer collectively to the entire group plan of a policyholder.

GROUP CONTRACT   A contract of health insurance made with an employer or other entity that covers a group of persons as a single unit. The entity is the policyholder.

GROUP INSURANCE   An arrangement for insuring a number of people under a single, master insurance policy.

GROUP POLICYHOLDER   The legal entity to which the master policy is issued.

GROUP REPRESENTATIVE   A salaried employee of the insurer whose principal tasks are to assist agents and brokers in developing and soliciting prospects for group insurance and to install and service group contracts.

GUARANTEED INSURABILITY OPTION   (See "Future Increase Option".)

GUARANTEED ISSUE   Amounts of insurance coverage offered on a one-time basis, not requiring the insured to provide evidence of insurability.

GUARANTEED RENEWABLE POLICY   A contract under which an insured has the right, commonly up to a certain age, to continue the policy in force by the timely payment of premiums. However, the insurer reserves the right to change premium rates by policy class.

H

HAZARD   The measure of risk assumed by an insurer. It can involve physical, moral, or financial elements.

HEALTH INSURANCE   Coverage that provides for the payments of benefits as a result of sickness or injury. Includes insurance for losses from accident, medical expense, disability, or accidental death and dismemberment.

225

HEALTH MAINTENANCE ORGANIZATION (HMO) An organization that provides for a wide range of comprehensive health care services for a specified group at a fixed periodic prepayment.

HIGH-LOW COMMISSION SCALE A commission scale providing for the payment of a high first-year commission and lower renewal commissions.

HOME HEALTH CARE A comprehensive, medically necessary range of health services provided by a recognized provider organization to a patient at home.

HOME OFFICE ADMINISTRATION The method of insurance plan administration in which the insurer maintains the basic records for the persons covered.

HOSPICE A mode of care provided to terminally ill patients and their families that emphasizes patient comfort rather than cure and addresses emotional needs, such as coping with pain and death.

HOSPITAL BILLING AUDITS Independent examination of hospital bills by a third party to determine if services and supplies charged to the patient were actually delivered and if the price charged was correct.

HOSPITAL EXPENSE INSURANCE A form of health insurance that provides specific benefits for hospital services, including daily room and board and surgery, during a hospital confinement.

HOSPITAL INDEMNITY INSURANCE A form of health insurance that provides a stipulated daily, weekly, or monthly payment to an insured during hospital confinement, without regard to the actual expense of the confinement.

I

IDENTIFICATION CARD A form provided to insureds that identifies them as members of a particular insurance plan and may provide basic information about their coverage. Although such cards do not guarantee eligibility for medical care benefits at any given time, they provide procedures for providers to follow to verify that a patient has health coverage.

INCONTESTABILITY   Result of incontestable clause, defined below.

INCONTESTABLE CLAUSE   The provision in a group life and/or health insurance policy that prevents the insurance company from disputing the validity of certain coverage under specific insurance conditions after the policy has been in effect for a certain time (usually two years).

INCREASE IN COVERAGE   An addition in benefits that becomes effective for an insured or a group of insureds as a result of a specific change in class, due to a wage or salary increase, occupational promotion, or negotiated enhancements to the benefits program.

INCURRED BUT NOT PAID CLAIMS   Claims that have not been paid as of some specified date (may include both reported and unreported claims).

INCURRED BUT NOT REPORTED (IBNR) CLAIMS   Claims that have not been reported to the insurer as of some specified date.

INCURRED CLAIMS   An amount equal to the claims paid during the policy year plus the change of the claim reserves as of the end of the policy year. The change in reserves represents the difference between the end of the year and beginning of the year claim reserves.

INDEMNIFY   To compensate for a loss.

INDEMNITY   A benefit paid by an insurance policy for an insured loss.

INDIVIDUAL INSURANCE   Policies that provide protection to the policyholder and/or his or her family. Sometimes called personal insurance as distinct from group insurance.

INDIVIDUAL PRACTICE ASSOCIATION (IPA)   An association of individual physicians that provides services on a negotiated per capita rate, flat retainer fee, or negotiated fee-for-service basis. It is one model of an HMO.

IN FORCE   The total volume of insurance on the lives of covered employees at any given time (measured in terms of cases, lives, amount [volume] of insurance, or premium).

INITIAL RATE   A premium rate that is charged on the effective date of a new group policy.

INJURY Accidental bodily damage sustained while a particular health insurance policy is in force.

INSTALLATION The process of assisting a group policyholder to set up the administrative practices essential to the proper handling of all initial and ongoing administrative activities of the plan.

INSURABILITY Refers to the physical, moral, occupational, and financial status of a risk and its acceptability to the insurer.

INSURABLE RISK The conditions that make a risk insurable are the following: (a) the peril insured against must produce a definite loss not under the control of the insured; (b) there must be a large number of homogeneous exposures subject to the same perils; (c) the loss must be calculable and the cost of insuring it must be economically feasible; (d) the peril must be unlikely to affect all insureds simultaneously; and (e) the loss produced by a risk must be definite and have a potential to be financially serious.

INSURANCE A plan of risk management that, for a price, offers the insured an opportunity to share the costs of possible economic loss through an entity called an insurer.

INSURANCE COMPANY Any corporation primarily engaged in the business of furnishing insurance protection to the public.

INSURED The person and dependent(s) who are covered for insurance under a policy and to whom, or on behalf of whom, the insurer agrees to pay benefits.

INSURER The party to the insurance contract that promises to pay losses or benefits. Also, any corporation primarily engaged in the business of furnishing insurance protection to the public.

INSURING CLAUSE The clause in a policy that names the parties to a contract and states what is covered by the policy.

INTEGRATED DEDUCTIBLE A high fixed amount (e.g., $1,000) or the sum of the benefits paid under a base medical care plan, whichever is greater, that must be exceeded before supplemental major medical benefits are payable.

INTEGRATED DELIVERY SYSTEM A system of managed care that brings together all the components of health care delivery into a single entity. They are usually organized by physicians and hospitals.

INTERIM COVERAGE   Initial coverage of an applicant between the date of premium prepayment and the date the insurer notifies the applicant of its underwriting decision.

INTERNATIONAL CLAIM ASSOCIATION (ICA)   An organization concerned with information and education in the area of life and health claims administration.

K

KEY-EMPLOYEE DISABILITY INSURANCE   Insurance designed to protect a business firm against the loss of business income resulting from the disability or death of an employee in a significant position.

L

LAPSED COVERAGE   Termination of coverage provided in an insurance contract because of the nonpayment of a premium within the time period.

LATE APPLICANT   An eligible person who applies for insurance after the normal 31-day open enrollment period.

LEGAL RESERVE   The minimum reserve that a company must keep to meet future claims and obligations as they are calculated under the state insurance code.

LEVEL BILLING   A method of billing that allows the policyholder to pay a certain set amount of premium on each due date during the policy year, based on an estimated annual premium, with an adjustment at the end of the policy year for coverage changes that have occurred during the policy year.

LEVEL COMMISSION SCALE   A method of assigning commission payments that applies the same commission rates to the premium each year, regardless of the policy year.

LEVEL PREMIUM   A rating structure in which the premium level remains the same throughout the life of the policy.

LIABILITY   The probable cost of meeting an obligation.

LICENSE Certification, issued by a state department of insurance, that an individual is qualified to solicit insurance applications for the period covered.

LIFETIME DISABILITY BENEFIT A disability income provision payable for an insured's lifetime as long as the insured is totally disabled.

LIMITATION A provision that sets a cap on specific coverage.

LIMITED POLICY Policy that covers only specified accidents or sicknesses.

LOADING FACTOR The amount added to the net premium rate determined for a group insurance plan to cover the possibility that losses will be greater than statistically expected because of older average age, hazardous industry, large percentage of unskilled employees, or adverse experience.

LONG-TERM CARE A wide range of health and personal care, ranging from simple assisted living arrangements to intensive nursing home care, for elderly or disabled persons.

LONG-TERM CARE INSURANCE A benefits plan that provides a specific dollar benefit or a percent of expenses charged for nursing home care, home health care, and adult day care if a covered person suffers a loss of functional or cognitive capacity.

LONG-TERM DISABILITY (LTD) INCOME INSURANCE A benefits plan that helps replace earned income lost through inability to work because of disability caused by accident or illness.

LOSS (1) The amount of insurance or benefit for which the insurer becomes liable when the event insured against occurs; (2) the happening of the event insured against.

LOSS RATIO The ratio of claims to premiums (claims divided by premiums).

LOSS RATIO (INCURRED BASIS) The ratio of paid claims plus change in claim reserves to earned premiums.

M

MAJOR MEDICAL EXPENSE INSURANCE A form of health insurance that provides benefits for most types of medical expense up to a high maximum benefit. Such contracts may contain internal limits and usually are subject to deductibles and coinsurance.

MALPRACTICE   Improper care or treatment of a patient by a physician, hospital, or other provider of health care, due to carelessness, neglect, lack of professional skills, or disregard of established rules or procedures.

MANAGED CARE   The term used to describe the coordination of financing and provision of health care to produce high-quality health care on a cost-effective basis.

MANDATED BENEFITS   Certain coverages required by state law to be included in health insurance contracts.

MANUAL PREMIUM   The premium developed for a group's coverage from the insurer's standard rate tables.

MANUAL RATE   The premium rate developed for a group's coverage from the insurer's standard rate tables, usually contained in its rate manual or underwriting manual.

MARKETING   The sum total of all corporate functions and activities directly or indirectly involved in the selling of products to the consumer.

MASS MARKETING   Technique used by insurers to approach a large number of prospects simultaneously.

MASTER POLICY (OR MASTER CONTRACT)   The policy issued to a group policyholder setting forth the provisions of the group insurance plan.

MATERIAL MISREPRESENTATION   A false or misleading statement of fact on an application for an insurance policy, that influences the insurer's decision as to the prospective insured's insurability. Such statements may serve as a basis for voiding the policy. (See "Rescission".)

MATERNITY BENEFIT   Benefits for a normal pregnancy are paid under this provision of the hospital or medical policy rather than the regular provisions that apply to sickness, since maternity is not normally considered a sickness.

MAXIMUM BENEFIT   The maximum length of time for which benefits are payable during any one period of disability.

MAXIMUM DAILY HOSPITAL BENEFIT   The maximum amount payable for hospital room and board per day of hospital confinement.

MEDICAID   Government insurance program for persons of all ages whose income and resources are insufficient to pay for health care. Medicaid is state-administered and financed by both the states and the federal government.

MEDICAL EXAMINATION   The examination given by a qualified physician to determine an applicant's insurability or whether an insured claiming disability is actually disabled.

MEDICAL EXPENSE INSURANCE   A form of health insurance that provides benefits for various expenses incurred for medical care. Benefits for prevention and diagnosis, as well as for treatment, are sometimes included.

MEDICALLY NECESSARY   Term used by insurers to describe medical treatment that is appropriate and rendered in accordance with generally accepted standards of medical practice.

MEDICARE   A federally sponsored program that provides hospital benefits, supplementary medical care, and catastrophic coverages to persons aged 65 and older, and to some other eligibles.

MEDIGAP   A term applied to private insurance products that supplement federal insurance benefits under Medicare. Also called MedSup.

MEETING OF THE MINDS   The agreement and understanding on the part of both parties concerning their respective obligations and rights under a contract.

MINIMUM GROUP   The fewest number of employees permitted under a state law to constitute a group for insurance purposes; the purpose of minimum group is to maintain a distinction between individual and group insurance.

MINIMUM PREMIUM PLAN   A combination approach to funding an insurance plan aimed primarily at premium tax savings. The employer self-funds a fixed percent (e.g., 90 percent) of the estimated monthly claims and the insurance company insures the rest.

232

MINIMUM PREMIUM RATE   The lowest premium rate that an insurer may charge a policyholder during the first year the group insurance is in effect, based on its field manual premium rates.

MINIMUM STANDARDS MODEL REGULATION   Promulgated by the NAIC in 1974, it sets categories for basic forms of coverage with required minimum benefit levels.

MISREPRESENTATION   A false or incomplete statement of relevant fact on an application for an insurance policy. (See "Material Misrepresentation".)

MONTHLY ADJUSTMENT BILLING   A method of premium billing by which the policyholder is billed on each premium due date for the insurance coverage on the actual number of persons covered by the group insurance plan.

MONTHLY INDEMNITY   Benefit amount paid monthly under a health insurance policy.

MORAL HAZARD   Risk from any nonphysical, personal characteristic or habit of an applicant or insured that may either increase the possibility or intensify the severity of a loss.

MORBIDITY   The frequency and severity of sicknesses and accidents in a well-defined class or classes of persons.

MORTALITY   The death rate in a group of people as determined from prior experience.

MULTIPLE EMPLOYER GROUP   Employees of two or more employers, such as trade associations of employers in the same industry or union members who work for more than one employer, covered under one master contract.

MULTIPLE EMPLOYER TRUST (MET)   A legal trust established by a plan sponsor that brings together a number of small, unrelated employers for the purpose of providing group medical care coverage on an insured or a self-funded basis.

MUTUAL INSURANCE COMPANY   An insurer in which the ownership and control is vested in the policyholders.

N

NATIONAL ASSOCIATION OF INSURANCE COMMISSIONERS (NAIC)   A national organization of state officials who are charged with the regulation of insurance. It was formed to promote national uniformity in the regulation of insurance. It has no official power but wields tremendous influence.

NET COST   In group insurance it equals claims plus reserves plus expenses.

NET PREMIUM   Amount paid or earned premium after discounts.

NEW BUSINESS   The sale of insurance coverage to a new policyholder or extending or adding new coverage(s) to an existing policyholder.

NONCANCELLABLE POLICY   A contract the insured can continue in force by the timely payment of the set premium until at least age 50 or, in the case of a policy issued after age 44, for at least five years from its date of issue. The insurer may not unilaterally change any contract provision of the in-force policy, including premium rates.

NONCONTRIBUTORY PLAN   A group insurance plan under which the employer does not require employees to share in its cost.

NONDISABLING INJURY BENEFIT   A benefit in some disability income policies providing payment for medical expense due to injury when medical care is necessary but the insured is not totally disabled.

NONDUPLICATION CLAUSE   A policy provision that results in a stricter application of coordination of benefits principles. When an individual is covered by two or more policies, this provision excludes expenses incurred that are covered by another policy.

NONOCCUPATIONAL INSURANCE   Insurance that does not provide benefits for an accident or sickness arising out of a person's employment.

NONRENEWABLE FOR STATED-REASONS-ONLY POLICY   A contract of health insurance under which the insurer has the right to terminate the coverage for only those reasons specified in the contract.

NONRENEWABLE POLICY   A policy issued for a single term that is designed to cover the insured during a period of short-term risk.

NOTICE OF CLAIM   A written notice to the insurer by an insured claiming a covered loss.

O

OCCUPATIONAL HAZARDS   Dangers inherent in the insured's occupation that expose him or her to greater than normal physical danger by their very nature.

OCCUPATIONAL RATE   A variation in premium based upon occupational class, due to differences among occupations in the incidence of accidents or illness.

OFFER   The initial proposal by one contracting party to another. It is one of several necessary elements of a contract in which one party makes an initial proposal. In insurance, the application is usually considered to be the offer.

OPEN ENROLLMENT   A time during which uninsured employees and/or their dependents may obtain coverage under an existing group plan without presenting evidence of insurability. Differs from a resolicitation in that a minimum number of applications are not required.

OPTIONAL PROVISIONS   Certain provisions of the Uniform Policy Provisions Law that an insurer may include in the insurance contract.

OPTIONALLY RENEWABLE POLICY   A contract of health insurance under which the insurer has the right to terminate the coverage at any policy anniversary or, in some cases, at any premium due date.

OUT-OF-POCKET EXPENSE   Those medical expenses that an insured must pay that are not covered under the group contract.

OVERHEAD EXPENSE INSURANCE   A form of health insurance for business owners designed to help offset continuing business expenses during an insured's total disability.

OVERINSURANCE   Coverage exceeding the probable loss to which it applies.

OVERRIDING COMMISSION   A commission paid to general agents or agency managers in addition to the commission paid the soliciting agent or broker.

P

PALLIATIVE CARE   Medical relief of pain rather than cure of illness.

PARTIAL DISABILITY   Inability to perform one or more functions of one's regular job.

PARTIAL DISABILITY BENEFITS   A disability income benefit payable when an insured is not totally disabled but is prevented from working full time and/or is prevented from performing one or more important daily occupational duties.

PARTIAL PAYMENT   A payment to a claimant where it is expected other payments will be made before the claim can be considered closed.

PARTICIPATION   The number of insureds covered under the group plan in relation to the total number eligible to be covered, usually expressed as a percentage.

PENDING CLAIM   A claim that has been reported but on which final action has not been taken.

PER CAUSE DEDUCTIBLE   The flat amount that the insured must pay toward the eligible medical expenses resulting from each illness before the insurance company will make any benefit payments.

PERIOD OF DISABILITY   The period during which an employee is prevented from performing usual occupational duties, or during which a dependent cannot perform the normal activities of a healthy person of the same age or sex.

PERMANENT AND TOTAL DISABILITY   A disability that will presumably last for the insured's lifetime and prevent the insured from engaging in any occupation.

PERSISTENCY   The degree to which policies stay in force through the continued payment of renewal premiums.

PERSONAL PRODUCING GENERAL AGENT (PPGA)   Person who works independently, under contract to an insurer, in the marketing of an insurer's products.

236

PHYSICIAN'S EXPENSE   Insurance coverage that provides benefits toward the cost of such services as doctors' fees—for surgical care in the hospital, at home, or in a physician's office—and X-rays or laboratory tests performed outside of a hospital. Also called regular medical expense insurance.

POINT-OF-SERVICE (POS) PROGRAM   Health care delivery method offered as an option of an employer's indemnity program. Under such a program, employees coordinate their health care needs through a primary care physician.

POLICY   The document that sets forth the contract of insurance.

POLICY ANNIVERSARY   The date that separates the experience under a group policy for dividend and retroactive rate purposes. The period is normally 12 consecutive months.

POLICY FEE   An amount sometimes charged in addition to the first premium as a fee for issuance of the policy—for example, group health conversion policies.

POLICYHOLDER   The legal entity to whom an insurer issues a contract.

POLICYHOLDER ADMINISTRATION (SELF-ADMINISTRATION)   Situation whereby the group policyholder maintains all records and assumes responsibility regarding insureds covered under its insurance plan, including preparing the premium statement for each payment date and submitting it with a check to the insurer. Under this method the insurance company, in most instances, has the contractual prerogative to audit the policyholder's records.

POLICY ISSUE   The transmittal of a policy to an insured by an insurer.

POLICY NUMBER   That number assigned to a group contract that contains both the account number of the policy and the policy code number.

POLICY YEAR   The time that elapses between policy anniversaries, as specified in the policy.

PREADMISSION TESTING   The practice of having a patient undergo laboratory, radiology, and other pre-screening tests and examinations prior to being admitted to a medical facility as an inpatient.

237

PREAUTHORIZED CHECK (See *check deposit billing.*)

PRECERTIFICATION A utilization management program that requires the individual or the provider to notify the insurer prior to a hospitalization or surgical procedure. The notification allows the insurer to authorize payment, as well as to recommend alternate courses of action.

PRE-EXISTING CONDITION A mental or physical problem suffered by an insured prior to the effective date of insurance coverage.

PRE-EXISTING CONDITIONS PROVISION A restriction on payments for those charges directly resulting from an accident or illness for which the insured received care or treatment within a specified period of time (e.g., three months) prior to the date of insurance.

PREFERRED PROVIDER ORGANIZATION (PPO) A managed care arrangement consisting of a group of hospitals, physicians, and other providers who have contracts with an insurer, employer, third-party administrator, or other sponsoring group to provide health care services to covered persons.

PREMIUM The amount paid an insurer for specific insurance protection.

PREMIUM NOTICE (BILLING) The statement requesting the policyholder to pay a premium on a particular due date. The insurer may enclose a premium remittance card that should be returned with the policyholder's check.

PREMIUM PAYMENT MODE (FREQUENCY) The number of times premiums are payable in a policy year. For example, a policy on which premiums are paid monthly is said to have a monthly premium frequency.

PREMIUM RATE The price of a unit of coverage or benefit.

PREMIUM REFUND Monies returned to a policyholder, usually because of favorable experience (i.e., an experience-rating refund).

PREMIUM TAX An assessment levied by a federal or state government usually on the net premium income collected in a particular jurisdiction by an insurer.

PRIMARY CARE   First contact and continuing health care, including basic or initial diagnosis and treatment, health supervision, management of chronic conditions, preventive health services, and appropriate referral.

PRIMARY CARE PHYSICIAN (PCP)   The network physician designated by an employee (and each of his or her dependents) to serve as that employee's entry into the health care system. The PCP often is reimbursed through a different mechanism (such as capitation) than are other network providers. This physician sometimes is referred to as the "gatekeeper."

PRINCIPAL SUM   The amount payable in one sum in event of accidental death and, in some cases, accidental dismemberment.

PROBATIONARY PERIOD   A period from the policy's effective date to a specified time, usually 15 to 30 days thereafter, during which no sickness coverage is provided.

PRODUCTION CREDIT   The new business volume and/or premium written on new and existing cases that is credited to an agent, broker, or group representative.

PROGRESSIVE CARE   A term identifying a method for providing the degree of health care that is medically necessary at any given stage in illness or recovery, ranging from acute care in a hospital to recuperation at home.

PROOF OF LOSS   Documentary evidence required by an insurer to prove a valid claim exists, usually consisting of a claim form completed by the insured and the insured's attending physician. Medical expense insurance claims also require itemized bills.

PROPOSAL   A quotation, submitted to a prospective group insurance policyholder by an insurance company primarily through an agent, broker, or group representative, that outlines the benefits available under a suggested plan and the costs to both employer and employees.

PROSPECT   A potential customer or client.

PROVIDER DISCOUNTS   An element of network-based managed care programs whereby financial arrangements are negotiated with providers to reduce fees for medical services rendered.

PROVISION   A part of a group insurance contract that describes or explains a feature, benefit, condition, or requirement of the insurance protection afforded by the contract.

PROVISIONAL PREMIUM   An estimated premium paid prior to the exact determination of the total amount due.

Q

QUALIFICATION PERIOD   The period during which the insured must be totally disabled before becoming eligible for residual disability benefits.

R

RATING   Determining the cost of a given unit of insurance for a given year.

READABILITY STANDARDS   Requirements that insurance policies use simplified language that an average consumer would be able to understand, as measured by an objective numerical scale.

REASONABLE AND CUSTOMARY CHARGE   A charge for health care that is consistent with the average rate or charge for identical or similar services in a certain geographic area.

REBATING   The illegal act of giving any valuable consideration, usually a part or all of the commission, to a prospect as an inducement to buy insurance.

RECORD CARD (REGISTER)   A card used by the insurer and/or the administrator of the plan to indicate a person insured, coverages and amounts of insurance, beneficiary, and any other information necessary to successfully administer the group plan.

RECURRENT DISABILITY CLAUSE   A policy provision that clarifies amounts payable if an insured is again disabled by the same condition for which benefits previously have been paid.

240

REHABILITATION   The process and goal of restoring disabled insureds to maximum physical, mental, and vocational independence and productivity (commensurate with their limitations). A rehabilitation provision appears in some long-term disability policies; this provides for continuation of benefits or other financial assistance during the rehabilitation period.

REIMBURSEMENT   An amount paid to an insured for expenses actually incurred as a result of an accident or sickness. Payment will not exceed the amount specified in the policy.

REINSTATEMENT   The resumption of coverage under a policy that had lapsed.

REINSURANCE   Acceptance by one insurer (the reinsurer) of all or part of the risk of loss underwritten by another insurer (the ceding insurer).

RENEWAL   Continuance of coverage under a policy beyond its original term by the insurer's acceptance of the premium for a new policy term.

RENEWAL UNDERWRITING   The review of the financial experience of a group case and the establishment of the renewal premium rates and terms under which the insurance may be continued.

REPLACEMENT   The substitution of health insurance coverage under one policy for coverage under another policy.

REPRESENTATION   Statement by insurance applicants as to some past or existing fact or circumstance. Such statements must be true to the best of the applicant's knowledge and belief, but are not warranted as exact in every detail.

RESCISSION   Voiding of an insurance contract from its date of issue by the insurer because of material misrepresentation on the application for insurance. The policy is treated as never having been issued and the sum of all premiums paid plus interest, less any claims paid, is refunded.

RESERVE   A sum set aside by an insurance company as a liability to fulfill future obligations.

RESIDUAL DISABILITY   A period of partial disability that immediately follows a period of total disability.

RESIDUAL DISABILITY BENEFITS   A provision in an insurance policy that provides benefits in proportion to a reduction of earnings as a result of disability, as opposed to the inability to work full-time.

RETENTION   That portion of the premium kept by the insurer for expenses, contingencies, and contributions to surplus (profit).

RETENTION ESTIMATE   A projection of estimated expenses on a particular group insurance case.

RIDER   A document that modifies or amends the insurance contract.

RISK   The probable amount of loss foreseen by an insurer in issuing a contract. The term sometimes also applies to the person insured or to the hazard insured against.

RULING   A judicial decision, or a decision of the commissioner of the Internal Revenue Service relative to a specific tax question.

S

SCHEDULE   A listing of amounts payable for specified occurrences (e.g., surgical operations, laboratory tests, X-ray services, and such).

SECOND SURGICAL OPINION   An attempt to verify the need for surgery by encouraging insureds to seek the advice of another physician or surgeon who will not perform the operation.

SELF-ADMINISTRATION   Maintenance of all records and assumption of responsibility, by a group policyholder, for insureds covered under its insurance plan, including preparing the premium statement for each payment date and submitting it with a check to the insurer. The insurance company, in most instances, has the contractual prerogative to audit the policyholder's records.

SELF-FUNDING   A medical benefit plan established by an employer or employee group (or a combination of the two) that directly assumes the functions, responsibilities, and liabilities of an insurer.

SELF-INSURANCE   A program for providing group insurance with benefits financed entirely through the internal means of the policyholder, in place of purchasing coverage from commercial carriers.

SHORT-TERM DISABILITY (STD) INCOME INSURANCE   Form of health insurance that provides benefits only for loss resulting from illness or disease and excludes loss resulting from accident or injury.

SICKNESS INSURANCE   A form of health insurance providing benefits only for loss resulting from illness or disease, but excluding loss resulting from accident or injury.

SOCIETY OF ACTUARIES   A professional organization of life, health insurance, and pension insurance mathematicians.

SOLVENCY   Ability to pay all legal debts.

SPECIFICATIONS   A detailed listing of the qualifying factors of a certain group of individuals (type of risk, complete census data, contributions, past experience if a transferred case), the coverages (types, amounts, schedules), and services (self-administration, draft book claims, level commissions) that an insurance company gathers in order to obtain the right to administer the program.

SPECIFIED DISEASE INSURANCE   Insurance providing an unallocated benefit, subject to a maximum amount, for expenses incurred in connection with the treatment of specified diseases, such as cancer, poliomyelitis, encephalitis, and spinal meningitis. These policies are designed to supplement major medical policies.

STANDARD PROVISIONS   Policy provisions setting forth certain rights and obligations of insureds and insurers under health insurance policies. Originally introduced in 1912, these provisions were replaced by the Uniform Policy Provisions Law (UPPL).

STANDARD RISK   A person who, according to an insurer's underwriting standards, is entitled to purchase insurance protection without extra premium or special restriction.

STATE INSURANCE DEPARTMENT   An administrative agency that implements state insurance laws and supervises (within the scope of these laws) the activities of insurers operating within the state.

STATE OF ISSUE (SITUS)   The jurisdiction in which the group insurance contract is delivered or issued for delivery.

STATUTE   An enactment of a legislature (state or federal) declaring, commanding, or prohibiting something.

STOCK   The outstanding capital of a corporation, represented by shares in the form of ownership certificates.

STOCK INSURANCE COMPANY   An insurer in which the legal ownership and control is vested in the stockholders.

STOCKHOLDER (OR SHAREHOLDER)   A person who owns shares of stock in a corporation.

SUBROGATION   The substitution of the insurer in place of an insured who claims medical expenses from a third party.

SUPPLEMENTAL MEDICAL INSURANCE   Health insurance policies that fill in the gaps of medical expense coverages (e.g., deductibles, coinsurance, maximum out-of-pocket expenses); provide additional benefits (e.g., dental, prescription drugs, and vision care); and cover additional expenses as a result of a severe accident or illness (e.g., accident medical expenses).

SURGICAL EXPENSE INSURANCE   Health insurance policies that provide benefits toward the physician's or surgeon's operating fees. Benefits may consist of scheduled amounts for each surgical procedure.

SURGICAL SCHEDULE   A list of cash or unit allowances up to a maximum amount an insurer will reimburse, based on the severity of the operation.

SURPLUS   The amount by which the value of an insurer's assets exceeds its liabilities.

SURVEILLANCE   The covert observation of an insured to determine the extent and duration of physical activity.

T

TEN-DAY "FREE LOOK"   A right of the insured to examine a policy for ten days and return it for a refund of premium if not satisfied with it. A notice of this right is required to appear on the first page of health insurance policies.

THIRD-PARTY ADMINISTRATION   That method by which an outside person or firm, not a party to a contract, maintains all records regarding the persons covered under the group insurance plan and may also pay claims using the draft book system.

THIRD-PARTY PAYER   Any organization, public or private, that pays or insures health or medical expenses on behalf of beneficiaries or recipients.

TIME LIMIT   The set number of days in which a notice of claim or proof of a loss must be filed.

TOTAL DISABILITY   Generally a disability that prevents insureds from performing all occupational duties. The exact definition varies among policies.

TRANSFERRED BUSINESS   A term used to describe a group insurance plan that is switched from one insurer to another.

TRAVEL ACCIDENT POLICIES   Limited contracts covering only accidents that occur while an insured person is traveling on business for an employer, away from the usual place of business and only on named conveyances.

U

UNBUNDLING OF CHARGES   The practice of making separate charges for components of a surgical procedure that results in a total fee that is higher than the usual fee for the procedure as a whole.

UNDERWRITER   The term generally applies to (a) a company that receives the premiums and accepts responsibility for the fulfillment of the policy contract; (b) the company employee who decides whether the company should assume a particular risk; or (c) the agent who sells the policy.

UNDERWRITING   The process by which an insurer determines whether and on what basis it will accept an application for insurance.

UNIFORM POLICY PROVISIONS LAW (UPPL)   Statutory policy provisions of health insurance policies that specify some of the rights and obligations of the insured and the insurer. These provisions, with some modifications, are part of the insurance laws of all 50 states and the District of Columbia.

UNIFORM PREMIUM   A rating structure in which one premium applies to all insureds, regardless of age, sex, or occupation.

UNILATERAL CONTRACT   A contract that contains legally enforceable promises by only one of the parties to the contract. An insurance policy is a unilateral contract.

UNPROVEN TREATMENT   A method or mode of treatment not approved by medical regulatory authorities.

UPCODING   The practice of charging for a service that represents more treatment than was actually given, either in testing, office procedures, or surgical operations.

USUAL AND CUSTOMARY CHARGE   (See "Reasonable and Customary Charge".)

UTILIZATION   Patterns of usage for a single medical service or type of service (hospital care, prescription drugs, physician visits). Measurement of utilization of all medical services in combination usually is done in terms of dollar expenditures. Use is expressed in rates per unit of population at risk for a given period, such as number of annual admissions to a hospital per 1,000 persons over age 65.

UTILIZATION REVIEW   A program with various approaches designed to reduce unnecessary hospital admissions and to control inpatient lengths of stay through use of preliminary evaluations, concurrent inpatient evaluations, or discharge planning.

W

WAITING PERIOD   The time a person must wait from the date of entry into an eligible class or application for coverage to the date the insurance is effective.

WAIVER   The voluntary surrender of a right or privilege known to exist.

WAIVER (EXCLUSION ENDORSEMENT)   An agreement attached to the policy and accepted by the insured that eliminates a specified pre-existing physical condition or specified hazard from coverage under the policy.

WAIVER OF PREMIUM   A provision that, under certain conditions, a person's insurance will be kept in full force by the insurer without further payment of premiums. It is used most often in the event of permanent and total disability.

WELLNESS PROGRAMS   Employer programs provided to employees to lessen health risks and thus avoid more serious health problems.

WORKERS' COMPENSATION   Liability insurance requiring certain employers (a) to pay benefits and furnish medical care to employees for on-the job injuries and (b) to pay benefits to dependents of employees killed by occupational accidents.

WORKERS' COMPENSATION LAW   A statute imposing liability on employers to pay benefits and furnish care to employees injured and to pay benefits to dependents of employees killed in the course of and because of their employment.

WRIT OF MANDAMUS   A court order commanding a regulatory officer, such as an insurance commissioner, to perform some specified act.

INDEX